Advance Praise for Unlocking Minds in Lockup

"The potential of prison education to protect future generations is real. This book is a must for educators, criminal justice professionals, students, child advocates and policy makers." (Excerpt from Foreword)

Alice Payne, Retired Deputy Director,
Washington State Department of Corrections
Criminal Justice Lecturer, University of Washington, Tacoma

"Walker in *Unlocking Minds in Lockup* makes an important contribution to our understanding of the critical need for meaningful education in our prisons. She makes clear that it is through education that everyone's humanity is recognized. It is time for everyone to realize the human capital locked away in our prisons and how it may be translated into an asset important to the future of our communities."

Faith E. Lutze, Ph.D.
Professor and Graduate Director
Research Faculty, Washington State Institute for Criminal Justice
Washington State University

"Jan Walker's book is a welcome and valuable addition to the literature on prison education. Across the political spectrum there is agreement that the U.S. experiment with hyper-incarceration has failed and that we need to engage in serious decarceration efforts. Critical programming of the sort that *Unlocking Minds in Lockup* describes so movingly, will play a key role in reducing the number of men and women who return to prison. Although Walker's book is a retrospective of the eighteen years she spent teaching in Washington State facilities, it also serves as a blueprint for our way forward. I hope state prison systems and higher education administrators will take seriously her call to create more education programs inside our nation's prisons."

Rebecca Ginsburg,
Associate Professor and Director, Education Justice Project
University of Illinois at Urbana-Champaign

"Jan Walker's portrayal of her experience teaching in prisons in America illustrates the hope, potential, and redemption that can, and should, be cultivated in the large population of incarcerated people in the U.S., the vast majority of which will be returning to their communities at some point in the future, many sooner rather than later. She deftly interweaves touching anecdotes with hard-hitting statistics and facts that forces the reader to reexamine his or her assumptions about the realities of the prison system and those held within it, and what a different approach and future could mean for society as a whole."

Emily Patka, Academic Coordinator
Hudson Link for Higher Education in Prison
Ossining, NY

UNLOCKING MINDS IN LOCKUP

Prison Education Opens Doors

JAN WALKER

Plicata Press LLC
Gig Harbor, Washington

Plicata Press LLC
P.O. Box 32
Gig Harbor, WA   98335
www.plicatapress.com
www.TeachInside.com

ISBN: 978-0-9903102-5-9 print
ISBN: 978-0-9903102-6-6 ebook
LCCN: 2015934799

Cover designer – Anita Jones

Publisher's Cataloging-In-Publication Data
(Prepared by The Donohue Group, Inc.)

Walker, Jan (Janet D.)
    Unlocking minds in lockup : prison education opens doors / Jan Walker.

    pages ; cm

    Issued also as an ebook.
    Includes bibliographical references.
    ISBN: 978-0-9903102-5-9

    1. Prisoners--Education--Washington (State) 2. Criminals--Rehabilitation--Washington (State) I. Title.

HV8883.3.U52 W37 2015
365/.66609797   2015934799

Printed in the United States of America

To Correctional Educators and Inmate Students
To the children of incarcerated parents . . .
They are doing time, too.

Also by Jan Walker

Romar Jones Takes a Hike: Runaway or missing person ... (fiction)

History Lesson: The Walls Know Where the Body Lies (fiction)

The Whiskey Creek Water Company (fiction)

A Farm in the South Pacific Sea (fiction)

An Inmate's Daughter (fiction)

Dancing to the Concertina's Tune: A Prison Teacher's Memoir

Parenting From a Distance: Your Rights and Responsibilities
(specialty text)

My Relationships, My Self (specialty text)

| Acknowledgments |

Writing and rewriting the stories in this work brought back memories of the struggles and rewards of an unusual career. I will begin with thanks to all the women and men who were my students inside prison classrooms, and who undertook the work required to reach out to their families, especially their children. I learned from them how to teach to their needs. I can hear Anna in *The King and I* singing, *It's a very ancient saying But a true and honest thought That if you become a teacher By your pupils you'll be taught.*

Special thanks to Alice Payne whose support for family programs inside prison planted the first seeds for the Residential Parenting Program at Washington Corrections Center for Women when she served as Associate Superintendent at that facility. She is a visionary and innovator. When she moved from the women's prison to serve as associate superintendent at McNeil Island Corrections Center she saw that men needed and deserved parenting and family classes. She fostered the intense orientation program, Project Social Responsibility, at McNeil Island Corrections Center and nurtured it to fruition. She asked me to transfer to the island to coordinate the program. I am grateful for the opportunities that opened for me. The tenets of that program and the challenges we faced are told beginning in Chapter 10 of this work.

I deeply appreciate Alice Payne taking time from her demanding schedule to read this work and write the Foreword. She continues to devote her knowledge and purpose to improving the correctional justice system through university level education and professional writing.

Thanks to Tom Rabak, education director at McNeil Island at the time I transferred there to work with the men, and to Gil Burton, shift lieutenant extraordinaire. He came from the "old guard" in the once federal penitentiary on the island, and helped make the orientation program work through his support and participation. Thanks to those correctional officers at both the women's prison and the island who treated offenders with respect while maintaining the demands of their positions.

My heartfelt appreciation goes to the volunteers with whom I worked at Rebuilding Families, Inc.: Audrey Shaw, Ric Cederwall, Pat Crawley, Jean Fernandez and Anne Delaney. They gave countless hours over several years to helping female offenders prepare for release to our communities. Thanks to Sharon Peterson for her work with women offenders and her insight into their special needs.

As both writer and publisher, I appreciate and herald the value of editing. Editor Ted Olinger's questions, comments, corrections and nudging helped make this work cohesive and readable. He did the first edit, and then he did a second edit to sharpen the changes I made after the first round. Colleen and Frank Slater did copy editing as they have for most of my books. Several early manuscript readers offered suggestions and support. They include Rebecca Ginsburg, Associate Professor and Director of the Education Justice Project, University of Illinois at Urbana-Champaign; Faith E. Lutze, Ph.D., Professor and Graduate Director at the Washington State Institute for Criminal Justice, Washington State University; Emily Patka, Academic Coordinator, Hudson Link for Higher Education in Prison, Ossining, NY; and Mary Schroeder, Owner, Brilliant Moon Bookstore, Shelton, WA.

Thanks to Sharon Castlen for helping put together all the parts that take a work from manuscript to published book.

Finally, my own family's love and support always sustains me.

Contents

| Foreword |

Alice Payne
MS Public Administration/Criminal Justice

When I first met Jan Walker I quickly discovered we shared a strong bond through our Scandinavian heritage. We both understood the importance of the family and the impact that those relationships had on family legacy. We had been taught the moral lessons of life through the writings of Hans Christian Anderson, the mystic tales of many Norwegian trolls and, of course, who can forget the teaching learned from the many storied antics of "Ole and Inga." Scandinavians love a good story.

Jan and I heard many stories told by male and female offenders throughout our careers, in our different capacities inside women's and men's prisons. We came to understand the impact incarceration left on families, especially children. Their family legacy often entailed a history of neglect, emotional and/or physical abuse and transiency and, most devastating, a sense of hopelessness that paralyzed their future.

Jan had been teaching the concepts of critical thinking, family relationships and parenting skills to female offenders for years in the women's prison where I served as Associate Superintendent, prior to working with the men housed at the McNeil Island Corrections Center. She had been successful in getting the women to critically examine their lives and the resulting consequences their actions brought to their families and children. What occurred in her classroom was the heart and soul of prison education at its best. Many offenders have bad memories of their early education years. That was often the place of their first and frequent academic and social failures. Jan created an atmosphere where offenders became students. They were able to leave their prior classroom experiences behind and reconnect with learning through guided reflection. They felt safe telling their stories in the classroom.

Do not underestimate the power of this document. The stories of these offenders are timeless. The potential of prison education to protect future generations is real. The stories of these offenders were groundbreaking and served as a foundation to further the development of additional programs for the children of incarcerated parents in Washington State. Jan Walker has created the foundation. It is up to you, the reader, to advocate for prison education to change lives and protect the future generation so that they, too, will have good stories to tell their children for their legacy. This book is a must for educators, criminal justice professionals, students, child advocates and policy makers.

Alice Payne, Retired Deputy Director,
Washington State Department of Corrections
Criminal Justice Lecturer,
University of Washington, Tacoma

A Note for Readers

There is a national dialogue on prison reform underway in our country, though too few of us are involved. I hope this book inspires you to join the discussion. There are approximately 2 million adults in prisons and jails in this country at an expense of about $30,000 per person per year. Over half a million of those prisoners are doing time for drug offenses. Most of them are not high-level players in the drug world, and most have no prior criminal record for a violent offense. They will spend five years or more inside prison. Many of them are fathers and mothers of young children; many will rarely see their children or other family members due to the distance between the facility where they're housed and the community where their loved ones live.

I didn't know anything about prisons or inmates before I reluctantly signed a contract to teach inside a small women's prison in Washington State. Now I know that our prison system is broken. Mass incarceration that began in the 1980s is costing billions in dollars and causing immeasurable damage to our society, especially to the 2.7 million children under age 18 with a parent in prison or jail and the additional millions of children with a parent under court supervision.

Going inside adult women's and men's prisons to teach any subject matter is both a challenge and a privilege. When the subject matter pertains to parenting, family relationships and social responsibility as my work did, it elevates to an honor. Every incarcerated student who did the work required for every course offered inside prison added to the humanity that is our society. Ask any correctional educator about the experience of teaching inside prison and you will likely hear something akin to *privilege* and *honor*. It's not easy to explain why and how. This book is my attempt to show you what I mean.

Jan Walker

Introduction

I believe in the power of story. This book is a story about women and men who spent time in prison for crimes punishable by removal from society. More specifically it's a story about how they used their time inside and what that means to all of us on the outside. I hope it provides food for thought and perhaps changes how you view the American criminal justice system.

Several of the resources listed at the end of this book refer to the collapse of that system, the plague of prisons in this country, mass incarceration and the imprisonment binge. The authors of those stories tell them from different perspectives. They are scholars, professors, journalists, jurists, proponents of sentencing reform, and concerned citizens.

I am a teacher who went inside adult female and male prisons for eighteen years. I learned what those inside needed and adapted materials to fit their needs while meeting the expectations of the community colleges that employed me. I used a purple pen to write notes on my students' assignments because they associated red with failure. I carried that pen behind my right ear. Setting it down made it fair game for theft. The pen left purple streaks in my white hair and that became part of my personal trademark.

I left when the criminal justice system focused on getting tough on crime campaigns, and three strikes laws led to education budget cuts that eliminated most college level courses. Before retiring from the system I rewrote parenting, family and chemical dependency class materials and syllabi for use with students at all education levels for continuing education rather than college transfer credit.

Once I saw the need and potential for change that would benefit future generations, especially offenders' children, it was an easy choice to teach inside as long as it was viable and then to volunteer inside later with a dedicated organization that focused on helping women prepare for returning to their families. All most all offenders are released from prison once they've completed their time.

The stated purpose of prison is retribution (punishment for the crime committed), incapacitation (keeping the offender from hurting others), deterrence (preventing future criminal acts) and rehabilitation (reforming behavior through education, skill development, psychological counseling and time).

Most prisons are now called corrections centers or correctional facilities. Being sentenced to prison is punishment; being held inside is incapacitation and deterrence at least for the duration of confinement. Being rehabilitated requires work on the part of offenders. They need to participate in programs and counseling to prepare for reentry, and they need to begin that preparation when they enter prison.

My work fell under rehabilitation. I taught classes that were categorized as home and family life and personal responsibility inside the Washington Corrections Center for Women (WCCW) through Tacoma Community College (TCC) for eleven years and McNeil Island Corrections Center (MICC), a medium custody men's prison, for seven. The classes focused on parenting skills, child development, family relationships and social responsibility.

I also taught simple things you might imagine most adults already know: sewing and clothing care, meal management and nutrition for college science credit. I developed curriculum for specific courses in behavior management, family history and patterns, chemical dependency and family issues, parenting from inside prison and a legal awareness course called Street Law.

At McNeil Island I coordinated an intense orientation program called Project Social Responsibility that dovetailed with inmate case management mandated by the Department of Corrections (DOC).

These stories will differ from popular images of life inside prison. They are based on my personal experience from untold hours spent in direct contact with incarcerated students in classrooms, visiting rooms, segregation units, and prison corridors.

Most of the crimes you read or hear about in the media are sensational cases. Most of the offenders you will read about here weren't mentioned on the evening news or written up in the daily paper. That doesn't make their crimes acceptable. I'm not telling their stories to excuse their behaviors, but to show the humanity I saw in my students. They are part of our culture; they were incarcerated at the time their stories unfold here, but now most are living outside the prison fence as former felons.

I think some facts are important to this story. According to the Bureau of Justice Assistance, a federal agency, there were 2.3 million adults in prison and jails at the end of 2012 at an annual cost of 70-billion taxpayer dollars. Their statistics say that 95 percent of all prison inmates get back out. That's currently over 650,000 persons per year returning to their communities. Around 70 percent of them are parents who have reunited or are working to reunite with their children. In addition to the 2.7 million children who currently have a parent in prison, there are another 7 million with a parent under the jurisdiction of the criminal justice system. It is well documented in research as a traumatic experience for the children. I taught adults inside with one eye always on their children outside.

In 2014 the Rand Corporation released a comprehensive study on the effectiveness of correctional education. The study stated that every dollar spent inside saves five dollars on recidivism. I have tried several phrases to state that fact but all of them sound trite. My students would have said, "Spend a buck on school inside and save five on the outs, Dude." Women and men who leave prison with more education and social awareness are less likely to be sent back inside for parole violations or new crimes. That's important to all of us and especially to their children.

When asked about my work inside, I tend to explain it as teaching parents how to reach out to their children and resume their role when they get released. Their time inside prison can serve as an opportunity to consider the acts that put them behind bars, to think about their own humanity and to prepare for reuniting with their families and communities as productive citizens.

In many ways prison serves as parents in absentia to offenders: the system provides food and lodging, establishes expectations and rules, metes out discipline for misbehavior, and gives them opportunities to grow toward independence. Prison education picks up where offender students gave up, dropped out, got suspended or got arrested the first time.

Some of the classes I write about in this story can be replicated inside prison classrooms today when the value of correctional education seems to be on the upswing. Many classes will have the benefit of advanced technology and the awareness that the tough on crime concept and three strikes laws are too costly in both tax dollars and humanity. All classes taught inside will need students who choose to think and to learn, and to reach out to their families and communities for the support they will need when they are released.

All inmates' names in this work are fictitious, created to protect their identification; all their stories are real. The professionals named and their titles at the time of the event are their actual names and titles.

1

| Going Inside the Prison Fence |

Most prisons are surrounded by chain link fences topped with spiraled razor wire designed to shred flesh to ribbons. That spiraled wire broadcasts its Keep Out message at first sight. It serves to keep criminals separated from the community for all the reasons prisons use for their existence.

My first trip inside the prison fence was as a visitor to the old federal prison on McNeil Island in Puget Sound, where cold salt water also served as an effective separation of the public and the prison. It was the last American prison accessible by boat, a twenty minute cruise from the mainland.

I was with my Tacoma Community College Personal and Family Relationships class, a night course for adults. One of my students worked in the prison as a correctional officer and arranged for our visit so we'd have a clearer understanding of his interest in the course work.

He was seeking career advancement, whatever that might have been in that environment at that time, and heard about the classes I taught, or perhaps my teaching style. I'd managed to make systems theory part of the course objectives. He believed that would be helpful in his daily interactions with inmates.

I'd never before met anyone who worked in prison, never known anyone sentenced to do time, never given prison or inmates, or their interactions, much thought. That made me a rather typical American. I had worked with a few other young men and women who attended the community college at night to further their careers through what they called human awareness classes. They'd liked some of the extras I crammed into the course that took it a step beyond family meaning only the people with whom one lives.

The federal government had purchased pristine McNeil Island in 1875, over a hundred years before that visit, and used it as a prison compound since, though there were rumblings about returning it to the state. I saw the compound as an ugly scar at the forest's edge. Dirty-yellow and non-color buildings with dingy barred windows stood on a hill above the dock where passenger ferries came and went twenty-four hours a day, carrying prison employees, inmates, and authorized visitors. Barges and tugs delivered food and all the other supplies the prison needed to another dock a short distance away.

While waiting for the locked gate to open we looked east across the Sound to the sleepy town of Steilacoom and the mainland dock where corrections officers, generally called prison guards in those years, had checked our credentials. Snow-clad Mount Rainier, skirted with thick stands of evergreen forests, loomed above the town and Sound. At sunset on sunny days, the mountain blushes pink for a time before disappearing into darkness. Shoreline property on the Sound is expensive and highly prized. The island has beautiful beaches, forested acreage, a small lake, and abundant wildlife on two-thirds of its 4,400 acres. Prime real estate now wholly owned by the state.

Our group moved through the sally port into a wide, high ceilinged corridor where we were met by an on-duty officer, and off we went into the dismal, almost dead interior of 3/4 cellhouse. We were subdued, reverent even, though our hard soled shoes announced our presence as we climbed steel mesh stairs and walked cellblock tiers. The blocks were sections within the cellhouse and were used to separate men by their crimes or patterns of behavior. They also served as security and control measures. Blocks that held men being disciplined had more security staff and the officers physically checked each cell more frequently. Men were released by housing block to mainline (mess or dining hall), yard or gym.

We walked the tiers, glancing into cells that were bedrooms, bathrooms, living rooms, and sometimes kitchens for men clever enough to rig electric wires to simple pieces of metal—perhaps a contraband fork in the days before plastic utensils—to cook stolen meat. Their dank cells, built for five men, had been double-bunked and housed ten by then. They reeked of overused toilets, under-washed bodies, and despair.

Somewhere, on one of those tiers in a high security block, we viewed what my student called the Lala cells. Lalas traded sexual favors for food or other commodities from the prison store, or art items created by inmates for sale and trade. Such men are generally called punks or any number of slang terms for their sexual role, but they will remain Lalas in my mind.

Though my student guide had prepared me for meeting them, I felt uncomfortable. I'd been taught not to stare at those who were different, and in my world they qualified as outside the norm. The Lalas were playing cards. Other cards, presumably from a worn deck, served as makeshift hair rollers, preparation for their late night dates. Some Lalas wore lipstick, blush, eyeshadow. The men, accustomed to visitors walking by, paid us little heed even when our guide said the Avon representative who sold them their cosmetics often achieved top sales recognition in her region.

In truth, hair rollers and makeup bothered me less than the sight of grown men sitting around playing cards during what I considered work hours of the day. I had no understanding then of what doing time meant, or how few jobs were available inside the prison fence.

From the cellhouse we went to prison industries, to me a much more appealing place. Daylight filtered through fly and dust specked windows. Men worked at physical tasks: welding, electronics repair, furniture making.

My dad, a carpenter by profession, had been adept in many crafts. As firstborn in a family of girls, I was strongly father aligned, a typical birth order characteristic. Dad taught me to see the artisan in all work. Men working with their hands to create or restore useful items gave me an odd sense of all being well in spite of the setting.

Those prison workrooms were male places, with vintage girly pinups, machine noise, and torch flames. Men wore safety goggles, work gloves, sturdy clothing and boots. None wore makeup. I hoped they wouldn't couple with the Lalas when night fell and further darkened the old cellblocks. If I'd had a better understanding of the large cellhouse and separate cellblocks I would have known that they were unlikely to be in the same space at any time.

I now know only a figurative handful of incarcerated adults ever get hired for prison industry jobs. Those who do are generally long-termers whose money goes home to support a family. They have their own inside fraternity and shun any they consider homosexual. I can also report that metal eating utensils were long since replaced with plastic spoon/forks (sporks) in prison dining rooms.

We made the rounds—the prison hospital and chapel, an open barracks like living unit for those who'd climbed the privilege ladder, the mess hall, staff dining room, mailroom, administrative offices. We heard stories of some famous men who'd done time there and whose names may be no longer recognizable to most: Gangster Mickey Cohen for tax evasion; Teamster president Dave Beck, convicted of racketeering; auto thief Charles Manson, who later committed the heinous Tate-La Bianca murders.

My student pointed out a ranking member of the Mexican Mafia and a man known as a kingpin in Hawaiian drug trafficking. Both were believed to be running their homeland operations from within the prison.

An officer holding chains told us about a man soon to be famous, at least inside the federal system, for information he revealed in an attempt to reduce his sentence. The body chains were meant for him, for his transport across the Sound, where he would be met by federal officials and flown to another institution.

"He's wearing a snitch jacket," the officer rattling the chains said. "Nowhere's safe for him now, and he knows it. Snitches make their own death row."

The male students in our tour group asked pointed questions about the move, including how many guards would accompany the prisoner into an airplane lavatory, and whether the cuffs would be removed while he urinated. The question reminded me I needed to use a restroom before we boarded the boat for the twenty-minute crossing to Steilacoom and our parked cars. I was reading door signs when one student, a male, asked if the officer would demonstrate the body chains on me. Without my agreeing to what my students considered a great laugh, the officer cuffed my wrists, snapped a chain around my waist and knelt to put ankle bracelets in place.

I remember a chill swept over me, and my stomach churned. Did I gasp for breath before the chill gave way to heat so intense it felt as if I stood in flames? I had the odd feeling my hair had caught fire. The officer must have seen alarm in my look, or felt it radiating from me.

"You claustrophobic?" he asked.

I hadn't considered myself so, but seemed to be in the throes of a panic attack. "Take them off. Get me out of them." My need for the restroom escalated to near-emergency. "Just get the damn things off."

"Key's lost," someone joked.

But it wasn't funny, not to me. It felt as though my essence, my spirit, had disappeared. Once we were outside the fence, my students' chatter seemed removed from me, like the noise of a radio in another room. The ferry approached, seagulls called, a blue heron waded in the shallows. Mount Rainier loomed. All was well in my world, but the lost feeling lingered. The memory lingers still. Perhaps it foreshadowed my future. I didn't know then that I would teach inside the prison fence, eventually on the island, or how many times I'd see men—and occasionally women—in body chains. Hundreds of men and several women told me they had experienced emotions similar to mine. It goes far beyond the humiliation of being handcuffed, which is bad enough, they say. It's worse than the finality of prison or the loss of self-control; it's the loss of individual essence, of being human.

Body chains—shackles—serve their purpose in just that way. Officials responsible for transporting prisoners need their charges to be subdued for reasons of safety—the official's, the public's, the prisoner's. It is an officer's duty and obligation to manage prisoners with dignity, but dignity takes a back seat to public safety every time. Even pregnant women must endure cuffs and chains, though most jurisdictions now cuff their hands in front of their bodies as added protection should they trip and fall forward.

My moment in shackles underscored a valuable lesson my mother lived by and taught: look at the person, not the chains. (She said look inside the person, or some such, but the message remains the same.) Her teachings, and Dad's strong work ethic, followed me through life and quite possibly prepared me for my unusual career as a correctional educator.

2

| Becoming a Correctional Educator |

Two years after that discomforting trip inside the prison fence, community colleges by legislative mandate became education providers inside all Washington State prisons. My department chair at TCC asked me to set up a Home and Family Life program at the women's prison near Gig Harbor where the college would be replacing courses provided by the local high school.

I asked, "Why me?" She said that I'd been innovative with the night courses I taught on campus, one of them the family relationships class that visited that old penitentiary on McNeil Island. That boosted my ego until she told me the rest of the reason—the prison administration wanted an instructor who could teach clothing construction as well as parenting and family courses. She knew I tailored most of my clothes.

"One year," I told my department chair. "I'll transfer out there for one year."

What she didn't tell me and likely didn't know was that I'd be teaching parenting and family classes, which relied on lecture/discussion, and overseeing a sewing lab at the same time. I'd never really taught sewing except as a 4-H leader, and I didn't think about prison inmates using scissors and seam rippers and steam irons. If I had given that any thought and turned down the offer, I would have missed out on a fascinating, frustrating, fulfilling opportunity to create educational materials that fit a need, not a formula.

The women's prison was relatively new when TCC sent in our teaching team. We all knew it was somewhere on the west side of the highway that connects the Tacoma Narrows Bridge to our end of the Kitsap Peninsula. The prison was hidden from passing cars' view by a stand of old evergreen trees. It's more visible now, with signs posted advising drivers not to pick up hitchhikers.

Our team was made up of instructors for classes in adult basic skills, high school completion, business and office management, home and family life, art and GED/learning lab. We met for the first time inside key control in the prison administration building where large windows overlook the compound. Single story red brick buildings were softened by lawns, shrubs and flowerbeds. There were towering evergreen trees along the perimeters and deciduous shade trees inside the compound.

Women were dressed in casual clothing, not prison uniforms. Most were free to move about, gather in groups, stretch out on a patch of grass to enjoy the sun, and even hit tennis balls on a small court. To my untrained eye, the setting looked like a small college campus that fit the treatment center persona. That was in stark contrast to our new-employee processing and training that let us know it was a prison.

We were finger-printed, photographed and given badges that identified us as contract employees by their color. We were told a prison riot was a matter of when, not if, and reminded to remain alert at all times. We viewed a video that included footage on searching a toilet for contraband, and on the danger of retractable pens that could become bombs. An officer had lost parts of his fingers to such a device packed with Tide detergent mixed with urine. I remember wrinkling my nose at that image. It all seemed surreal.

We toured the education building, centrally located on the compound. Double doors opened into a corridor between the library and school office. A long hallway ran from the office reception window to another entry corridor at the far end of the building, with recessed doors to classrooms along both sides.

One room near the office end of the hall housed Pooh's Corner, a cooperative preschool room where children and their parents from the outside community came in weekday mornings. The preschool teacher was already on staff.

The Home Economics lab was at the far end of the hallway from the school office. That recessed door opened into a sewing lab with two four-by-eight foot cork-topped cutting tables in the middle, each with dressmaker cutting shears hanging from heavy chains on one corner. File cabinets, a curtained dressing room and makeshift sewing stations lined the left wall. One steel file cabinet was crammed full of sewing patterns, many of them for apparel not seen since the 1950s and '60s; another held manila folders with assorted lesson plans and miscellany, none of which fit the community college course requirements. It looked like the former tenant had left in a hurry.

Built-in sewing stations lined the far window wall; floor to ceiling cabinets created a room divider that separated the sewing area from a dining room. A small, dark kitchen was tucked into the inside corner, also separated from the dining area by ceiling hung cabinets above a counter and under-counter cupboards deep enough for industrial cookware. An old wood teacher's desk and chair stood just inside the recessed hallway door. It was positioned to oversee the sewing area and kitchen, but not the dining room. Sitting at a desk had never been part of my teaching style. I made it a place for students to complete written class assignments while they waited for their turn to use a sewing machine.

The first time I drew keys for the room, the key control officer said, "Good luck with all those hidey-holes," handed me a ring with eighteen keys, and a grin that said I'd need more than luck.

Eighteen keys on an industrial key ring do not fit neatly into pockets of personally tailored clothing. I carried them in suit or blazer jackets, or on a hook on skirt waistbands, with the keys shoved inside, out of view. Only correctional officers and maintenance staff could wear keys dangling from belts.

The nearly hidden dining room served as lecture/discussion classroom for all the courses I taught. A large dining table and more chairs than could fit around it, a portable green chalkboard and a two-seat steel-framed orange sofa with orange cushions overfilled the room. Students tripped over the blackboard's feet on their way to a preferred spot at the table; I tripped in my attempt to position the board for use or get it out of the way so I could tend to students' needs in the sewing room area.

Our TCC team was given transition time to become familiar with our classroom spaces, equipment and materials so we could adapt existing course syllabi to meet continuing education or college transfer course guidelines. We'd been told there wasn't room in the budget to purchase new books. Textbooks meant for my use were stacked on the dining room table.

The clothing and textiles handbook would serve the purpose if students were interested in learning basics about fiber and fabrics.

The child development and family relationships texts were decades out of date. The parenting manual was based on a popular effective parenting program that required parents to practice its tenets with their children on a daily basis. I mentally amended my one-year commitment to one quarter.

The prison's open campus/free movement concept included access to the education building where women came to check us out during that transition time. They were apprehensive about changes taking place in course offerings. Those who had been students of the gregarious home economics teacher I replaced made it clear that she'd been their friend. She had always let them bring items from Store, the prison commissary, to the classroom to lock inside cupboards or the refrigerator/freezer until they wanted them.

I had been instructed to flush my keys down a toilet if a riot broke out, but nowhere in my training did I learn what to do when an inmate dropped by with six ice cream bars and asked me to unlock the freezer so she could store her stash.

The refrigerator was 1960s gold with a steel plate surrounding the upper refrigerator and lower freezer door handles. A padlock with a foot-long shackle kept them locked. One of the large keys on my key ring was for that padlock.

The woman reached for the keys as though accustomed to handling them, then pulled her hand back and pointed. Several former or would-be students observed my interaction with the woman and her six ice cream bars. There wasn't a correctional officer in the building to check with, so I did as she asked, relocked the beast and told her she'd need someone from custody side to unlock it. She didn't like that and repeated the statement about the former teacher always letting her put her ice cream in the freezer and other items in the refrigerator.

I was on stage. I shrugged. "She's gone; I'm here," and left it at that.

My next challenge came from those who'd spent most of their time in what they called "the sewing room." It was their place of refuge, a fact they were certain I'd understand. They flocked to the room with stories about fabric and supplies they'd been promised by the departing teacher—the blue linen, the flannel with pink roses, the white eyelet trim, packets of needles, spools of thread defined by color. They knew riches lurked behind the locked cupboard doors.

The first time I unlocked those sewing lab cupboards I stepped back in shock. Shelves held enough fabric, thread, zippers, trim, hand and sewing machine needles, tape measures and other notions to rival the dry goods section of a community variety store. Contemporary dressmaker patterns, including expensive Vogue designs, spilled from a shelf.

I learned to unlock one cupboard at a time, even when the

classroom door was locked and I was alone in the space. Still, supplies disappeared. The women had their ways, as one told me. Correctional officers or other staff could draw the classroom keys from control, procure items requested by an inmate in exchange for a favor, and no one would know.

"A favor?" I raised my left eyebrow and got only a cocky grin in return.

Word that TCC instructors would do a complete inventory of classroom equipment and supplies, with trace sheets going to all areas of the prison for missing items, swept across the campus and brought more women flocking to the sewing room, some to return items that could bring an infraction if found in their living unit rooms, others seeking a signed permission slip for the items they carried. I had them list everything they returned, locked the goods in a dining room side cupboard and gave their lists to the education director. She, not me, could give them permission slips or tell them their glory days were over.

Several women claimed to be the departed home economics teacher's aide, seemingly unaware that records left behind with the new education director indicated they were not. I gave them credit for trying, thinking I would do the same thing in that situation. A woman named Sherry returned a missing sewing machine. I'd been told she would be the sewing lab inmate assistant during our transition and for the first quarter of classes, though one black woman could be called on, too. That seemed to be for racial balance, Sherry being white, though Sherry sewed for indigent inmates and the other woman did not.

Racial tension existed, though it wasn't discussed during our transition.

There was an element of truth in Sherry's claim that she needed a sewing machine in her living unit room—she occasionally crafted garments or repaired clothing for oversize indigent women, oversize being the operative word for any size the clothing room couldn't accommodate on any given day. (The clothing room relied on donations from the community.) Staff told me Sherry had to do her work for other women in the sewing lab, but staff also let her into the room to take a machine back to her unit. The machine Sherry preferred went missing on a regular basis.

That's when I realized I'd learn more about how the prison functioned by observation than through training. Officers on day shift tended to have more experience, a shift lieutenant or sergeant on duty, corrections unit supervisors and offenders' primary counselors in the living units, and administrators in offices that overlooked the compound. Women did not ask day shift officers to procure items from locked cabinets in the maze known as the home and family classroom. Sherry always got the sewing machine she considered hers when night staff were on duty.

The transition period ended, women registered for fall quarter, many of them seeking classes that helped them stay connected with their children and families. My classroom, now jokingly called a designated security nightmare by other teachers, soon hummed with sewing machines operating on one side of the partition wall, parenting and family lecture/discussion classes on the other. We were warned that we exceeded capacity as per the fire code in the dining room, and should move some students into the sewing room if word came down that a fire inspection loomed. I recall only one such inspection in eleven years.

Students bumped elbows on the dining/lecture room table top and fought for hip space on the chairs. Several mentioned the "Purdy thirty," the thirty pounds most women gained early in their incarceration. Though they blamed the weight gain on the lack of activity, the staff said it had to do with being off their drugs of choice and purchasing sodas, chips and candy from Store. The clothes they'd been allowed to bring from home no longer fit.

The first Positive Parenting class I taught inside used the Systematic Training for Effective Parenting (STEP) textbook, with students allotted brief observation time in the cooperative preschool inside the prison education building. The program had an outstanding reputation in the greater Gig Harbor area. The families who chose it over other cooperative preschools knew the inmate assistants were minimum security level offenders who had committed nonviolent property or drug related crimes.

One woman, for example, had stolen a boombox worth less than two hundred dollars. She'd committed prior petty thefts; the judge seemed to believe he was sentencing her to a treatment center that would teach her to stop stealing.

I discovered that most of the mothers who brought their children to Pooh's Corner had at least some college education and an interest in the welfare of incarcerated women. They came inside to prison control where the professional preschool teacher met them and escorted them through locked gates, across the prison compound to the education building, and into the locked preschool center.

The space was open and sunny, with Winnie the Pooh figures painted on the walls, two child-size bathrooms, and all the activity stations necessary to provide a complete learning environment for children. The adjoining outdoor area had age-appropriate playground equipment, tricycles, wagons and assorted toys, all segregated from the rest of the prison grounds by fences.

Mothers of children enrolled in the cooperative program assisted on a rotating basis, and interacted with parenting class students. The STEP program worked adequately to teach basic parenting concepts though it didn't address many of the women's specific needs.

That program showed me how much incarcerated women value the presence of children. If they were outside when the children were escorted across the compound, they stood still and quiet to watch, their faces telling their stories: children mattered to them. If they were in the education building hallway while preschool was in session, they ducked into the recessed entry door to look through the window. Some smiled; others got teary-eyed. If a corrections officer came along the woman moved. It was considered loitering.

The Family Relationships text left behind by the high school program was written for ninth or tenth grade. The book's introduction went something like this: *Now that you are dating …*

A large and aggressive woman I'd identified as overbearing, possibly a trouble maker, said "Dating? Is that like doing it in the back seat?"

She may have been thirty, though she could have been much younger, weatherworn by a life on the streets. By her own account, she'd been a hooker in a tough Seattle neighborhood and turned tricks wherever she could. A customer pulled up to the curb, they agreed on a price and service. If it was more than a blowjob, which she characterized as "Over and done, take the money and run," they might find a safe place to park and get into the backseat. That was worth a bigger bill. She called it a date.

She was testing me. We both knew it. I told the class to keep the obviously inadequate textbook they'd been given for what information might be helpful, while I prepared supplemental material from the college level course I'd taught on campus. Several students frowned or narrowed their eyes. They hadn't expected a new teacher to say the textbook was a poor fit for their needs, but they rose to the challenge of new material coming in batches rather than one bound book.

So began the work that eventually became my textbook designed specifically for incarcerated students. An independent publisher produced *My Relationships, My Self,* and marketed it as a nontraditional text for prison classrooms. I owe thanks to all those women who enrolled in that first Family Relationships class, to those who followed, and to the editor of that book who said only "Hmm," when he read the unit on deprivation homosexuality. Some women develop close relationships inside prison even while maintaining marriages or partnerships outside.

Sherry became the sewing room teaching assistant (TA). She was an accomplished seamstress and remained in that position through my first year. She was an attractive dark haired woman, though exceedingly thin with sunken cheeks and damaged teeth associated with long-term bulimia. Women in my classes talked about her binge and purge episodes. I soon learned that Sherry had her own little industry going. In addition to the garments she made for indigent women, she also sewed for inmates who hired her for items they wanted and paid her with food from Store.

I suspected early on that Sherry had an accomplice trained to help her remove sewing supplies from the one cabinet left unlocked during class time. That cabinet held some fabric scraps, all of them noted on an inventory sheet Sherry had to check daily. It also held plastic storage boxes filled with sewing notions that had been donated when such donations were permitted, and that were unlikely to be consumed by current students.

Sherry knew I could see enough from the my post in the dining room to know when she went to that cabinet, and that I often moved between both areas. That's when she enlisted help from Penny, a large woman who always wore elastic neck peasant blouses and elastic waist pants.

The first time I noticed that Penny's blouse front had bulked up and looked lumpy at the waistline, I asked if she was hiding anything that belonged in the cupboard. She pulled the blouse hem up out of her waistband and said, "How did those get there?" as assorted notions and small fabric scraps dropped to the floor.

Her living unit staff told me they routinely patted her down and checked her room, and sent back what they found. Bias tape and other trims could serve as rope, they reminded me. Thankfully my job description didn't include searching students or possessions, but I did manage to stop her transport of items some of the time. Other times she wandered off to the restroom with Sherry's permission, and handed off items to whomever Sherry had waiting somewhere in that long hallway of recessed doors.

Penny was labeled as "mentally certifiable," and was on a list of inmates who would be moved to a locked Special Needs Unit as soon as such a unit could be set up inside. She was one of many offenders I met who needed and deserved special help. A mentally challenged offender in an open living unit is an easy mark for predators and often a disruption in class. Penny's kleptomania served assorted purposes for many women who plotted schemes and let her take the fall if caught. The sewing lab cupboards weren't her only picking grounds. She also ferried teachers' tests and answer keys, notebook paper, pens, blackboard chalk … anything that fit between an elastic blouse neck and sweatpants waistband.

Penny did her time and returned to Tacoma to a group home. I ran into her one night several years later in a hospital emergency room where I was waiting for one of my sons to be seen for a back injury. Penny was being treated for headaches and was waiting for someone from her home to pick her up. She seemed excited to see me and told the nursing staff that we'd been in school together in Purdy. The nurse startled, frowned and scooted her chair back from her desk. I said we had indeed been there together, but in somewhat different capacities.

All the members of our teaching team struggled through those early days when we were working toward moving students into college-based programs designed to help them prepare for their return to their families and communities. We met over lunch in the education staffroom, and in planned sessions with administrative staff, to learn more about our students and the prison system. The women ranged from adult basic education to precollege level. We were learning how to adapt our materials to reach all of them.

The prison associate superintendent, Alice Payne, worked closely with us to help prepare women for their return to their families. She wanted to establish a living unit inside for incarcerated moms with newborns or young infants to spend time bonding. I supported her in that goal but didn't see it during my years there. It's now in place as the Residential Parenting Program at Washington Corrections Center for Women (RPP at WCCW).

I went inside the women's prison to establish a college level continuing education program, and found humanity in a microcosm. Over half of those incarcerated women were doing time for property crimes. One of my students said she perfected the art of rip and run, and would have been okay if she hadn't been set up in a sting—a customer who bought some of her stolen goods was an undercover policewoman. Her sister, who was minding her kids while she was down, refused to bring them to prison visiting because it was such a hassle. Getting them ready to leave home and make the drive, and then going through prison control where their shoes or clothes made the security alarm go off, exhausted her and the kids.

"How you gonna help me deal with that?" she asked. That became the root of my next nontraditional textbook, *Parenting From a Distance: Your Rights and Responsibilities*, written for incarcerated adults, now in its third edition.

I had agreed to teach in the women's prison for one year, clipped on a badge that let me go inside the prison fence, and found a need I couldn't ignore.

3

| It's About Time |

The learning curve was steep for a prison outsider like me. I didn't know enough about criminal law or sentencing practices to understand the legalities of doing time, but I could pick up on the vibes.

My students helped me with the lingo. It didn't take long to hear that a student with a dirty UA (urinalysis) was in the hole (Administrative Segregation or Ad Seg) and would need her assignments sent down. Or that someone's EPRD (earliest possible release date) was coming up so she'd be short and shitty, might as well not expect her to pay much attention in class, she's just showing up to stay out of trouble. Or that nothing much would be accomplished on Board Day when the big wigs came from Olympia (the state capitol).

Two members of the state parole board traveled to the prison to interview inmates who were eligible for parole or a review status. Some would get immediate release; some would learn that infractions for assorted offenses meant they lost some of the earned time they'd gotten for good behavior. In their lingo earned time and good time meant the same thing. Current law in Washington clarifies it as Earned Release Time that includes good conduct time and earned time, and explains eligibility by crime classification.

Time is what inmates do. They can be overheard saying, even singing, "If you can't do the time, don't do the crime." As many former students said, "Real time stops when you enter prison, and doing time begins."

One of my first women students called it "doing prison." She considered the idea of registering for classes while in the hole a ludicrous expectation. Her primary counselor and case management team gave her a choice: enroll in education or get infracted and have more Ad Seg time added to the year she knew she'd do from the date of her entry. That long stay in the hole was due to her crime classification as a sex offender for abusing children in a day care facility. Chatter on the prison grapevine said the classification didn't seem to fit. She might be covering for a teenage son, or possibly for the husband who divorced her while she was going through the court process.

Regardless of rumors circulating, she'd had a jury trial, been found guilty, and sentenced to prison where she had to serve a specified number of months in Ad Seg. Official word from prison administration was that she suffered from depression and staff believed she needed class assignments to change her focus. Mental health care was still limited at that time.

Looking back, I can say that much of what we did as teachers provided some level of mental health support. Offenders who had proper diagnoses, therapy and medication fared well in most classes, but there were always some convicted felons that staff believed belonged in a state mental health hospital. The question of whether to incarcerate for the crime or treat for the condition remains an ongoing problem for all of society.

In one case a student who started her coursework in our open classrooms had to continue assignments from Ad Seg, where she was sent for aggressive behavior. She worked on the grounds' maintenance crew, and reportedly used a shovel for something other than digging in the dirt. Education staff suspected she suffered bouts of schizophrenia. She sent class assignments to us under two different names and with very different handwriting. Ad Seg staff said she was clever, her names and handwriting were ruses, just grade her work and record it under her Department of Corrections (DOC) name.

Birth names, arrest names, conviction names and preferred names frequently differ, leaving DOC to select the relevant one and use the others as AKAs. Some offenders are unaccustomed to their DOC name, though they assumed it when they committed their crime. That was back when. "This is me doin' time, not that name someone typed on my badge."

Offenders talk time all the time. "How much time you get?" "I don't have much time." "Me, I gotta lotta time to do." "I lost some Good Time." "I'm trying to get credit for jail time served." (Weeks or months served in county jail prior to a trial or hearing are credited against the sentenced time.) "I only got thirteen, I could be outta here in under nine, that don't leave me much time for programming." "I got sixty-eight months, I figure I can knock that down to fifty with earned time by doing my programming and staying clean." Programming includes classes, job assignments and individual therapy.

Years later a teaching assistant at McNeil Island brought it to light when he told the men in orientation, "It's a giveaway. You get out, you meet a lady you want to impress, she asks how long you've lived in the area or been at a job, thirteen months or twenty-one months pops out before you think. If she's a little streetwise she says, 'Where'd you do your time?' Learn to say, 'Little over a year, almost two years,' forget the months, even in here. Answer like civilians."

I tested his theory when I joined three women relatives who'd been beachcombing on the Washington coast. Guys from a work crew in the area were chatting them up at the motel when I got there, asking where they planned to go for dinner. One man had the lingo and the moves that said not long out of prison. "Where'd you do your time?" I asked. "Texas," he said. "How'd you know?" I shrugged. "Just checking."

Long before that interaction on the coast, I'd looked up state laws that pertained to prison sentences, copied the Sentencing Grid and kept it on hand in the classroom. Though my students taught me lingo and gave me glimpses of life on the other side, most of them had never seen or read criminal law. They studied the grid and accompanying information on crimes included in each seriousness level and the sentencing range. More than once a woman said, "Nothing I did matches anything I'm seeing here in this list."

"Read the next highest seriousness level," another woman would say. Or "Look at your paperwork for mitigating circumstances." Or "Who's your lawyer?"

My advice was to request time in the law library. They needed a lot more information than can be found on the sentencing grid.

Prison sentences are administered in months based on the grid, where each offender is assigned a seriousness score for the crime committed and an offender score for the number of prior convictions. Seriousness ranges downward from Aggravated First Degree Murder as the most serious, carrying a sentence of life without possibility of parole in most states. First Degree Murder, the second level down in seriousness, if committed without any prior convictions (an offender score of zero) carries a sentence of 240 to 320 months in Washington. The time increases incrementally for each prior conviction.

Drug trafficking in the first degree (or Trafficking 1) in Washington ranks in the third seriousness score level, with a sentence range of 123 to 164 months with no priors. Drug related convictions almost always include other crimes, all of which factor into determining sentencing. Several students over the years told me the real traffickers never got caught, just the mules who crossed borders illegally and users who shared what they scored. When I asked if sharing involved an exchange of money, someone would say "Duh." That was a teachable moment. They could be charged with trafficking when all they wanted was to get high with someone who paid them for a share of their score.

There's a long laundry list of the least serious crimes on the grid, including one that caught my attention: Unlawful Fish and Shellfish Catch Accounting. There have been times when razor clam digging on the coast with my family was almost too good to be true. It was difficult to stop when we reached our limits but, thankfully, we did, and not just to be on the right side of the law. Cleaning those clams isn't nearly as much fun as digging them.

I once heard a female TV news reporter say a man just arrested could get up to fifty-eight years in prison for his crimes. She must have determined what time he could receive for each separate crime, but that would also have given him three strikes, which automatically meant life without parole. She emphasized the time, "Fifty-eight years," as though it were written in bold and underlined. I've read extensive criminal justice research that claims prison sentences are based on society's fear factor instead of time deemed reasonable for rehabilitation.

Prison sentencing laws underwent major changes from the late 1970s to the mid 1990s, starting with determinate sentencing based on the sentencing grid rather than judges' decisions. Many judges still maintain that the grid is unduly harsh in some cases and too lax in others. Prior to this change, the time for murder was 20 years with one-third off for goodtime. I often heard "Thirteen-four" bandied about inside in those early days.

"That's 'Life?'" I said to the education director, a long-time DOC employee who moved from overseeing a living unit to overseeing the education program.

She nodded and shrugged. "Not many lifers get out in thirteen-four. They pick up infractions along the way and lose some earned time." Still, most of them got out in well under twenty years.

Truth in sentencing laws ended the chance of doing thirteen-four for murder with the enactment of mandatory minimums and myriad enhancements for firearms, other deadly weapons, and a long and growing list of specifics used by both prosecutors and defense attorneys.

Mandatory minimums were enacted to limit or override earned or good time and enhancements to increase time beyond the maximum on the grid. Drug related crimes were most impacted by mandatory minimums. During the years I taught inside and later, when I went into the women's reentry prison as a volunteer, I met offenders who correctional staff considered exemplary and highly likely to reintegrate without reoffending, but who would remain locked up due to the mandatory minimum rule.

The other change in sentencing legislated in the mid-1990s was the Tough on Crime movement that led to states enacting three-strikes laws for most felonies. A third conviction meant life without the possibility of parole. Strikes were assigned retroactively for incarcerated offenders who were soon complaining in orientation programs and classrooms. It's often up to teachers to help students sort out bad news. That's true from preschool on. We learn how to filter information for our students and direct them to proper sources for more information.

One student voiced the three-strikes concerns of all when he said, "Cops'll jack up guys like me, hang something on us, get us off the streets forever. Our public pretenders ain't gonna care one bit; they're driving on overload, they'll be glad to get rid of the tough cases."

Assigned counsel or public defenders were referred to by a variety of euphemisms but most of those who complained the loudest had to admit that their assigned attorney helped them plea down—plea bargain in court to a lesser charge with a lower seriousness score. As that student said, those attorneys have large caseloads, work long hours and have been known to resort to euphemisms themselves when discussing their toughest clients: street rats, scumbags, thugs. In the end they do their best by their clients in court. It's their sworn duty.

In Washington State one of the first offenders to 'strike out' received his third strike for robbing a sandwich shop of $151. His prior strikes were for similar robberies. He'd done time, gotten out, reoffended, returned to prison. The court considered his case, concluded he would continue to offend and sentenced him to life without parole under the law. An outgoing governor commuted his sentence, citing time served and cost as her reasons.

It currently costs this state $40,000 per year to keep an adult in prison. There has to be a better way to address the problem of repeat offenders who continually commit property crimes. Public safety is always the first concern, and the delicate balance between paying to keep repeat offenders in prison and protecting the public from them remains a challenge. The state is reexamining the three-strikes law and close community supervision of property crime offenders when they're released. It would save taxpayer dollars and could get those offenders back into the workforce where their earnings would help support their families and pay restitution fees.

Prison inmates are reminded daily that they're doing time. Every program activity inside the fence ceases when an officer announces "Count time, count time," over the prison intercom. Prison rules may require inmates to stand in a certain place until count is declared clear, or they may simply be counted in place as in the classroom or on work detail. If the number count clears, activity or class resumes. If it doesn't clear, a recount is called and might require name and picture verification. If that doesn't clear, all inmates will be recalled to their living units with the intercom blaring "Lock up for count, lock up for count."

Lockup can become Lock Down if the final count reveals someone is missing. Everyone at every level dreads that. Investigations ensue, even if the missing person is found somewhere inside the fence. It's assumed, until proven otherwise, that someone knew or saw something. It's known that most inmates aren't going to say anything; repercussions for snitching out another inmate are harsh. An inmate who does talk, or who is suspected by others of talking, might be placed in protective custody, an unpleasant experience that differs only by name from being locked in the hole. And that is a lonely place to do time.

Much is made of time in poetry and prose. Time is teacher, healer, comforter, counselor, friend, and bridge. I believe doing time can teach and heal, and build a bridge back to a meaningful and productive life for those who use their time effectively: those who register for education and job training; those who reach out to their families and help their children deal with the reality of prison; those who work in prison industries to pay restitution and child support; those who take care of their physical and mental health, and help other offenders make their way through the system.

But after two or three years, many offenders have taken every class they're permitted by state law, they're on a waiting list for a correctional industries job, they've run out of things to talk about during phone calls to their spouse and parents and children, and they're still doing time.

Even after working in prisons for eighteen years, after listening to countless men and women describe their lives inside, I do not understand the reality of doing time, of being confined to a prison cell or locked housing unit, of always looking out through chain-link fences topped with razor wire. Prison gates opened to let me in at the start of my work day, and opened again to let me leave at the end.

When does doing time stop working for the good of the incarcerated, and therefore society, and become a negative return? How much time does a felon need to spend in prison to be properly punished? How many more prisons will we need to build, how many more tax dollars will we spend before we learn to look at the inmate arc—the climb to a personal peak of learning, growth, and behavioral change, and the descent to a point where much learned and garnered is lost to time?

Prison is about time. How many years, days, and minutes make time served enough?

4

| Women Doing Time |

There are more than 200,000 women in prison and more than one million on probation status in the United States, most of them for substance abuse related crimes. About 70 percent of them are mothers; almost 90 percent of them have been victims of physical and sexual abuse. That's information only, not an excuse for criminal behavior, but it should be considered when we lock up women.

Studies of sex-differences indicate females score higher in verbal skills, males in spatial relationships. Men are generally better at mapping and map-reading, though not at following verbal directions when reading the map results in getting lost. A popular book suggests men and women are from different planets. Correctional officers, especially male COs, who have worked with both men and women in prison say men are easier; give them males to guard any day. When pressed for how they differ or why men are easier, they fall back on clichés, most of them having to do with hormones and emotions, most of them unkind to women.

We know there are differences in male and female brain wiring in areas that control thought, memory and emotion. Studies show that men tend to think in a linear fashion while women's thought processes are more circular; males' emotional responses tend toward systemizing or analyzing, women's toward empathizing.

Recent research by the U.S. Department of Veterans Affairs on Post Traumatic Stress Disorder (PTSD) found these disparities create differences in how to treat the disorder. Their work focuses on "fear learning" and "extinction learning." Fear learning is part of human fight or flight behavior, and is a vital conditioned response for war combatants. Extinction learning, according to psychologists, is reconditioning to gradually decrease the response to such conditioned stimuli.

The VA research, and that of psychologists studying brain activity, determined that women have deeper or longer held emotional memory retention. It takes more work and more time for women to accomplish extinction learning.

A woman who has long volunteered inside Washington's women's prisons, where she leads both faith-based and secular programs to help women make prison time work for them, told me she believes all incarcerated women suffer some level of PTSD. Research shows that women who have suffered long-term physical and/or sexual abuse, like most inmates, have stored enormous levels of fear. They need guided learning to decrease their response to fear provoking stimuli. Much of that can be self-guided once their awareness is increased.

For example, Washington State DOC now provides sexual harassment and prevention training for all employees and volunteers. Though I don't recall the trainer mentioning extinction learning per se, he did explain that such simple comments as "I like your hair," or "You have pretty eyes," can send the wrong message to an abuse victim. The sergeant who conducted the training I attended made it clear that reporting led to counseling for inmates who were involved, and that becomes part of their extinction learning.

In my early days in the women's prison when it was still knwn as the Purdy Treatment Center for Women, a male unit counselor was known for snapping offenders' bra straps if they put in a request for new undergarments. He would be placed on administrative leave for that behavior today and investigated by DOC officials. He might get transferred to a men's prison if there was an opening and if he could prove he'd only done that one time. I spoke with the man after hearing the complaint from more than one woman. He defended himself by saying he just grabbed a hunk of clothing at a woman's shoulder; he wasn't groping.

Here's another example of sex differences I saw firsthand inside prisons. Women tended to refer to their living unit rooms as their house, as in "I left my homework back in my house." Men tended to refer to their living unit rooms as cells long after the old cellhouse was a memory, and they resided in two-man rooms off large well lighted dayrooms.

Many women formed and joined family groups inside prison. I considered them their family of survival, as important while doing time as their family of origin and family of procreation had been outside the fence. I learned a little about how they functioned, though I didn't probe too deeply, just as I wouldn't ask prying questions about their families in the real world. Some women talked openly; others said little.

Their prison family tended to fit a pattern. Mom was usually a mature woman who had successfully reared children and had extensive life experiences not associated with criminal behavior. She described her crime as one of passion or need, carried out to protect or provide for her real world children. In her real world life she was a traditional mother who also performed traditional father roles out of necessity rather than choice.

Dad was usually a woman younger than Mom, without children of her own, and with an aggressive crime she described as getting her share, or evening the score. Some women who assumed the father role also declared themselves lesbian, but most did not. Dad's relationship with Mom was not sexual—it was about mutual respect. The families crossed racial lines. Older white women often acted as mentors for young black and Hispanic women. The older women answered to "Mom," much as you see several women turn their heads in a crowded store when a child calls. One older black woman mothered everyone who entered her orbit, though she didn't answer to "Mom." Offenders and staff alike addressed as "Ms." and her last name. I considered her a classroom assistant and resource.

Mom and Dad's prison family children were young inmates, many of whom had children of their own, but who had little emotional or financial support from outside the fence. They relied on their prison Mom and Dad to help them cope with crises inside prison and out. As children will do, prison-children acted out when they didn't like their parents' advice. Their prison parents used consequences for such behavior, often ignoring their children to the point of shunning. Children do not like being ignored; those inmate-children changed their behavior to find ways back into the family circle.

Though I never suggested women enrolled in my classes should consult their prison mom or dad, or talk things over with others in their survival family, I knew they did. They told me about their discussions. In several instances, I had moms and children in the same parenting class. I provided information and stimulus for thinking through decisions, urged those who needed help beyond education to get psychiatric counseling, and photocopied materials for prison dads who dropped by the classroom to ask questions.

This unscientific study, or perhaps I should say observation, fits much of what is known about sex-differences. Women's lives tend to center around family.

Many female offenders formed other significant relationships inside, though most didn't consider themselves homosexual. Pairs usually developed within races. They maintained their heterosexual relationships through phone calls and letters, and occasional visits. Many of them sought the closeness of hugging and touching that looked sexual to observers, though the women called it "sisterly."

The prison librarian told me she often disrupted cuddling in the library, a meeting place for women who formed significant relationships but lived in separate housing units. In short, women did not exhibit the extreme homophobic reactions I saw with men, and will describe later in this work. Most women were comfortable with hugging and even kissing in public, sometimes for shock value. The prison staff viewed such behavior with varying degrees of acceptance from telling them to knock it off to issuing major infractions.

One white woman whom I'd identified as rather judgmental regarding prison family groups and cuddling sought me out during period movement for a private discussion. My students left the room. Altheda said it had to do with sexual issues and another teacher. I shook my head, said I didn't listen to such complaints, though she didn't hear me. She talked louder, shaking her own head. In a heavy British accent, she said, "The keyboarding teacher is depraved. She makes us type the most ghastly sentence over and over: 'The penis mightier than the sword, the penis mightier than the sword.' I shot my husband in his, you know."

She shoved her typed exercise sheet in front of me before I could say I didn't know her crime, and would not discuss it with her. Indeed she had typed that line the length of the page. I changed 'penis' to 'pen is,' explained it was a quote, assured her the typing teacher was not supporting male superiority, and listened to specific details of the ghastly husband who had used his penis in a rather sword-like way until she shot him there. Her only regret, at the time she described the shooting, was his survival and recovery from the wound. She realized, after the fact, a shot through the heart would have served better, but she'd long since decided the man was heartless so really, what else could she do?

I did not laugh. I handled the situation with the aplomb of a confessor, made all the students lingering outside the classroom remain there, locked the door, walked down the hall with a stride that said move aside, unlocked the staff room door, and then the restroom door. Safely locked inside, I turned on both faucets, flushed the toilet, and laughed until tears ran. Then I washed my face and carried on. I didn't tell Altheda's story until several years later when it seemed to fit a meandering discussion in an orientation program at McNeil Island. A couple men laughed; most stared. A male colleague later said men do not like women to say penis, regardless of what they might like women to do with one. However, he did laugh at the idea of that statement typed the length of a page.

Many women doing time had used a gun to retaliate against a controlling or abusive man. When they talked about shooting, they said things like, "I wouldn't be doing time if I hadn't reloaded the gun, but five shots weren't enough." "I shouldn't have shot him when he was asleep." "Shooting him at work wasn't the smartest." They had been passive women, victims of physical, sexual, and emotional abuse that escalated until they ended it by killing the abuser. Most of those women said they knew at some level it was him or them.

Abuse continuums say the same thing. What starts with conventional or routine slapping or pushing will lead to more dangerous abuse. If not stopped, there's a high likelihood the victim will die. The emotional abuse continuum can reach the same end: death.

During my tenure at the women's prison, a decree came down ordering all women convicted of murder to be confined in the maximum security unit (Max) for a percentage of their sentence, and to wear the standard orange coveralls male inmates wore during transport. Before that, female inmates dressed in civilian clothes they brought from home or procured from a clothing room filled with donations from the community or left behind by prior inmates.

The orange coveralls didn't fit women's curves, but rules were rules. At first the women were allowed to wear undershirts, and zip the top as far as they could. Someone found an unzipped front provocative, even with a state-issued undershirt to the neck. A new zipped-front edict came down. Coveralls drooped from women's shoulders like shrouds, sleeves clumped above their wrists, waistbands settled around hips, crotches at knees, and six or eight or ten pant-leg rolls ballooned around their ankles.

"This is ridiculous," I said to the male unit supervisor. "I understand the reason for uniforms, but they need to be made for women's bodies."

"Or use another solution," he said. "Line 'em all up and shoot 'em. That's pretty much what they did to their men."

I'd grown accustomed to such comments, tossed about to see the listener's reaction, and didn't give him the pleasure of responding. Instead I lined those women up, so to speak, and taught them a college-level family relationships course.

We were locked in Max dayroom, a narrow room with one barred window to the grounds, one small window to the corridor. Their individual rooms along the same corridor also remained locked at all times. They pushed a button, or more often yelled, when they wanted out. I understood why they resorted to yelling; more than once I waited, and waited, after ringing for an officer to come unlock the dayroom door.

Officers in Max control also answered phones, oversaw movement into and out of Ad Seg, took restroom breaks, and in some cases didn't give a damn about women who wanted out of a locked room. Those doors, in those years, couldn't be buzzed open; someone had to walk down the hall and insert a key.

The Max dayroom had a spider table—a large round metal table with attached stools. As there were more of us than stools, students carried in chairs from their rooms, but that defied regulations. Chairs could be used as weapons or battering rams. If we couldn't all fit around the table, some had to sit on the floor. Suck it up; education is a privilege.

Hall mirrors were positioned so a control officer could see what transpired within the room at all times. One officer, in an attempt to unnerve me, joked about locking me in with murderers and leaving me there. (He, like the unit supervisor, considered educating female felons a waste of money.) Prior to taking on the group, I'd been briefed on their criminal history. All had committed one crime: murder. None had prior arrests. They came from cities, small towns, farm communities. They were white and black, intelligent, interested and interesting women. I loved teaching them. Unfortunately, my enthusiasm must have been too evident; I was permitted to go into that situation only one quarter. We had a new male education director onsite at the prison who said those women had plenty of time to do. They would be out in open population sooner or later and could take my classes then. We viewed time differently; he'd fled Uganda in a bloody uprising and patiently waited for a safe time to return to his roots. Though I understood his reasoning, I disagreed with his decision. That disagreement gave him a good laugh.

I left those students with a lengthy list of books and materials they could request from the prison library, and they shared information they garnered with new offenders sentenced to Max. They passed along their knowledge and understanding with other women in their living unit, one of the best ways to enhance learning. They engaged in thoughtful discussions with any staff willing to participate. Teaching never stops at the classroom door.

I do not condone murder, but do understand those women considered it their only recourse. Until they killed to escape violence and abuse, the women in that group had not been violent. To a woman, they felt freer inside the prison fence than they had felt in their own homes, and they used their time to advance their education, improve skills, grow in awareness, nurture their children as best they could from inside, and help other women struggling with similar life patterns. And to a woman they agreed that victims can't be helped out of abusive relationships until they're ready to abandon all hope for change, risk the fallout their children experience, and leave behind, perhaps forever, life as they have known it.

Ellen made such a choice. She moved her young children to a relative's home, continued working to support them, and lived in her car parked different places every night. The man found her parked in an underground garage. She emptied a gun into him. Her case didn't go well in court. The arresting officer said there were no signs of struggle, no evidence she'd been assaulted then or ever. It was her word against the evidence—a man dead of multiple gunshots. Witnesses who testified to her fear were discounted. The restraining order she had against him wasn't proof he intended to hurt her the night she shot him. Prior beatings didn't prove he would beat her again. He didn't have a gun. She should have gotten help. She should have gone to a shelter rather than risking her life in a car parked in an underground garage.

"Shoulda shoulda shoulda," she said. "It means 'Fuck you.'"

Over the years I listened to female felons' stories, I also studied the abuse continuum, talked with professionals who operated shelters and safe havens, and kept hearing that line, "No one can help victims until ...." There were always women students who had ended the abuse continuum by ending their abusers' lives. Later I taught men doing time for domestic violence, and pondered anew what makes a man choose to batter the woman he claims to love. It always came back to a basic fact: abuse is a learned behavior and being a victim of abuse is a learned response.

I see those statements as both oversimplified and profound. We learn who we are, and how to be, in the family where we grow and develop. All these years later, I still promote the study of family patterns, and quote as a reminder Alexander Pope's *Moral Essays* line which reads, "Just as the twig is bent the tree's inclined." I still wonder what events in those women's childhoods inclined them to victimhood, and to killing their victimizers. I still wonder if their crimes and the time they served broke the cycle of abuse—if their children and grandchildren got help.

Women convicted of murder made up a very small percentage of those doing time. Most of my students had committed drug or property crimes (robbery, burglary, embezzlement), or both as drug use often led to theft. Some of my first students claimed to be riding their 'old-man's' beef, particularly drug-delivery charges, because women received lighter sentences. That was in the time of indeterminate sentencing laws, when judges used their discretion rather than a sentencing grid, and knew full well that the women pleading guilty were allowing a man to avoid incarceration.

Members of the parole board came to the women's prison once a month to review cases of those whose time and crime earned them a hearing. "It's Board day," echoed across the compound, and women scheduled to meet the visiting board members came to class dressed to the nines, makeup applied (often over-done), fingernails chewed to the quick.

They came out of hearings whooping or crying; their friends waited to cheer or console. Soon another woman appeared in the same nice suit or dress worn earlier that day by a friend. "You want to look your best. No way do you want to go in front of the board in ratty old clothes."

For some looking their best meant sexy. One young blonde woman wore a sheer blouse the honey color of her hair over a bright turquoise bra. She was granted immediate release, rearrested for prostitution within hours of being dropped off in Tacoma, and returned to prison.

"I was just looking to make a little money," she said. "The cops set me up."

Another woman, Luanne, came back from Board fuming. Many women used English slang quite creatively, and she was a master. The very air turned blue. No amount of hushing stopped her diatribe. I'd been teaching there so short a time I didn't know who she was calling 'bitch,' until another student explained the board had 'bitched' her. She'd been named a habitual criminal and sentenced to remain in prison indefinitely for accumulated property crimes over several years. (A habitual criminal finding under indeterminate sentencing guidelines is similar to three strikes laws in determinate sentencing.)

As she spewed invectives, I learned about her crimes: she stole to order. If a client wanted a new TV set, a special garment or shoes, any small appliance, Luanne procured it. Her clients came from all walks of life, including parole officers. So she claimed.

When she calmed down we had an interesting discussion about

her level of expertise. I knew little about such an operation, or about those who chose to commit crimes. After she'd schooled me, I said it sounded like she lacked adequate skills for her chosen profession and asked her if she was ready to quit and earn a living some other way.

"You don't get it. I've been bitched." More colorful language followed. I felt like I was wading through a garbage dump, but oddly that it was important to trudge on.

"You also said you're appealing to Olympia (DOC headquarters) to get it overturned, and just want to go home to Alaska to take care of your mom."

"Yeah, what of it?"

She was enrolled in a traditional clothing construction class that was part of the vocational education programming of the time, had completed textile manufacture and care theory quickly and with outstanding grades, and sewed well enough to show me she had capabilities beyond what she called her 'ripping and running' career. She was making a pair of flannel pajamas for her mother, and mastered flat-fell seams, not an easy task, on her first attempt. She had determination and skill, and love for her mother.

A clothing manufacturer set up a sewing industry called Inside Out in the prison and Luanne was one of their first and best employees. She earned enough money to send home. Though I wasn't fond of a sweatshop industry in the prison, it did help many women earn enough to support themselves, give them employment when they got out, and work history for their resume when they job searched. And it helped with their self-esteem, that immeasurable quality that makes a difference. Working in that industry helped Louanne win her appeal. She was granted release on condition she leave the state and never return.

How many courses taught in prison include a component on self-esteem building? The answer is probably few that use the term, but every program inside the fence offers opportunities for inmates to increase their sense of self-worth. That improvement is difficult to measure and impossible to record on forms and grids, but it can make the difference between reoffending and making it in the real world.

5

| Moms in Prison Parenting Classes |

One of the first things I learned about teaching parenting and
family concepts inside prison was that I needed to understand laws
that addressed family issues. Delving into criminal law and
sentencing guidelines wasn't enough. I enrolled in a night class for
paralegals and with the instructor's permission, asked him
innumerable questions, kept the textbook as a reference and turned
to the Revised Code of Washington (RCW) to read specific laws.

Sentencing law seemed clear-cut in comparison to juvenile court
law and family law. Child custody and dependency laws are
addressed in two separate chapters of the RCW. I learned enough
to answer basic questions and to know what to ask professionals
when a student needed more information.

In a nutshell, when mothers of underage children go to prison,
legal arrangements must be made for their children. Fathers of the
children may not have been involved in childcare or, if involved,
were unable to provide daily care. In some cases both parents were
incarcerated at the same time. Incarcerated moms who had been
their children's primary caregiver often arranged for relatives to care
for their children, though they rarely thought through the
ramifications. How does the relative get medical assistance for the

child, especially in an emergency? Does the child's school administrator know how to reach the relative? Does the school have a correct address?

I had all students complete a simple Affidavit of Legal Guardianship form as part of their parenting coursework. They needed to understand that granting guardianship until they resumed physical custody of the child was in the *best interests of the child*. That terminology is used in the law, and all legal determinations are made on that basis. The caregivers should have a notarized affidavit of legal guardianship from the parent who had custody at the time of arrest/incarceration.

Grandparents or other relatives often step in as primary caregivers. There were cases where a child's grandparents already had custody by court order or by default—they had taken over care of the child at birth and assumed all the responsibilities of rearing the child. If there isn't a responsible relative available to assume care of the children at the time of incarceration, the state will declare the children dependents under the law and make provisions for foster care. Relatives may be declared foster care parents to make them eligible for social and health services funds for the children's needs.

States currently provide financial aid through federal Temporary Assistance for Needy Families (TANF), which succeeded Aid to Families with Dependent Children (AFDC). TANF was instituted in 1996 to provide temporary assistance to families while aiming to get them off of that assistance, primarily through employment. An employable adult is required to find a job within 24 months. The change from AFDC to TANF gave states more discretion in providing the funds. TANF sets a 60 month maximum for benefits within one's lifetime. States may stop TANF payments for adults in a family while continuing funds for the children, or they may eliminate payments entirely. The funding by either title is generally referred to as "welfare."

Incarcerated moms in my classrooms needed AFDC information for their edification, sense of responsibility to their children, and some peace of mind. Moms in prison during and after the change to TANF in the late 1990s need that information. They arrive in prison with crime classification labels, but they remain mothers.

Too often I heard staff (usually males) make comments like, "They should have thought about their children before they committed the crime." My students said they heard it all the time from certain corrections officers.

One black woman spoke for herself and others when she said, "I was thinking of my children. I was thinking about getting money to get food and clothes for them. Yeah, okay, I wasn't stealing clothes in their sizes; I was stealing things I could sell so I could buy milk and cereal, and stuff like that."

"And drugs," another student added. "Don't be lying in parenting class. You stole to support your old man's habit, or maybe your own. We all did, and we all know who's getting welfare and who's using it to buy shit."

Too many of those prison moms came from a sorority of sorts—streetwise insiders who'd been where I would never go. Every class discussion taught me more about what that special population needed, and their needs revolved around legal issues.

Most of the laws concerning parental rights, children's rights, dependency, custody, and child support fall under Juvenile Court laws and Domestic Relations laws. A large percentage of mothers enrolled in prison parenting classes had never married the fathers of their children; some hadn't named the father of the children until they sought what they called welfare. We cut to the chase.

Whose names are on your children's birth certificates?

Were your children living with you at the time of your arrest?

Who is caring for your children while you're in prison?

Have the children been named dependents of the state, thus eligible for assistance under the law?

Has the state filed for termination of your parental rights? If so, what is the date of the filing, and when will your case be heard in court?

Who will represent you?

Those questions remain pertinent.

My foray into juvenile and family law wasn't enough to serve my students' best interests. I had to wrestle with titles, chapters and sections of Washington's criminal code to better understand what crimes would make it more difficult for students to regain custody of their children. There was a set of the RCWs inside the prison library, and a copy machine available for limited use. I've always been good at taking notes and retracing references, so I managed my self-education well enough, photocopying only what my students needed to see in print.

That was before states' laws were available online. Now everything is easily accessible if not easily understood. Read a section of state laws and consider how much sense they make to an offender who reads at fourth grade level.

When the community college granted me the right to pilot the course that became Parenting From a Distance (PFAD), we opened with a session on Rights and Responsibilities. Too many women believed that being sentenced to prison automatically terminated their parental rights. They'd heard that on the prison wireless (their term for information bandied about and accepted as truth), or from the father of their children who'd resurfaced when he thought her welfare payments were his due, or from foster parents who refused to bring the children for a visit, or from someone in their own family who'd grown tired of dealing with a loved one inside.

There were also women who had supportive caregivers for their children and maintained contact with them, though sometimes in roundabout ways to keep the fact of prison a secret. (My young adult novel, *An Inmate's Daughter*, deals with the consequences of keeping such secrets. An overview of that work appears in Resources.)

Students felt encouraged after lecture/discussion sessions on parental rights and responsibilities, but the course work that garnered the most interest was explaining incarceration to children. Women not enrolled in the course stopped by the classroom to ask for a copy of the chapter. I communicated with correctional educators doing similar work in California, Texas, New York and other states who were helping women with the same concerns. Here's the condensed version of how parents can explain being in prison:

I broke an adult law (or rule).

Prison (or jail) is my consequence.

It's not your fault.

Of course it's not that simple, nor was it that simply accepted by my pilot class students or later by the men at McNeil Island. The explanation has to fit the age of each child. That means learning about ages and stages of development, how to properly deal with children's anger or disbelief at each age, how trust develops in children and what happens when they've been deceived. Some women said, "lied to," others said "misled" or "fooled with." One said, "Hoodwinked, plain and simple, done to cover up my shame."

That made my task easier. One student admitted feeling shame, the others nodded, and we took time to talk about feelings and how to help children deal with theirs. Talking in class helped, but writing helped more. Every chapter in the PFAD book has Write to Clarify Thinking prompts as part of the Chapter Review. Some students found it easier to tell the truth on paper before trying it aloud. They wrote it out and read it in class to practice.

Creative inmates set up lies about where they are and why they can't come home. They keep the lies going, getting in deeper, until they have no news to write the child, nothing to say on the phone, and communication doesn't work at all. Or as with one former student, the children visit but are told prison is a hospital, the parent ill.

Sally was doing time at the women's prison when it was called Purdy Treatment Center for Women, and programming included outings with community sponsors to swim at the high school pool, ride horseback, even shop at a major mall in Tacoma. The prison was new, the population small. Over 60 percent of the offenders were doing time for property crimes; they weren't much danger to the community. Sally walked away from an outing. Literally and legally, she escaped, though offenders say "went on escape" or "walked away" if the escape occurs on an outing. She was with a volunteer, not a correctional officer, but it still made the prison administration look incompetent.

Sally remained on escape status for several years. She married and had two sons, and said she fretted continually about being found someday, arrested in front of her children and hauled away in shackles. She and her husband talked with an attorney who helped Sally turn herself in. She was returned to prison and placed in the maximum security unit where she spent twenty-three hours a day locked in a single-person cell with a combination toilet-sink fixture. She and her husband told their sons she was sick, and in the hospital.

Sally registered for a parenting class. She had to do most assignments on her own, though I was permitted to meet with her once a week to go over her work. I stood in the corridor of the administrative segregation side of Max and communicated with her through the cell's tray door, about waist high on me. I squatted or bent over to speak and make eye contact from my side of the door; she did the same on her side. Neither of us were allowed chairs.

When her husband and sons visited, which they did most weekends, Sally was transferred to the Max visiting room with its thick glass window and old black phones. She wore orange coveralls. Visiting time was limited and there was no physical contact. She and her husband and sons touched while they talked by putting their hands on their respective side of the window. You've seen it portrayed on TV or in a movie. The boys were five and three; holding the heavy phone receiver tired the younger boy.

I urged Sally to tell her boys the truth. She said she couldn't. How could they understand?

I recited the three simple sentences. "Give it a try. Say it to me."

She did and said, "That sounds phony."

"A lie is better?"

"I can't tell my sons I'm in prison, I just can't. They'd never forgive me."

"What message are your boys getting about hospitals? About your health? They come here, wait for electronic doors to open to let them inside a fence with razor wire stretched along it, walk through a device that sounds an alarm if their shoes have metal supports in them, wait for another locked door to open, and another, and yet another. The hospital staff here all wear blue uniforms with walkie-talkie radios dangling in leather cases from their hips. How do those look to a child?"

It took her a long time to decide, but finally she told them just as we'd practiced. "This isn't really a hospital; it's a prison. I broke a rule a long long time ago, way before I met your daddy, way way before you were born, and I have to live here a while longer as my punishment. I love you both." Tears streamed down her face and fell on the shelf where her phone rested. She waited for the shock of the truth to settle. Her husband was there to console the boys; at least they had him on their side of the window.

Her five-year-old son said, "Oh, Mom, I'm so glad they finally told you. It was hard to pretend."

She sobbed over the burden her older son had carried. He knew, but didn't talk about it to his dad, his grandparents, his younger brother or friends. He assumed the role so often shouldered by firstborns: he kept a secret to protect those he loved.

Another woman who created an interesting but untrue story for her child was a federal inmate transferred to Washington State in a move to reduce overcrowding at the federal prison at Pleasanton, California. Transfers generally stress inmates, but Carla tried to take it in stride. She'd been enrolled in a good education program there and wanted to continue working toward a college degree.

Carla was doing time for delivery of controlled substances, and mourning her husband's death. He was a bush pilot who went down in his plane somewhere in Florida. She'd been involved in his drug deals and received a rather lengthy sentence. Her parents, in another southern state, accepted custody of her daughter, aged four at the time of Carla's transfer, and agreed to do all they could to help mother and child remain in touch.

Carla wrote her daughter creative letters and illustrated stories. She made cards and inexpensive gifts in a program we called parenting lab, and mailed them with lovely little notes. She talked to her daughter weekly about going to school, and what she was learning. The phone calls were paid for by her parents. Carla's daughter believed her mother was in college somewhere far away.

One Sunday, while they talked on the phone, her daughter said, "I'm never going to college. College is mean. They won't let little girls visit their mommies."

Tears welled as Carla told her story. Women could cry in class and be comforted by their peers in those years. Rose, one comforter, had regular extended family visits with her children. They spent two days together in a trailer inside the prison fence, played in the yard by the trailer, did board games, read books, prepared meals, watched television, and talked about worries and joys. She talked to them on the phone between visits, told them about her classes, her schoolwork, and asked about theirs. They talked about serious things and silly things. They communicated.

Carla's parents said they would bring her daughter for such a visit, if she chose to tell the truth. She wanted her parents to do the telling, and then bring the child. Her parents, already burdened by her life choices, gently said no. It was her responsibility. They would pay for the phone call, no matter how long it lasted, and they would comfort her daughter afterward.

Carla wrote out what she'd say, and asked me to read it—a handwritten document ten legal pad pages long, a detailed explanation of drug running from Colombia to Florida, with all sorts of ruses and dodges to make the trip work. It said nothing about breaking laws. I found it fascinating. She bit off a couple fingernails while she waited for my response.

"Shred it," I said.

"I won't remember what to say. I need to read it on the phone."

"Okay, take a clean piece of paper and start with the simple explanation we discussed in class: 'I broke an adult rule called a law.

Sometimes, when adults break rules, they go to jail or prison. I am in a prison. I go to a special school inside prison.'"

She wrote. We practiced pausing for her child to ask questions. She was certain her daughter would ask, "What rule?" Most children do, and the parent needs to be ready to answer honestly without terrifying a child. Carla could answer she sold drugs but did not use them. She believed the distinction would matter to her daughter. It would, someday, and including it made telling the truth easier. When we finished practicing, she said, "Should I send this?" She waved the legal pad. "Or just keep it for when I see her? For future reference, so to speak?"

"Do you want it read by the officer who examines mail before it goes out?"

"No!"

"Do you want it with your personal items during a shakedown?" (Officers are trained to watch for such items.)

"No, you know I don't." She picked at her fingers, looked out the window, everywhere but at me. "It's a lot to tear up and flush. And that's a major." (Inmates often got rid of unwanted items, including notes, by flushing them down the toilet.)

I went back to my first suggestion. "How about shredding it?"

We went together to the school office, a place out-of-bounds for inmates. Carla felt uncomfortable. Staff conversations ceased. I explained we had a little project. She did the shredding; staff members watched, wondering why I didn't just shred the pages for her. It was important for Carla to do it herself for two reasons: she knew they were shredded, and she symbolically ended the justification of an illegal act.

"Okay," she said when we left the office, "I'm ready to face the music."

Later Carla told the parenting class her conversation with her daughter went quite well. Of course her daughter forgave her; she was only four, and so longed for her mother that anything could be forgiven. Their relationship began to change. They talked about fibs and lies, and telling the truth. At four, children are learning about identity and power in relationships and need parents who are secure in their own identity, and who provide accurate information about the child's world. Carla had started parenting from a distance.

Sally and Carla had bonded with their children at birth and been with them up to the time they were sent to prison. Not all prison moms are so fortunate, especially if the children live too far for caregivers to make the drive to and from prison in a day. Further, not all caregivers are willing to cope with the hassle regardless of distance from the prison. The Washington State DOC policy states "Visits help to preserve healthy relationships between inmates and their family and friends. The Department strives to make these visits comfortable and pleasant."

Every facility has its own guidelines that begin with requiring all visitors to be on an approved visitor list, have a driver's license or other state identification to show on entering the prison, and have approved adult caregivers accompanying all minor children. Visitors need to plan travel to fit the time stated for the individual they are visiting. Prison crowding often means inmates will be assigned visiting times, and their visitors need to arrive and leave according to the schedule. Visitors need to follow all the facility's guidelines including dress codes, and prepare for electronic scanning to enter.

Visitors may be subject to pat searching. They can refuse, but that will deny them entry. Most prisons have vending machines in visiting rooms. Visitors may be allowed to carry in limited cash, or they may have to purchase chits for the machines before entry. Visitors need to know that the facility can go into lockdown at any time due to security issues, thus canceling visits in progress or denying entry on arrival.

I have observed long lines of family members waiting to be processed through security. It can be tense, especially if someone causes a delay by having unacceptable items in their pockets or on their person. A man didn't want to leave the keys to his motorcycle with security or in a locker; a mother tried to sneak homemade cookies in for her daughter and endured a lecture that her visiting privileges could be revoked; a young child had a meltdown during the process, screaming and flailing. The caregiver, who may not have wanted to make the trip in the first place, was warned that she would need to keep the child under control in the visiting room.

That caregiver, the child's grandmother and offender's mother, had traveled via ferry from Seattle, an hour-long trip that cost close to fifteen dollars each way. She said she had a thirty-minute drive to the ferry, and then from the ferry to the prison.

Washington's two women's prisons are on the Kitsap Peninsula, one in Purdy (near Gig Harbor), the other in Belfair. Both have towering evergreens in the near distance and saltwater vistas along the way, but those views of nature are often not enough to assuage weary visitors. The grandmother in this circumstance said she felt like she was being punished.

"I'm not the one who committed the crime, but I'm sure paying a price. Not just transportation costs … everyday costs of seeing to my grandchild. She's a handful."

Extended Family Visits, generally called Trailer Visits by inmates, have been available at the women's prison since the early 1980s. Approved family members, including legal spouses and fathers, arrived at the prison with approved personal effects and supplies for meals for a one or two-night stay in a two-bedroom trailer inside the prison fence.

The trailers were fully furnished and included extra amenities such as children's books, board games and toys. Women occasionally borrowed a few age-appropriate items from Pooh's Corner preschool, and prearranged for specific items to be carried in by visitors. Young children were also permitted to use the fenced preschool playground and equipment on weekends. The inmate had to stand count, which could be accomplished by answering the trailer phone.

Visiting, whether in designated spaces where offenders and guests are continually viewed by correctional officers or in structures equipped for overnight stays with limited sight counts, is highly valued by the prison population. Correctional professionals acknowledge the correlation of visiting rights to inmate behavior, and the benefits it provides for the well-being of all. It serves the greater society by preserving the family, strengthening relationships, and helping children adapt to the reality of an incarcerated parent.

Carla was granted a two-day visit with her parents and daughter. She gave the parenting class a full report, emphasizing that she knew she was lucky—her parents could afford to make the trip. They flew to Seattle, rented a car for the trip across Puget Sound to the women's prison, and stayed in the background as much as they could so Carla and her daughter could get reacquainted. Once the child was asleep, Carla and her parents managed to progress past their superficial weekly phone conversations to serious long-range plans. Her parents made it clear that they expected Carla to focus her reentry plans on employment opportunities close enough to her parents' home to maintain their relationship with their granddaughter. Further, they would "take steps" if she renewed contact with her dead husband's partners or friends.

"They didn't need to spell out the steps they'd take," Carla said. "My daughter's needs come first. They would turn me in to protect her."

When asked how she felt about that she said "Relieved. Thankful. I'm still working out why I went along with the things my husband was doing. One thing about prison … there's lots of time to think about falling in love. Did I violate my own values to help my husband commit crimes because I loved him? Or because the money part sounded good?"

"Okay, what'd you decide?" a student asked.

Carla shrugged, pushed her hair behind her ears, and looked out the window as though she could see all the way to that distant southern state where her daughter lived with her parents. "I love my daughter. That's really all I know right now."

Another student separated from her daughter came from a community within a thirty-minute drive of the prison, but with a background on the other end of the supportive family continuum. Dee was 16 and pregnant when arrested and housed in a juvenile facility where she remained until she turned 18, legally old enough to be transferred to the adult women's prison. A judge, who considered her an escape risk, ordered her chained to the birthing table during delivery. Just ankle chains ... the delivery staff insisted her upper body remain mobile. (I was then, and remain now, appalled at such treatment.)

No one in Dee's family wanted the child. Dee's daughter went from the hospital nursery to foster care without Dee holding her, a move that is deemed harmful to both mother and infant who benefit from first-touch bonding. The judge may have considered the decision to be in the best interests of the child, as the law requires. In this case, the mother's parental rights were not being terminated. Bonding time could have been helpful to both when they spent time together during prison visitation.

When I met Dee, the first thing she said was, "I need help." Her ability to voice that need became her saving grace, and would benefit her relationship with her daughter.

Dee was an attractive teen quick to admit she'd been in trouble and, she guessed, could be labeled troubled if that's what being rebellious was called. She wasn't certain what she'd been trying to prove, or to whom, but running with a small-time gang, getting sexually involved with a gang member and becoming pregnant hadn't been part of her long-term plan. That was part of the problem she saw ... she didn't have a plan at all. She fit the part of what another student classified as "Just a girl having some fun."

Though she never said anything negative about her family, enough information came out to create a picture of a teenage girl with a very young divorced mother and a couple of relationships that introduced other children into the household for short spans. Call it serial blended family relationships. Children got blended for a time, there were new rules to follow from the new adult in the household, and there was a change in the entire family structure.

Firstborn children accustomed to certain privileges and responsibilities got thrust into situations with other firstborns. Youngest children accustomed to being the attention-getting baby had to battle against another child equally positioned. Middle children were created out of first born or youngest, and had a whole new set of issues to battle. Call it dysfunctional, the catchall word that describes most families, but think about the dynamics.

Dee and her daughter had an assigned social worker from the church affiliated foster care agency that placed the child with a family who accepted newborn infants. The social worker and foster mother both visited regularly at the prison to help build a mother-child relationship with the plan for the baby to be returned to Dee on her release. A family court judge ruled that Dee and the child should be granted an extended family visit without the foster mother.

Picture a young woman, still a teenager in years, who's been arrested, jailed, gone through a court process with a public defender who managed to get her a plea-bargained sentence that sent her to prison but would get her back out in a relatively short time. Though she's held her baby daughter in a visiting room filled with other offenders and their families, she's never been alone with her child, never been coached in caring for a baby, and accustomed to running away when she's uncomfortable in a home situation. The baby is just beginning to navigate on her own—that stage between crawling and walking that involves pulling herself upright with furniture, but not yet ready to let go and take steps on her own.

Picture this mother and toddler-to-be alone in a strange setting. Now add one more complication … an ear infection. The foster mother knew the child was fussy when she delivered her to the prison and left her; she allegedly thought the fussiness was typical for the child when her routine was interrupted. Mother and child were escorted to the trailer in early afternoon and left alone to accomplish the bonding that had been denied at birth.

Dee reported that things went well enough for a while. The child fussed, but the simple food provided, along with a properly warmed bottle, calmed her. Dee rocked her to sleep. She called that experience wonderful. The baby wakened, still fussy, though she allowed her mother to distract her with age appropriate toys and storybooks. Most things found their way to her mouth. Dee had been told that she might be teething again, and that rubbing her gums would calm her, and she could be expected to sleep six hours. Instead, the baby's fussiness had escalated, though she dozed off for fitful moments, only to waken and cry.

By midnight, there was no pretense of sleep, and no way to calm the screams. Dee thought the child's forehead felt too warm, but that could have been from crying. She walked the floor of the small trailer, trying things she'd been told might help if the baby fussed. Nothing helped. The screams escalated. The child tugged at her ear.

"I was about to lose it," Dee said later. "Thank God we'd talked in class about the horror stories … Shaken Baby Syndrome, where the brain gets battered against the skull; a baby thrown at a wall; worse things than that. When my baby screamed in spite of all I did to calm her, I suddenly understood how an adult could do that. Even an adult who's the parent. The baby was screaming, I was getting hysterical, begging her to please stop, and suddenly I remembered what we talked about in class. Ask for help. I was ready to shake her, I could feel it in my arms. I wanted to shake all the noise out of her, and … and that's when I picked up the phone that's in the trailer so the COs can check on you whenever they want. I dialed the number on the phone and said, 'I need help.' The guy in control sent a woman staff. She's a mother, she said 'Ear infection' within the first couple minutes.

"She told me to take a deep breath and calm down as much as I could. From there she took over, using a warm towel over the baby's ear, sponge-bathing her while keeping her mostly covered to bring down her temperature, calming both the baby and me. She called control, reported the situation and told the officer to tell the shift sergeant that she'd be staying with me until the foster mother could be reached in the morning to come for the baby. She said it was an emergency, and the sergeant should treat it as such."

Dee had students in tears and giving her hugs. By the time she told her story in class, she knew the outcome: the foster mother arrived early in the morning to take the baby to the doctor who prescribed antibiotics, warmth on her ear, and sponge baths until the temperature normalized.

Dee taught the class several lessons that day including one about a correctional officer who demonstrated concern and care for Dee as a person and mother. The power of such teaching cannot be measured and charted; neither can it be denied.

Recent studies state one woman in seventeen is pregnant when she enters prison. In 1999, after years of planning, the Washington Corrections Center for Women (WCCW) instated a Residential Parenting Program (RPP) that allows women who are pregnant at the time of admission to keep their newborn babies with them if they meet certain criteria, one being a sentence of 30 months or less. RPP has a proven success record for reduced recidivism, mother and baby wellbeing, and related childcare programs for the mothers and other offenders who can work in the nursery while the birth mothers enroll in classes or job training. The trend for such programs is growing, though not yet nationwide.

There are other options being discussed and Washington State has implemented alternatives to prison time in which the pregnant female offender or the mother (and in some cases father) of minor children may remain in the community under electronic monitoring supervision. Washington's program is referred to as the Family & Offender Sentencing Alternative (FOSA). Nonviolent offenders are eligible for consideration. The decision rests with the court hearing the presenting crime, and it can be revoked if the offender doesn't meet established guidelines

The state also has a DOC alternative called the Community Parenting Alternative (CPA) that allows nonviolent offenders with minor children to be considered for release 12 months prior to the end of their sentence to complete their time in the community under electronic monitoring. When presenting proposals for these alternatives to the state legislature, the proponents cited research that shows children of incarcerated parents are significantly more likely to end up in the criminal justice system themselves due to the risk factors they face during their parent's incarceration. The goal is to help stop that cycle of criminal activity.

There are many organizations offering information on the needs and rights of children of incarcerated parents. Some are listed in the Resources section of this book; others may be found in an online search. They include the Children of Incarcerated Parents: A Bill of Rights, which includes the following:

> I have the right to be kept safe and informed at the time of my parent's arrest.
>
> I have the right to be heard when decisions are made about me.
>
> I have the right to be considered when decisions are made about my parent.
>
> I have the right to be well cared for in my parent's absence.
>
> I have the right to speak with, see and touch my parent.
>
> I have the right to support as I struggle with my parent's incarceration.
>
> I have the right not to be judged, blamed or labeled because of my parent's incarceration.
>
> I have the right to a lifelong relationship with my parent.

These rights can be negated if the parent and child relationship is legally terminated and the child is made available for adoption or court ordered to a juvenile care facility. It didn't take long for me to become an advocate for children of incarcerated parents.

6

| Moms Facing Termination of Parental Rights |

Termination of the parent and child relationship is always a tough call. Think about the 2.7 million children under age 18 with at least one parent in prison or jail on any given day, and the additional 7 million or so with a parent under court-ordered supervision. Most of them benefit by ongoing contact with their incarcerated parent, though some will need the courts to intervene.

A few parents will have their rights terminated by a court determining that to be in the best interests of the child. Children can be permanently removed from their parents by legal termination of the parent-child relationship when the court finds there are clear and cogent reasons for doing so. The court can cite a parent's imprisonment as a clear and cogent reason, but it is rarely used without other evidence such as continued abuse, egregious neglect, or abandonment.

The court must consider the relationship of parent(s) and child prior to incarceration, length of a parent's prison sentence, the child's physical and mental health, and availability of an approved relative or long-term foster care parent willing and able to provide care for the child for the length of incarceration.

The state attorney general's office is most likely to initiate filing for termination of the parent-child relationship in cases where the child has witnessed a parent's crime or where the child is a direct victim of the parent's crime.

States' departments of corrections acknowledge the importance of family in inmates' lives, and work to support the family unit by providing visitation (simply called Visiting) and communication opportunities. Education and training programs also work in offenders' favor when termination is considered.

All children of incarcerated parents suffer the trauma of separation, stigma accompanying crime and punishment, and a sense of shame. Primary caregivers, non-incarcerated relatives and friends, teachers, social leaders and the community in which the children live can help the children adjust to the loss of the incarcerated parent. Children need understanding and support, an opportunity to talk about their feelings and assurance that it is okay to feel angry, sad, lonely, afraid and even guilty. Young children tend to believe they did something that caused the separation. They need adults willing to intervene if they're being ridiculed, teased, or shamed in any way for their parents' imprisonment. They may need professional psychological intervention.

Children whose parents face termination of the parent-child relationship need legal representation and emotional support. That may be provided by a court-appointed guardian ad litem, who represents the child's interests only as long as the legal case is active.

Guardians ad litem may be attorneys or professionals with child psychology backgrounds. The position is usually voluntary, or low paid, and can be time consuming and fraught with legal difficulties for the guardian, especially when a parent is unhappy with recommendations for the child's best interests.

The very possibility of termination strikes terror in the hearts of incarcerated mothers and sends them running to prison personnel who might help them prove they're staying in touch with their children. More women than I can count came to me when word spread of an inmate receiving a petition to seek termination of the parent child relationship.

"Where are those RCW laws you talked about? The petition to take our children away from us? The part about the child's best interests? And whether prison can be a just cause for termination?"

A male corrections officer discounted their concern, saying it was just typical gossip. One of my students asked me to get the RCW volume with the laws regarding termination and copy the entire chapter. The prison librarian was swamped with requests to use the law library, an area sectioned off from the regular library and available to only one inmate at a time.

We'd come to one of those teachable moments that underlined what a widely accepted effective parenting program lacked when it came to teaching parenting to students locked inside prison.

Most of the women who enrolled in parenting classes maintained contact with their children through the children's primary caregiver, usually a relative, and weren't in danger of losing their parental rights. Some saw their children at weekend visiting inside the prison. Some spoke with the children by phone as often as the caregiver agreed to accept collect calls. Most who were permitted contact wrote letters, though they complained in class about having too little to say, and about getting stamps sent in or having enough money on their books to buy postage.

The children's caregivers were also expected to supply their incarcerated loved one with stamps. Women hand-weighed little packages they were sending out to their children to decide how many stamps an item would require. It wasn't like going to the post office and paying the exact cost; they applied first class stamps and left envelopes open for the mailroom officer to inspect. If they didn't have envelopes available, they made them out of scrap paper.

Most jails and prisons now offer electronic communication and money transfer to offenders' funds by JPay. They also have provisions for prepaid phone calls, making it easier for incarcerated parents to reach their children on a regular schedule. The cost of phone calls, still high in many prisons, is supposedly reduced through such prepaid accounts, but someone has to provide the funds for the incarcerated parent.

One tenet of the termination filing is that the child has been removed from both parents and been a dependent of the state for at least six months. Another tenet is a declaration that there is little likelihood the dependent status will change, due to the parent's incarceration and crime classification. Crimes that carry lengthy sentences, especially those where both parents are in prison, can be considered due cause for proceeding with termination of the parent-child relationship. Incarcerated mothers who can show the court that they have continuous contact with their children through prison visits, phone calls, and written communication are less likely to face termination.

My students started keeping records of contacts they made with their children through letters, telephone calls and visits. They accepted additional assignments that became part of Parenting From a Distance before the college approved it as a course. Women who had long sentences but frequent contact with their children, thanks to relatives, learned ways to be helpful to the caregivers.

Some students said they got their heads on straight regarding their expectations, and remembered to say thanks. Some families received welfare funds to offset child rearing costs, including health care. Students discussed the ramification of that, and told each other to remember the caregivers had to report to social workers.

"Don't you go axing for too much cuz the social worker's gonna be knowin'," one woman said, mocking the street lingo they used.

Those families who assumed the financial burden without financial assistance through AFDC or TANF were pleased when their incarcerated loved ones wrote a note of thanks for all the support they offered. It was a simple class assignment that required students to think about how crime impacted their families.

Inevitably several women students had termination papers filed. Their assigned attorneys, acting on their behalf, contacted me to discuss their clients' progress in parenting class, and advised me I would be subpoenaed to testify at the hearing. DOC primary counselors were accustomed to testifying, but it was a new experience for me. I went to court several times, found it emotionally draining, and developed a lasting empathy for those caught up in the process.

Most of the women maintained their parental rights by showing that termination would not be in their children's best interests, and by explaining how they could contribute to their children's physical care and/or emotional well-being in the near future. They were women who had been writing letters to their children on a regular basis, and had been fortunate enough to have someone bring their children to visiting.

In my experience with Petitions to Terminate the Parent-Child Relationship cases, I learned that attorneys for the state's Office of the Attorney General had little admiration for corrections staff who oversee the inmate's programming, or for those of us who provided education. They had studied the cases they brought, followed the parameters of the law and arrived in court determined to free the child or children for adoption.

The state's attorneys denigrated testimony made by corrections staff, and continually interrupted me when I was on the stand. I felt like a nuisance ... a buzzing fly they wanted to shoo out of the courtroom. Several times judges banged gavels while I was on the stand, and ordered attorneys to permit me to answer. When attorneys for the state (the child) argued I was feeding the court information not requested, judges invariably replied that they were, in fact, the court, and indeed wished to hear what I had to say.

I'm neither maligning attorneys nor exalting judges. State attorneys who filed termination cases believed such an outcome would be in the best interests of the children. They hadn't come to that decision lightly. They had reviewed caseworkers' findings of the children's and parent's history, and seen little hope for reuniting the family in a timely fashion. They knew everything recorded about the parents' criminal behavior. Judges, who must suffer the weight of rulings they make, wanted all the information they could gather, including corrections employees' views of the inmate-parent, and parent-educators' views of children's developmental needs.

Unless they had been victims of the incarcerated parent's crime, I generally knew little about the children. Other evidentiary findings were confidential and not included in inmates' DOC records, which I rarely read to avoid tainting my opinion and view of the inmate as a student. My testimony was strictly held to course content, my trained expertise in that field, and my evaluation of the student's class performance and completion of specific assignments.

I did not ever say or suggest that the incarcerated mother would be the best parent for the child. I tried to remain objective and speak only to academic evaluation of the mother as a parenting student, and to professional views regarding what constitutes the best interests of the child. One widely held view is that children benefit by ongoing contact with birth parents, even if the contact is only by letters sent through the courts or a state designated social services provider.

My first court appearance as an expert witness was for Judith, whose daughter, then eleven, had suffered neglect, including malnourishment in early childhood, and some degree of physical abuse. The child had been placed in a group care facility because she "failed" in foster care. The state sought termination of parental rights of both parents so she could be put up for adoption.

The child, a girl well beyond average adoptive age, seemed to have adjusted to the group home. The attorney representing Judith (my student) said she'd worked closely with the group home administrators who informed her that adoption was highly unlikely; the child had emotional problems. Still, the case fit the parameters of termination of the parent-child relationship, and it was Judith's attorney's responsibility to argue against termination for adoption and for continued care in the group home where she was comfortable.

"I don't think she's adoptable," Judith's attorney said, "but I understand why the state feels compelled to terminate. The child has been bounced around. Terminating will give the state more muscle. They want her in a permanent home for disturbed children. They don't want Judith to continue writing to her or sending her greeting cards. They want both parents gone."

That's all I knew going into court. I testified to children's needs for ongoing contact with birth parents they'd lived with through their early years; stated ongoing contact could be by court-determined timing of correspondence and phone calls; agreed the child needed a primary caregiver, a role the mother could not fulfill while incarcerated; explained specifics of children's physical, emotional, intellectual, and social development at age eleven. The state's attorney objected repeatedly, calling my testimony irrelevant; the judge, who knew it was relevant to the child, overruled her.

The attorney then badgered me about child abuse. "Do you know this child's history? Do you know what this mother has done to this child? Yes or No?"

She knew my knowledge of the child's history would be sketchy at best since Judith was not doing time for child abuse. Judith had told me there were times she neglected to protect her daughter from the child's father. Though I kept my eyes on the attorney, I could see that Judith kept her shoulders square, but let her chin fall to her chest.

My head ached as though hit by the judge's gavel. I wanted my educated information about children's needs to be helpful to Judith's daughter's future, though I'd never met the child and wouldn't be privy to her progress.

The state's attorney may have been angry about the abuse the child suffered, or she may have been angry with the judge for overruling her objection, but her next question hurt her case against Judith. "Do you know this child described ejaculatory fluid to her caseworker? Do you know the child remembers ejaculatory fluid from when she was six or seven years of age? Yes or No?"

"No," I said, "but that would have to be male abuse."

"Yes or no, just answer yes or no," she shouted, while the judge hammered his gavel.

"My answer is No, I did not know." I wanted to shout, but

settled for encasing "No" in a longer reply. The attorney's disdain for education inside prison was palpable.

Two or three weeks later, word came from Judith's attorney and spread through the prison. The judge did not terminate her rights, but ordered the child to a state facility for psychiatric care. All correspondence would be monitored. Visiting, once Judith was released from prison, would be determined according to the child's needs and progress.

Judith remained a mother, but with little chance to participate in her daughter's life. Still, it gave her hope, as important as food and water to someone doing time. It also gave her daughter an opportunity to learn more from her mother as the years went by. Judith began writing a personal family history that helped her as she wrote, and would be helpful in her daughter's care through the ensuing years.

I was wiser about termination cases and better prepared for the courtroom drama the next time a subpoena reached me. State attorneys had their job to do, and I had mine, which I saw as disseminating generic information about children's needs at various stages of their development along with specific information about what the parent facing termination had accomplished in parenting and family courses.

More than one attorney sneered, "It's prison, not college," or some similar comment to impugn the integrity of prison classes, but it didn't work. Defense attorneys asked me to restate my educational background, additional certification, and the prison's academic accreditation.

The most difficult case in which I participated involved an immature mother of two girls, an infant and toddler. She had moved to Washington State from the deep South with a man who was not the girls' biological father. Betty Lee enrolled in parenting classes though her crime classification, listed as child neglect, denied her lab participation in Pooh's Corner preschool. A viewing window to the preschool allowed her to complete observation assignments. She whined about being "locked out," but she worked to complete the course requirements. Whining annoys me.

"Turn that complaint into an 'I feel' statement," I'd say over and over. My students were well acquainted with the five simple feeling words they could use (mad, sad, glad, lonely, scared) when they got tongue-tied.

Betty Lee's primary counselor and her prison psychiatrist both urged me to read her records before going to court. They believed I needed to know what they knew but wouldn't discuss as part of their professional integrity. In the middle of reading the findings, I dashed to a restroom and threw up. Both girls had suffered heinous sexual abuse by the man, who had mental disabilities due to shrapnel lodged in his brain. Betty, who was the family breadwinner, left the children in his care while she worked at a minimum wage job. She hadn't protected her children from him, and was found guilty of neglect to render physical assistance to her children in a time of need.

When her attorney called to brief me about my role in the hearing, I suggested he ask questions that would establish support for Betty Lee to maintain contact through supervised annual visits, and why I believed such contact would be in the children's best interests. They would need to hear explanations directly from her. They would want to know why she hadn't protected them from the abuse. The attorney said he wouldn't touch that with a ten foot pole.

There were six attorneys in the courtroom, one who represented Betty Lee and five who represented others: the children, their foster parents who wanted to adopt them, the male abuser who wanted his sentence commuted due to his war record and mental disabilities, social and health services who would have to supervise continuing care of the girls regardless of guardianship, and the state attorney general's office.

To my surprise, Betty Lee's attorney opened with a question he'd told me he wouldn't touch. I answered briefly, concerned I'd misread something in his question. He rephrased; I answered; five attorneys jumped to their feet, shouting, "Objection, Your Honor," with requests my words be stricken from the record.

My heart pounded. I struggled to swallow rising bile. I knew what the children had suffered.

The judge overruled; Betty Lee's attorney asked me another question. I introduced more information about children's ages and stages, emotional needs, and added philosophical comments about open adoption which didn't exist as a law in Washington State, but which could be arranged by legal agreement.

Again five attorneys were on their feet. The judge banged his gavel, issued warnings, reminded the attorneys they would all have an opportunity to question me, and asked me to continue with my answer. I left feeling badgered and wrung out. Betty Lee's attorney followed me into the corridor, offered an apology for changing his line of questioning without warning, and escorted in his next witness. I later learned a respected child psychologist from the area had offered opinions similar to mine before I was called in, thus opening the door Betty Lee's attorney needed.

The judge did not terminate her rights, though he reportedly admonished her at length for her choice of male partner, and advised her to have nothing further to do with the man. He named the foster parents legal guardians of the girls with all the rights and responsibilities of the role until the children reached legal majority, but ordered supervised visitation for Betty Lee. The state social and health services agency, in cooperation with the Department of Corrections, transported her from prison to the community where the children lived, over two hundred miles east, four times a year until her release.

She planned to settle in that community after completing her sentence, though the children would not be returned to her. I learned that the legal guardians treated her like a family member, nurturing her along with her children. The man who abused the children was granted an early release from prison based on findings of mental disabilities due to severe war wounds. He was transferred to a veterans' hospital in the area.

Judith's daughter went into a care facility where she was to remain until age eighteen. Then what? Betty Lee's daughters fared better. They were granted guardians who wanted to provide care and love. Two former women students lost one child each to termination. In both cases, the foster family who'd cared for them since infancy legally adopted them. Both women had other children with whom they'd bonded and attached prior to committing their crimes. Both resumed care of those children. Both sets of adoptive parents permitted the birth mothers to stay in touch with their "lost" child.

Judith, Betty Lee and one of the two women who lost a child to termination were white women. The other woman who lost her parental rights to one child, but had her other children returned to her, was black.

Another young white woman who left her newborn infant with a babysitter and went on a crime spree lost parental rights before the child reached eighteen months of age. Most cases aren't filed that early in a child's life. Someone intervened for the foster parents, who wanted to adopt the baby they'd seen through an early struggle with drugs in her system.

The inmate's primary counselor said, "The child's better off." He knew the inmate's background and crime, and may have helped move the case through the courts. I would still argue that children taken from their parents will need information about them, and the best persons to supply such information are the birth parents themselves.

7

| Teaching Inmates the Meaning of Discipline |

The prison rumor mill poured out stories about children yanked away from parents who spanked them to teach them right from wrong. I countered with long discussions on discipline and how it differs from physical punishment. There were always students in my classes who had attended or would soon be attending a disciplinary hearing where they received infractions for breaking prison rules. I wove that into teaching discipline as a major component of positive parenting. My students turned it into an argument for parents' rights to spank a child.

As a parent-educator, I define discipline as a method of teaching children appropriate behaviors and using reasonable consequences for inappropriate behaviors. Spanking a child tends to teach them that an angry parent or other adult can hit them.

If I had been in a classroom during the current unrest over police killings of young black men, I would ask my students what role anger played in those events. Were the police involved doing their sworn duty to serve and protect the citizens of their communities? If anger entered the picture, what fueled it? I heard a policeman say none of these events would have happened if the now dead citizens had simply obeyed police orders. That makes it sound like the deaths were the victims' own fault. As I've listened to and read the news about the events, I've tried to consider when anger entered the equation, and when an officer fired a weapon to protect his own life. Only the officer involved in a case can answer.

I've listened to students argue that they weren't angry when they spanked a child, and watched them become angry when other students said they didn't believe an adult who wasn't angry could hit an infant, a two-year-old, or even a teenager similar in size to the parent.

Spanking that involves more than a swat on a child's bottom is considered child abuse under current law. During my years teaching and volunteering inside, I heard hundreds (possibly thousands) of spanking stories. Students were spanked with switches they had to cut themselves and bring to the parent, generally the father. They were lashed with belts, slammed into walls, hit with a clock for not learning to tell time, whacked with firewood meant for the kitchen stove or fireplace, beaten with extension cords; they had their hands held over open flames on a gas cook top or forced onto the rings of an electric one. Women showed me scars of cigarette burns; men pulled off shirts to show me lash scars on their backs.

Too many of them called those acts discipline. Too many of them said the law against spanking is crazy.

The saddest parent-child termination case involving one of my students resulted from spanking. It involved a woman student I'll call Tanya, and her belief that spanking children when they misbehaved was an absolute necessity. She spanked her toddler daughter to death over "pooping in her pants."

Tanya took one court-ordered positive parenting class from me. She was pregnant with that daughter at the time, and had other children in foster care. She was a difficult student who argued vehemently that black children must be spanked; my "white-ways" didn't work in black families. She turned a deaf ear to reason, logic, research, and other students, including other African Americans in the class.

It remains the most heart-wrenching case of my career, the only case where I failed to develop any sense of trust with my student.

Trust is essential in all relationships and interactions. I relied on a trust bond to grow, teacher to student, student to teacher, as part of my work. In my career I encountered only two students (one female, one male) who rejected everything I taught as worthless, discredited every textbook and source of information as unreliable, and considered child psychologists, social workers, and related professionals as conspirators in a scheme to control their lives and all social interaction. Both exhibited racist tendencies, one against whites, one a white supremacist. It is destructive to have such a student in class. I still hear Tanya in my head.

"Who says? Maybe for your white ways but not for blacks. All that stuff was written by whites who never asked blacks about their children." I wonder if she heard the nationwide protest chant, "Black lives matter," and thought about her dead daughter.

I didn't ignore Tanya's concern. Cultural differences must be taken into account in all teaching, especially in areas of social sciences and human relationships. So must stark realities of individual lives before prison, possible mental illness left unidentified and untreated, and the aftermath of long-term drug abuse. I sought ways to connect with Tanya, who had been court-ordered to complete a parenting class she didn't want to take but that I was contracted to teach.

Tanya had babies without fathers. When she enrolled in parenting class she was pregnant for a fourth time, uncertain who impregnated her, uncertain who'd fathered her other three children, and unconcerned. They were her children, not some man's, she wanted them back, and she would fight the system to get them returned to her custody. All three children were in a foster care home; Tanya did not have a relative deemed capable of caring for them while she did her time.

In those years before federal assistance for dependent children was managed by TANF, social workers tried to connect responsibility for pregnancy to males, but too many mothers applying for funds wouldn't, or couldn't, give courts or social workers names of potential fathers. Relatives were sought only in the mother's extended family. That has since changed. Women seeking state and federal financial assistance for their children now must name the father(s), and blood tests are ordered to determine paternity if a woman names more than one possible dad for a child.

Did Tanya want her children returned so she could nurture them, provide for them, protect them from evils she saw in the social services system? The criminal justice system? Or did she, as one child protective services employee suggested, just want the "welfare money" that was given rather freely in those years?

Conception dads dropped off sperm in women like Tanya. Maybe they didn't know they'd impregnated a woman, not for certain, but they wondered. They lived in the same neighborhoods, saw those women's bodies changing, saw them with babies. I listened to women in prison tell their stories. Those men came back around to beg, borrow or steal the proceeds of those women's welfare checks, to sleep in their apartments or houses, to take liberties with those women's bodies.

Later, I listened to a few men in prison tell the same stories, with a different slant. "The bitch owed me my share of the welfare check, man, the kid was mine, too."

Of course I confronted such thinking with facts about the intent of welfare, moral and personal responsibility, integrity, children's need to know birth parents, but the child-as-property mindset is difficult to change in a few brief encounters. Most who used it avoided parenting classes, and me, until the system started pursuing fathers and enforcing child support laws.

When court-ordered blood tests found them in prison, and the Office of Support Enforcement began demanding child support payments, they came to me with their paperwork. They heard I helped dads complete forms to keep their support obligation at a minimum during incarceration.

I'd met men whose accrued debts were so high they said they'd just get new social security numbers when they got out, thus avoiding the debt, and then get new families, too. I gave them a generous serving of information while we completed their paperwork. Many came back for more: a parenting class, open door sessions, another personal lecture, help writing a letter to a child they'd been identified as fathering.

In Tanya's case, there was no attempt to locate fathers. Her 'fatherless children' were to be returned to her one at a time when she was released from confinement as part of her parole plan, a common one for mothers whose children were declared dependent and placed in the care and custody of the state.

There were rarely enough foster care homes available to meet the demand; returning children to a mother who had met basic requirements of the law was standard procedure. But Tanya's older children didn't want to leave their foster home, where they felt loved and knew what was expected of them. There they experienced a healthy balance of nurture and structure, the elements necessary for trust to develop, thus permitting them to grow through ensuing stages. The social services caseworker responsible for Tanya's children opted to reunite her with her youngest child first, and then return the other children as Tanya demonstrated her ability to resume her parent role.

Tanya's daughter had been placed with a foster mother within hours of her birth. The infant bonded with a woman who looked, smelled, felt, and acted nothing like Tanya. The infant accomplished her earliest developmental tasks, including trust, with a foster mother who loved her, cared for her, and kept her safe well into her toddlerhood. That woman was an experienced caregiver.

A caseworker, representing the state, took the little girl from the home and foster mother with whom she had bonded and formed a healthy attachment, and gave her to her birthmother.

The transition was disastrous. Tanya, who so mistrusted the world, lacked skills necessary to cope with the demands of a very young child she'd never known. It might have been easier for Tanya and the infant if the oldest child had reunited first, and then the others in order of birth, but since they resisted, the easiest remedy to meet the intent of the law was to start with the youngest child.

The decision was a tragedy in the making. Word came down from within the social services' ranks that someone lost a job, or was demoted, as an internal reminder that repeating such a mistake would not be tolerated.

Reportedly Tanya and her daughter engaged in a power struggle from the beginning. I wonder still how the little girl coped with swats and spankings for misdeeds that are part of a toddler's development. How did potty training become the focal point of their struggle? How many times had the child been spanked for wetting or soiling before the battle that culminated with the defiant child pulling off her pants and defecating on the floor right in front of her mother?

I imagine Tanya's rage, not just at the mess that had to be cleaned up, but at the child's stubbornness. Tanya told authorities she spanked the child to teach her a lesson. Just spanked. Spanked until the child was comatose. Then, in a panic, she took the child to a children's hospital emergency room, left her at the entrance without identification, and fled.

How did Tanya define spanking? In parenting class she insisted she meant swats on the bottom, maybe the legs. By then no others in her class agreed. Many had been beaten to teach them a lesson; all had at least swatted a child. They wanted to succeed at using consequences for misbehavior and other methods of discipline without invoking physical force. Still, they all suspected they would swat a bottom again in life, when they got out.

Tanya got out. I'm sure she swatted, but her daughter did not die of swats; her daughter was beaten—battered and bruised from head to toe according to the hospital report.

A prosecuting attorney subpoenaed me to testify in Tanya's case, the only case during my career where I was subpoenaed by the prosecution and seen as an "enemy" by the defense attorney, a public defender who didn't want me there. He tried to block my testimony before I spoke. He knew in advance that I would contradict what he considered Tanya's strongest justification for her actions: she didn't know any better.

"No one ever told Tanya spanking was wrong," he said, his eyes on the judge. "No one taught her how to discipline."

It was a weak defense, but how could anyone find a reasonable excuse for such an event? The female prosecuting attorney, a mother of young children, spoke with me only briefly prior to my testimony. It seemed to take her forever to ask if I had directly addressed the issue of spanking with Tanya. When I finally got to answer, to say yes, Tanya's attorney attacked the course materials and my credentials.

The court and both attorneys had subpoenaed my course curriculum and grade book, and copied them. Prosecutor and defender batted my curriculum and teaching methods back and forth, with me there as observer, unable to speak unless directed to by the judge.

Tanya's defense attorney belabored the fact that I'd written the material, suggesting it had no foundation in fact, interrupting my explanation that it was material used nationwide in parent education programs, but adapted to prison circumstances.

In the real world, or free world, parents practiced what they learned on a daily basis. Prison mothers had to practice theories of positive parenting in the classroom, and through communication they were permitted with their children. Personal and extended family visits provided opportunities to use what they'd learned, and even telephone calls and letters gave mothers a chance to change how they responded to their children's behaviors, questions, and needs. But Tanya had not participated in such interactions with any of her children.

I found myself explaining and defending what I taught to a judge who would decide Tanya's fate, and in so doing would also render judgment on me, my work, and the worth of prison education. Tanya glared at me. The judge banged his gavel when the defense attorney interrupted my answers.

By then I had enough experience in courtrooms to expect the

shroud of sadness that dropped over me after testifying. Though I usually went to court for the defense side, to speak for a child's needs for some level of ongoing contact with a birth parent, the immediate aftermath remained the same. I was excused, the next witness called. Someone would let me know the judge's decision when it was rendered.

The headache that began in the courtroom built to a migraine that made the drive from Tacoma across the Narrows Bridge to Purdy a challenge. I had classes to teach and an education director who reminded me I would need to make up the time missed for court. I was neither compensated for my court appearances nor reimbursed for travel expenses though he seemed to think I was making money on the side.

The judge found Tanya guilty of murder in the second degree, meaning the act was not premeditated. Though she didn't intend to kill her child, she did knowingly beat the child, and the act caused death. Tanya added to her culpability by taking flight to avoid arrest and thereby delaying emergency services for her child. Her prior felony convictions, added to her offender score, increased her sentence to fifteen years. She returned to the prison where she'd been my student, but was held in the maximum security unit.

Prison authorities assured me I would not encounter Tanya, even when I went inside Max to teach other women, as if that would somehow allay any pain I felt over the child's death. She was held for a time in Ad Seg for her own safety due to inmates' reactions to crimes against children, but she soon crossed the prison campus with other escorted Max inmates for meals in the dining room. I saw her often, and endured her glares and barbed comments.

During the months that Tanya's story played out, WCCW was planning for the now active residential parenting program inside the minimum security section of the prison. New York State had such a program, and other women's prisons worked toward similar goals.

A mother-child bonding program, I believe, could have given Tanya a chance to learn parenting methods beneficial to all her children, prevented the tragedy of her young daughter's death, and served society far better financially and morally.

Further, I believe there were places in Tanya's life where tax dollars invested in her long incarceration could have been better spent on intervention. Someone must have known about her life. Tanya had been spanked in her childhood. Beaten with a belt "for her own good." Hit upside the head to knock some sense in her. Repeatedly told how no-good and worthless she was. She lived up to the expectations of the adults in her world. No-good, worthless Tanya got into trouble with drugs and street crime early in her youth, got pregnant more than once in her teens. And she parented much as she'd been parented.

Such patterns, such learned behaviors, are difficult to overcome without help. Learned behavior is not an excuse for choosing to commit crimes, and certainly not a defense for violent behavior. But it is a facet of a person's life.

Tanya's case was one of many that pushed me to delve deeper into family systems theory, the psychology of the child, and the psychology of the criminal mind. All theories come back to the reality of choices. At some point the person who commits a crime chooses to do so.

In my research I found many felons tended to have similar ruts and holes in their early childhood. Still, other persons with such backgrounds do not offend against society. Stories abound of individuals rising above abuse and neglect they experience to become successful members of their communities. What makes the difference? Even psychologists can't say for certain.

I believe early childhood education programs, and early intervention with children and youth who exhibit inappropriate behavior, do and will reduce tragedies such as Tanya's daughter's death.

While early childhood education is becoming the norm in many communities, other intervention programs are frequently under attack. They are costly and have no success guarantees. The alternative—housing troubled children and adolescents in detention centers—is also costly, and the outcomes predictable. Most will continue being troubled; most will eventually do time in an adult facility.

I remain an advocate for prison programs designed to help inmate parents improve their parenting skills before they return to their families. If parenting classes cannot be offered inside, the concepts should be incorporated into adult basic education classes.

Because many young women are pregnant at the time they enter prison, I continue to advocate for mother-infant bonding programs inside the prison fence such as RPP at WCCW. New mothers are taught how to care for their babies and other inmates are taught the early stages of child development by working inside the program.

There are no longitudinal studies yet available, no proof that children fare better, but the lower recidivism rate for these moms means they are continuing to care for their children when they're released. For those who would argue such programs are too expensive, I say think about Tanya's daughter, beaten to death at age two-and-a-half by a young woman who never learned how to be a mother.

8

| Inmates Reparenting Themselves |

Tanya was abused as a child by the adults in her life and clung tenaciously to her belief that her childhood was normal for blacks. She had come to the court-mandated positive parenting class armored in anger and pain. While other students—African American, Hispanic, Filipino, Native American and Caucasian—completed assignments including "write to clarify thinking" that I made part of the coursework, she alternately stewed and spewed.

Her classmates gave up on her. She'd settle into her shell, a scowl on her face, until something triggered her suppressed anger. The reparenting concept was one such trigger. She dismissed it as "more of my white ways."

Though the word reparenting may not be in your dictionary, the definition is self-explanatory. It's a way to evaluate how you were parented, and identify areas where you may need to heal from parenting practices your family and other caregivers used with you. It involves recognizing what you know about yourself, admitting your mistakes and failures, and moving on to try new things. It requires taking time to improve your cause and effect thinking so that it becomes part of your decision making process. Take a deep breath and think before swatting a child or lashing out verbally.

The concept has known several names, some of them considered suspect by academic and political hardliners. Nurture your inner-child, grow up again, heal the child within, and reparent your self are among the more common. All are based on the awareness most of us face in adulthood when we realize we missed something we needed to make our lives rewarding, fulfilling, satisfying; something to help us achieve a goal or complete the person we intended to become back when we dreamed big and perhaps boasted a bit about our future.

It followed on the heels of family system theory used in counseling children of alcoholic or drug-addicted families, children of divorced parents who felt lost or forgotten during and after the proceedings, children who had been abused or neglected, or who came from other dysfunctional family backgrounds. That covers most families to some degree, as each family member experiences a level of dysfunction in one area or another.

If you look up dysfunctional family information, you will eventually find the translated opening line from Leo Tolstoy's *Anna Karenina* (1878)—"Every unhappy family is unhappy in its own way."

Before you dismiss individual issues as part of the reality of adulthood, and say "Grow up," to those who lament what they missed without showing appreciation for what they received, take time to consider the tenets of a basic reparenting program. When meshed with positive parenting, so parent and children grow together, its strengths are clear. I first learned the concept at a professional training session based on the book, *Growing Up Again: Parenting Ourselves, Parenting Our Children,* by Jean Illsley Clarke and Connie Dawson. Rather than "dysfunctional family," they use the term "uneven parenting." I found it vital in my work with inmate parents. It fit the work I was doing with women at WCCW, where I used the book as a supplemental text in teaching Family History and Patterns. Later, it served as part of the mandatory Project Social Responsibility orientation program I coordinated at McNeil Island.

The concept now is widely touted in self-help therapies, some of which are part of therapeutic community work being done with offenders in reentry prisons. It includes peer counseling for chemical dependency issues. I hope Tanya had the opportunity to be guided through such programs during her long reincarceration.

Though many incarcerated adults were physically abused in childhood, many more were neglected. Neglect is often referred to as passive abuse by a parent who is absent or too distracted to show concern for the child's needs. Offenders' stories of neglect centered on absent parents. Physically absent parents, who left their children behind to fend for themselves; mentally absent parents, who had children because their bodies were capable of reproduction; chemically absent parents, lost in alcohol or drug abuse; emotionally absent parents, incapable of coping with their own daily lives, often expecting their children to reverse roles—to become caregivers to the parents and other children.

A woman I'll call Anna, one of my first Family Relationships students in my earliest months at the women's prison, said she didn't know her father, and her mother fit all four absent parent categories. "I won't live to see twenty-five," Anna said. "I just won't. I know it in my bones."

Though I urged her to avoid such negative thought and to use her intelligence to climb up out of the miasma of her mother's life, Anna said she started too far down. "My mother's a hooker. My dad was a trick gone wrong. She got pregnant. She did drugs long before becoming pregnant, and continued doing them after I was born. I remember she slept most of the day. When I was old enough for school, and nagged for clothes and lunch money, she started shooting me up in the morning to keep me quiet. I was a heroin addict at age six, a prostitute not much later. I'm worn out."

I remember Anna as a pretty woman of Italian heritage, with dark hair and big eyes, a bright though undereducated person sadly resigned to what she considered fate. She was in prison for a rash of petty crimes committed to support her insatiable drug habit. She earned a GED, applied for education grants, enrolled in a community college before her release, and left prison drug-free. She hugged other inmates and some staff goodbye, and went back to her world. Several months later, Anna's picture was in the area's major newspapers as yet another murder victim of an unknown person dubbed the Green River Killer.

In the ensuing years another five former inmate-students were found dead, presumed victims of the same killer who preyed mostly on prostitutes working the streets near Seattle-Tacoma International Airport. Forty-five identified victims, and four unidentified, were considered probable victims of the Green River Killer. Most victims' remains were found along the Green River, which begins on the slopes of Mount Rainier and empties into Puget Sound south of Seattle. A suspect in those crimes was arrested in late 2001, almost twenty years after the first body was found. A picture of the woman I've called Anna appeared among those identified as his victims.

Gary Leon Ridgway, who had long been a suspect in the murders, evaded arrest until DNA technology reached a level usable to implicate him. In April 2003, when he was facing aggravated first degree murder charges in seven women's deaths, Ridgway began bargaining for his life. He confessed to murdering the forty-nine victims, and worked with the Green River Task Force detectives to lead them to "disposal sites." In exchange, the King County prosecutor did not seek the death penalty.

Ridgway's court hearing was televised in November 2003. The judge read forty-eight confessions Ridgway had prepared, and asked him if they were true. The screen displayed the then forty-four known victims, one at a time. I studied Anna's picture while Ridgway admitted he killed her. I heard him say he hated prostitutes and set out to kill as many as he could. Though he lost count, he thought it might be sixty or more. He said he stopped killing for a time when detectives seemed to be drawing too close to him.

He was sentenced to life without possibility of parole. Officials in two other Washington counties and in Portland, Oregon, have talked with him about unsolved murders in their areas.

A Seattle nonprofit, the Organization for Prostitution Survivors, is working to raise money to build and maintain a permanent memorial to the Green River victims. Their effort has the support of U.S. Congressman and former King County Sheriff Dave Reichert. In a mid-March 2013 article for *The Seattle Times*, he was quoted as saying, "When you collect remains for years and years and years, and sometimes multiple bodies in a week, those thoughts and visions never go away ... This is about the victims, the families and the relatives—they're the ones who have lost loved ones—but this has meaning for the detectives, too."

The article further stated that Reichert said the Green River killings were "the worst serial murder case in the nation," with 51 confirmed victims at that date in 2013, and dozens of other slayings believed to have been committed by Ridgway. More than half of his victims were 18 or younger.

Reichert noted that 90 percent of Ridgway's victims were on the streets because of the abuse they suffered in their own homes. Reichert himself ran away as a teen from an abusive alcoholic father. He understands why children run away from home; he knows the potential for those children to become crime victims on the streets, and/or to engage in criminal behavior. That's a powerful statement to support programs to help abused and neglected children to deter them from crime. It also supports helping them learn and grow inside prison.

Anna's story influenced the curriculum I developed for the prison population. In a sense, Anna spoke to inmate students for the remainder of my career. Students who weren't ready to work on their own uneven parenting issues could think about Anna, and how she might have reparented herself, given the opportunity. Though she became a stellar student inside the prison walls, she returned to prostitution when she reentered society. Students studied the ages and stages of reparenting and concluded that Anna didn't know how to trust her own abilities and skills. She quite likely continued numbing her emotions with drugs, and prostitution is often the easiest way to get money required to support a drug habit. She needed someone to help her learn how to nurture herself. Her mother hadn't been capable of caring for Anna, though she reportedly grieved her death.

I don't know what could have helped Anna find her way to a different life when she left prison. Reentry is a difficult task. Reparenting while inside is a self-help undertaking that can benefit incarcerated students willing to do the work. That's the caveat; it requires doing the work.

The "Ages and Stages" section of *Growing Up Again* explains the developmental tasks children need to accomplish from birth through adolescence. The authors include helpful and unhelpful parent behaviors to consider, clues to a need for adults to grow up again, suggested activities that can be helpful, and affirmations related to each stage. The section is broken down into six stages from birth through late teens.

Many of the authors' suggested activities wouldn't work inside prison (warm bath, therapeutic massage, exploring your surroundings in ways that use all your senses), so I created alternatives for incarcerated students. Affirmations were easy to use; I typed them out and copied them on colored paper for use as bookmarks. Students asked for extra copies so they could send them out to children, parents, spouses and friends, and so they could share them back in their house (living unit).

Soon, someone asked me to space the affirmations out more so they could draw or write notes on them. When I was warned by education office staff that my classes were deleting the paper supply for my program's use, I purchased reams of colored paper to donate to the cause, and pointed out that adding space on the page used more paper but the same amount of toner.

"You can find a way of doing things that works for you," is an affirmation of the Structure stage, ages six to twelve, of *Growing Up Again*. I found affirmations from every stage of development fit my needs at times, and I openly shared that information with my students. The first stage, birth to about six months, focuses on developing trust. The moms in parenting classes thought they'd fulfilled that stage with their children and, therefore, with themselves. If anything, they'd tended toward being too trusting of their men, and too often denied their own feelings.

Men at McNeil Island saw the whole trust thing as "not gonna happen."

"Trust who? I trust me. Ain't nobody else gonna see to me."

I heard those words so often I can still picture the delivery. Head forward, forefinger jabbing chest, eyes squinted, hair short or long, combed or wild, or no hair at all. That gave me an opening to discuss prison as surrogate parent ... the "three hots and a cot" reference to prison, and their individual need to make it more than a roof over their heads, a bed, and chow. Their comments and attitude set up the opportunity for the Reparenting for Self-growth lecture and discussion.

Trust develops when physical, mental, emotional and spiritual needs are met. How, I asked those men, will you accomplish that while you're inside, so that you will be healthier when you leave?

Physical's easy. Get out to the yard or into the gym every chance you get ... every time your unit's released. Work out, get on the weight pile if you're cleared, run track, shoot some hoops, swing a baseball bat of you're on the prison team.

Mental's not too difficult. Take a class, talk with your teachers or crew bosses about real world stuff, watch educational TV when you catch a chance.

Spiritual, well, there's chapel services inside.

I urged them to look beyond the fence as a way of thinking beyond the moment. We talked about the ever-changing patterns on Puget Sound. For those willing to focus on preparing for release the view became a metaphor. With some help, they practiced looking beyond the crumbling walls of that old classroom to notice deer browsing, an eagle overhead, blue heron feeding at low tide, sea gulls drifting on air currents. They looked through the fence to watch boats on the water, Mount Rainier on clear days, and the silhouette of evergreen trees. There were flowers on the grounds, and mowed lawns.

As for emotional needs, hey, you put them away, leave them

behind when you fall.

When discussing reparenting, I always recapped with a strong message about the importance of education, repeating a message written on blackboards and later on whiteboards: "Most teachers here are so in tune with life, they can answer questions you don't know how to ask."

One day, when I said that, a young black man with his hair in cornrows lingered after class. "I gots a question I knows how to axe. You be knowin' Tanya, right? From when you taught the womens?"

"No, I don't recall anyone named Tanya, and I don't discuss students, former or present."

"I knows you be knowin' her cause she done tole me 'bout you." His body swayed and dipped while he spoke his street lingo. He could have been Tanya's brother, the dead child's father, another relative, former boyfriend, current prison pen pal. His eyes and the way he stood too close for normal casual conversation told me he wanted to put me on the defensive.

I narrowed my eyes, studied his, and did what he called a change-up. "What's your personal view on spanking?" He knew how I felt.

"Huh?" he said. "Why we be talkin' 'bout that?"

"Why are you choosing to use poor grammar in an education department?"

"I ain't." He grinned, dipped, did a little soft-shoe. Yes, he could dance. "I just wanted to know . . . do you know her?"

"Same answer as before. I don't talk about students."

"Okay, okay, so you know her but you ain't . . . aren't talking. I knows . . . know her too, see, and she was messed up on drugs. Somebody else messed up when they gave that baby back to her, you see what I'm saying?"

I waited a beat, two beats, thinking about my answer. He had some connection to Tanya, and some lingering interest in what happened. Denial of my involvement wouldn't resolve what bothered him. "I do know something about her case, and I do see, and hear, what you're saying. If it's any comfort to you, Child Protective Services investigated the decision to return the baby before the older children. I expect they will be more careful in the future."

I watched him try to decide whether to trust me, and warned him off. "If you supplied her with drugs at any time, I'd rather not know. If you're the dead child's father, I'm sorry, and I urge you to enroll in a parenting class."

He shook his head, swept his tongue over his lips, and moved a step back. "No, it ain't nothin' like that. I just knew her on the streets, that's all."

A whisper of icy air brushed my back, arms, and face. "If you were her pimp, don't tell me. I'd rather not know."

He shrugged, noticed the officer waiting to clear the floor, and sashayed out. At the doorway he turned. "I'm just takin' a Time Out from the streets, you see what I'm sayin'? A little R & R. My homies, they be keepin' things cool for me."

I called after him, "When you get back out, use some of the information you've been given here to help a child. Start with just one. You'll be amazed at how you feel."

After the officer locked up, he stopped by my office. "You can't save 'em all, Jan."

"I'm not trying to save them. I'm trying to give them some thinking tools so they can start saving themselves." I could get so indignant, so impatient with officers who seemed to think I was wasting my breath.

The officer laughed. "You're so serious. Well, that's okay. I figure it this way. Even some of the smart-ass punks are going to remember something you said, whether it was in class or what you shouted down the hall to them to get them thinking. Right now they've got nothing but time to think."

True enough, and more of them thought about reparenting than I hoped. That young man and many others at MICC came to Open Door/Parenting Lab sessions to make something for a child, or for Mom. Simple things similar to art projects children do in grade school. They stopped by my classroom or office, said they were just hangin', then asked a question that opened a door enough for me to give them more information, and steer them toward Learning Lab or Adult Basic Education teachers who knew how to teach them at their learning level.

That, too, was adults reparenting themselves. They sent themselves to school.

| The Parenting Experiment – MICC |

Before reparenting became part of the orientation program with male offenders at McNeil Island Corrections Center, I taught a test run parenting class there one evening a week, summer quarter. Summer, when men can be outdoors until nine o'clock recall for count. Yard time is prized for fresh air and exercise, and the opportunity to talk without being overheard—no small thing in prison.

They did enroll, the maximum twenty-five, all interested in the material or curious about the instructor. If a couple of them hoped I'd carry messages back to the women's prison, where I taught days, they abandoned the notion in the first few minutes of questioning me.

"Do you know Jane . . . Audrey . . . Connie . . .?"

I shook my head.

Descriptions followed. I kept shaking my head, and tried to stop the grin tugging at my face. I'd advised those women not to play dress up and spend their photo chits on Polaroids, the only photographic choice of the time, for male inmate pen pals they found through an incarcerated friend.

"Do you know what they do with those pictures?" I asked those women. "Do you want to be some inmate's fantasy? You can do better."

"She thinks they use our pictures to jerk off," one woman said.

"So?" said another. Some women didn't care. They were looking for attention, someone who could write a stimulating letter, and who could blame them? Days are long and nights lonely in prison. They bought photo-chits, a dollar per photo in those days, fussed with hair and makeup, and did things with their clothes to make them look good, sexy. I'd seen dozens of such pictures before they were sent off.

I studied those twenty-five men, all dressed in khaki, all clean and combed. Nice looking men, some close to my sons in age. When they entered the classroom and took seats they became my students, and I'd treat them with the same concern and respect I gave the women.

"No," I told those men, "I don't know any of those women."

One man snorted. "She knows them, but she's too smart to give anything up."

I walked to where he sat, dead center in the room. He'd been slumped in his seat, eyes down, when I took attendance, but he sat up straight now. He had light brown hair, sad brown eyes, and little resemblance to his badge photo.

"You're right," I said, "personal information remains private. I don't carry their names to the streets, as they say, and I won't abuse yours either. If they ask about any of you, I'll shake my head and say I don't know you."

He smiled, and some sadness left his eyes. Ted enrolled in the class because something troubled him, and he hoped I could help. I have a knack for reading need in faces and posture, in simple gestures and words. Those men were all there for a reason, but some hurt more than others.

We met in an ugly old classroom with battered chair-desks, a blackboard still dusty from haphazard erasing, evening sun baking dirt on windows that didn't open enough to air out cigarette breath. Stained acoustical tiles drooped from the ceiling; faded institution-yellow paint covered the walls, except where plaster chunks had chipped off. A scarred and bulky instructor's desk, gunmetal grey, stood front and center. I pushed against it with hip and thigh to get it out of my way. Men jumped to help, and shoved it into a far corner. Testosterone and male chivalry, I learned, often worked to a female teacher's benefit.

I wove through the narrow spaces created by those desk-chairs lined up in rows, five across, five deep, and cramped. "Spread out if you like. I'm going to wander around and get acquainted, put names with faces. Tell me about your children. Gender, ages. No names unless you choose. I know it's risky to say too much inside."

The air in the room changed as men relaxed. We spent the first hour in informal discussions of children and course content. By period movement at seven o'clock, I had a good sense of their needs and could begin to do my work on patterns in families. During the ten-minute break I wrote notes on the chalk board, almost a century old by then. One note, "About 75% of our parenting methods are those we unconsciously adopted from our parents or caregivers," stirred up conversations with those who hadn't left for break. Some itched to get their hands on the photocopied materials I'd stacked on the shoved-aside teacher's desk, but they waited. They were more polite and patient than most of my women students, but that may have been because we were on trial, in a sense. Those inmates would determine whether parenting and family classes would be added to the education schedule.

After break I distributed the photocopied material that would serve as their text, and a syllabus and notebook paper. Precious notebook paper, carefully guarded by education office staff. (I learned that night to bring in more paper for the writing tasks I assigned so they could write to children, caregivers, any person or agency involved with their families.)

We looked through the material, traditional positive parenting information I'd adapted from texts written for parents who lived with their children. I packaged it in ten chapters or units to fit the ten-week study/one-week-final format community colleges followed.

I explained Positive Parenting as a lecture/discussion course, and told them the more they discussed, the less I lectured, and the ten assignments, one due each week, was homework, not to be completed during class time.

Much of the education program at MICC, provided by Pierce College, the nearest community college, was self-paced in a learning-lab environment. A night class where all worked on the same topic at the same time, exchanged opinions and stories, talked out loud and even laughed, was a departure from the norm.

We went over the course syllabus. One man said, "You serious? Twenty-five percent of our grade's based on class participation?"

"Absolutely. That's as much as Pierce College would permit. This is a college course, so they get to call some shots. I hope it's one of the most important life courses you ever take. It's about your children." I am a staunch believer in the teaching power of discussion where students learn by forming and positing thoughts and questions. I returned to the board, pointed at the statement there. "It's about what *you* can do to change any negative parenting behaviors you picked up from those who reared you so *your* children don't use them when they're parents."

It's almost frightening how much angst an experienced teacher senses in her students. I could see all of them remembered unpleasant moments in their childhoods, and how they felt years later when they'd done the same thing to a child in their care. I spoke of something from my own experience. Self-disclosure, so important in teaching parenting and family classes, was imperative with this group. There was a strong possibility I'd been oversold to them. We needed common ground on which to connect as adults equal in humanity though distanced in so many other ways.

"We're not here to blame our parents for what we've become," I said. "We're here to learn about positive parenting. I believe parents do the best they can in their given circumstances. It's a difficult task most of us undertake without any formal training. We're here to remedy that."

Twenty-five men nodded. Ted was the first to trust me enough to disclose his personal struggles as a dad in prison. He spoke with pride and love of his two sons. Then his face changed, his chin dropped, and he slid down in his seat.

"Their mother changed their last name. She let some asshole move in with her. Told the boys he's their new dad, I'm a convict."

"Were you ever married to their mother?" I'd grown accustomed to marriage as the rare exception over the years I'd taught incarcerated women.

"Still am," Ted said. "She wants a divorce, but she's waiting until I get out so I can pay for it. Says the guy's adopting the boys."

The man in front of Ted turned around. "She's your legal old lady and she's got some other dude living with her? That's cold, man."

"Living with her, calling my boys his, living on support I send through my mom. I always supported my kids, I got money set aside, my mom helps some."

And so began the discussion part of the course, which veered from basic positive parenting skills to legalities. I drew on the *Parenting From a Distance* text I'd written, and on years of experience with incarcerated women, but I had to stick to the course I'd contracted to teach. I concluded neither Ted nor his wife understood much about family law.

Ted slumped deeper. "She's their mother, she takes care of them and all, she needs the money. It's not about the money. It's about my name."

The room went quiet. The men watched to see how I'd react. Would I shrug it off as many in the system did? Inmates often heard, "Sounds like a personal problem to me," or "Shoulda thought of that before you did the crime."

I went into lecture mode. Or perhaps I preached. "First, unless your parental rights have been legally terminated, your sons cannot be adopted." Ted's eyes showed he'd known that at some level, but fear blurs awareness. "Second, most schools require children's birth certificates to enroll them, and use the last name on their birth certificate, though teachers will sometimes bend to a parent's request."

Ted sat up a little. "I'm on their birth certificate. I was there when they were born." A hint of smile touched his sad brown eyes. "Doctor let me catch the younger one."

Such first-touch bonding is considered powerful, a strong deterrent to future child abuse, a strong tie for parents of the child. What had happened between Ted and his wife? Was she using the children as pawns now for her own gain or for revenge to further punish him? Rather than ask in class, I went with what I knew.

"You have several positives going for you. If you don't have a court order preventing you from contacting the children, you can check with the school about the names they're using. If you do . . ."

A man at the back of the room growled, "Oh, yeah, sure, he can just call them up, say 'Hey, Dude, what name my kids go by?'" All calls from Washington state prison inmates were made collect at that time, and the recipient is advised the caller is in prison.

"I don't have any orders against me," Ted said. "I never hurt those boys."

Except by going to prison, but I didn't say that. We would get to that reality soon enough.

Ted's eyes, and the eyes of every man in the room, were on me.

"I wouldn't recommend calling. I'd suggest a letter—an honest letter introducing yourself, your situation, your questions about their school progress. You have a right to do so."

Ted slumped again. "My wife says I gave up all my rights when I fell."

"Unless you signed a paper voluntarily giving up your parental rights, they're still intact, and so are your responsibilities, which include financial and emotional support."

Ted was shaking his head. He hadn't signed any such documents. At least twenty men were talking at once, building a raft of questions and floating it my way.

"Hey, guys, the course I've been hired to teach is positive parenting. If we get too far off task, you'll have more homework to do. I expect you to become familiar enough with the course material to spout sections of it to the MICC education counselor. I'm a contract employee; I walk a narrow line."

"We'll handle it, we'll handle everything you can give us."

"Man, it's about time somebody other than some old con said we had some rights."

"Anybody gives you any flack about this class, you let us know."

And so began parent education at McNeil Island Corrections Center. Twenty-five men completed the course with high grades. Many of them took several other courses with me through ensuing quarters. Ted, whose crimes were drug related, took every class I taught, some more than once.

Those twenty-five dads or step-dads had over fifty children waiting for them to come home. Over fifty children there, seventy-six in one class one quarter during my career, and over two million nationwide at that time.

I explained that the state must have clear and cogent reasons to file for termination of parental rights, and the parent must be given due process in the form of legal representation and a court hearing. Though incarceration could be declared child abandonment, which is considered clear and cogent, it's rarely used. I'd been through it enough times with incarcerated mothers to know. Most inmate parents go home to their families, their children. That fact remains my strongest argument for teaching parenting inside prison fences. It benefits the children.

As for Ted, he had legal and emotional rights to the benefits of a relationship with his sons, but the relationship was defined by his incarceration. He needed his wife's cooperation, or a court order, to so much as talk to them on the phone. Ted, like many incarcerated parents (fathers more often than mothers) had given in to a sense of powerlessness. His children suffered for it. With his new understanding of parental rights and responsibilities, he took the risk of contacting his sons' school.

Getting information about children's school records and performance can be a long and humbling process but many inmate-parents have undertaken it with satisfactory results. There were those in the general populace outside prison who didn't think inmates should have such rights, and criticized me for teaching and writing guidelines for contacting school officials. But many teachers have thanked me. Most school administrators and teachers want to hear from incarcerated parents, if the parents contact them in an appropriate manner. They understand the emotional and scholastic impact an incarcerated parent has on a child, and welcome an open and honest relationship with the parent. Still, schools must err on the side of caution when information is requested by anyone. Parents have to show proof of the relationship. Those incarcerated generally have to get a notarized affidavit about their crime and sentence from the prison administration.

The principal of the school Ted's sons attended was pleased to hear from him. Ted's wife wasn't so pleased, but it did generate more open communication between them. She sent Ted a letter ordering him to call her. He wrote down things he wanted to say. He told her it hurt him when he learned she threw out the letters he wrote to the boys. Then he said, "They'll find out. Someday they'll find out."

He told me later he knew it was a threat, and it bothered him. On the scale of threats from prison, that one wouldn't cause a ping.

Before the quarter ended, Ted's wife started giving their boys the letters Ted wrote, and agreed they could accompany their grandmother (Ted's mother) to visit. The boys wrote back. The first-grader printed his name and drew a picture of himself. The third-grader said he played T-ball, and wanted his dad to come home to help him.

Ted, and all the experimental class students, gained information they had a right and responsibility to have. For the remainder of his incarceration, Ted wrote to his sons every week, and sent them things he made: cards, small puzzles, simple crafts that were part of parenting course work. He left MICC once for work release, got sent back for a dirty UA, and spent some time berating himself. According to him, he'd smoked one joint. "Stupid," he said. On his return to prison, he was housed at the MICC Annex, then an honor camp, which gave some credibility to his claim. He worked construction on the fifty-plus island homes during the day, and came inside the main institution for whatever class I taught at night. Annex students were subjected to strip-searches to come inside. "If they want to look at me naked, let 'em," Ted said, "if it means I get to keep being a dad."

Teachers often don't know if they've made an impact on students. Ted said he'd keep me informed when he got out, and called when he was back in court over child custody. He was divorced by then. Yes, he paid the court costs.

"Me and my ex are still duking it out over child custody and visitation," he said. (Remember, I taught parenting, not English.) "The boys like spending time with me, which pisses her off. The court wants verification of my parenting classes and grades, even though I gave my attorney everything. He says he needs a deposition."

Ted had given his attorney the parenting and family course syllabi, graded papers, official college transcripts, and a record of when he sent cards and letters to his sons. His attorney called me, said it looked good, and took my recorded statement. Then the judge called, swore me in on the phone, and listened to my testimony.

Ted called a few days later. "I got shared custody, liberal visitation rights, and the boys keep their names." He laughed, sniffed a couple times, laughed again.

I sniffed, too, and still do when I remember Ted's joy at being reunited with his boys.

Ted's story is a nice one for a prison teacher to be able to tell. It was an easy case. Ted was legally married to the boys' mother when they were born. He'd financially supported the family until he went to jail and most of the time he was incarcerated. His crimes, all drug-use related, were low on the seriousness level of the state's criminal code. He had a supportive mother. All in all, Ted was a decent sort who got into drugs and learned a hard lesson.

One last note on the experimental class: Someone at Pierce College questioned me about the official grade sheet. Where was the curve? How could every student do superior work?

What could I say? Parenting and family courses are not filled with absolutes—problems with only one correct answer. I didn't deduct points for spelling, punctuation, or grammar. They were outstanding students, all twenty-five of them, including those who'd received pictures of my women students, and used school notebook paper to write sexy letters. They earned their grades; I just recorded them, and replenished paper in the education office.

| Project Social Responsibility – MICC |

Welcome to Project Social Responsibility, an innovative 20-hour prison orientation program that tested education premises and demonstrated the value of involving students in the learning process through open classroom discussion. The success of the parenting experiment helped prepare McNeil Island staff for the undertaking, which was offered by the education department with participation of personnel from all areas of the institution. Then Associate Superintendent Alice Payne, with whom I had worked at the women's prison, and then Education Director Tom Rabak called the program PSR and asked me to serve as its coordinator and to facilitate the segments related to family and community relationships. The project also addressed basic education requirements, employment preparation, and physical and mental health issues.

An intensified case management program developed at DOC headquarters was being enacted at the same time, and dovetailed with PSR. Counseling staff members were already coping with an inmate population explosion that had resulted in overcrowding with as many as ten men in four-man cells. We knew the logistics of Project Social Responsibility would be met with resistance, but

William Callahan, then MICC Superintendent who wanted to see reform during his tenure, stood firm. He said, "I will not warehouse men," signed off on the project, and declared it mandatory for every man on every new chain. Chains arrived at McNeil Island on Thursdays, came to the education floor on Friday for a brief overview of the week ahead and returned on Monday, most often angry to a man.

We undertook planning Project Social Responsibility with two major goals in mind. We wanted inmates to reexamine their crime related behavior through critical thinking and introspection, and we wanted them to set goals for their time inside that would help prepare them for release. That's what we stated in our program overview, and that's what I continually restated in words that made sense to men whose education level ranged from below fourth grade to college graduate. The men needed to know what we were talking about.

When I look back at our program overview, I recall our struggle to meet college department requirements for measurable objectives, and pre- and post-test results that could be cited in evaluation forms. The college was awarding participants continuing education credits and course completion certificates that would be recorded in their permanent DOC record. That, in turn, could make a difference to case management when men registered for classes or sought employment inside prison. It could be considered by the parole board at six-month hearings, or when they applied for early release. It could factor into getting extended visitation privileges with family members.

I discovered that inmates were more confused about the critical thinking concept than about introspection, once I'd offered synonyms for that long word. Self-analysis worked for some of the men, soul-searching or looking inside your heart worked for others. I almost always ended up drawing Five Feelings Faces on the board ... Sad, Mad, Glad, Scared and Lonely ... and explained that introspection required looking back on events that brought on those feelings. They could see that introspection required thinking, and agreed that it would quite likely be critical thinking. Good enough for a starting point. We would have them think critically about several general topics during the week. We would also have them read along, listen to and discuss the George Orwell essay, "Shooting an Elephant." There's more on that and the critical thinking concept in Chapter 13.

Our second stated program objective was to assist inmate students in setting their own goals for their incarceration and their reintegration into society. That met the expectations of DOC for Program Managers, Unit Supervisors, and Primary Counselors. Education staff reported that they often heard inmate students say they didn't know their primary counselor's name. The exploding prison population had created large caseloads that made it easy for some inmates to avoid meeting with their primary counselor, and thus avoid educational programming or taking a prison job. When confronted, the inmate transferred responsibility onto the living unit staff. PSR changed that. Appointments with counselors/case managers were scheduled for the week following completion of the program. In most cases, the inmate students registered for classes on Friday afternoon of PSR week.

We knew some of the men would be nearing the end of long prison sentences, arriving at MICC as transferees from close custody or maximum security facilities. They subscribed to the old convict code, the stuff prison movies use to let audiences know who really runs the joint. Old cons don't do "mandatory." They're doing prison, get out of their way, leave them alone, but make sure the chow's good, there's plenty of yard time, the phones are working, and mail gets delivered six days a week. "Orientation?" they said. "To prison? Five days straight? Twenty hours? Man, this place sucks." Most of them used somewhat more colorful language.

I soon discovered that dealing with old cons routed through PSR to their new confines in what was yet another old prison was easier than cajoling DOC and education staff to participate in the program's delivery. Staff comments were more printable, but no less contemptuous. I faced a complex challenge.

The launch of PSR came shortly after three highly publicized horrendous crimes committed by men at work release facilities, and a full-blown riot at the state penitentiary in Walla Walla. The tax-paying populace, fired up by politicians using the news for their own ends, demanded that the Department of Corrections get tough on crime. PSR was broad and futuristic in its approach to preparing incarcerated felons for reentry to society. It sent the message to all who entered the confines of MICC that doing time wasn't about playing cards, watching TV and buffing up on the weight pile. It was goal oriented. Slackers wouldn't be tolerated, and getting sent back from the island to another facility would include a serious infraction and probably loss of Good Time.

Those old cons, accustomed to running things at the penitentiary, were now housed with young streetwise toughs from low-income, inner-city areas where they sold drugs and generally did the rip-and-run. They joined forces with their homies who were already inside to stake their claim to prison territory. They were a different breed with a different attitude.

Sprinkle in some white-collar offenders, some domestic abusers, some vehicular homicide convictions, stir them up and confine them in a medium custody prison on an island in Puget Sound, keep them in lock-step Chain Day (Thursday) and Orientation Day (Friday) while they hone their attitude. Warn them to stay cool over the weekend, round them up again on Monday morning, deliver them to Education, and give them one week to figure out how they're going to make prison work toward release and reintegration into a society that would just as soon throw away the key.

Therein rested the crux of my job: show them how to use prison time to prepare for successful reintegration into the real world. I was no longer just the Parenting Teacher, my favorite role. I was now Project Social Responsibility Coordinator and Chief Confronter of Attitude at McNeil Island Corrections Center. I met every chain on Friday, right behind the sergeant who said, "Listen up. It's mandatory. You mess up, you go to the hole, when you get out you go to PSR. Simple as that."

I met them again Monday morning, and delivered eight hours of the twenty they spent in the week-long program. I earned a reputation early on as being tough but fair, opinionated but interesting, old but not bad-looking. Looks are relative anywhere, especially in prison. Some called me the teacher with white hair; others the silver fox. No matter their games and cons, they didn't get much past me. I'd taught female felons for eleven years by that time—a good training ground. Every corrections officer I met who had worked with both female and male felons said dealing with men was "a piece of cake" after coping with "the ladies."

I had help: twenty-nine MICC staff members from DOC and Education, plus inmate teaching assistants (TAs) chosen for their prison moxie, education test scores, and ability to translate for the growing Spanish-speaking population. TAs are critically important in prison classrooms. Many could do the teaching, and with tightening education dollars they managed more of those responsibilities. My first PSR teaching assistant, Rafael Gomez, spoke fluent Spanish and English, and was a decent and gentle man who knew his way around the system. Inside the fence there are some things only inmates can accomplish. He served as a role model for new inmates without losing the respect of the old cons; he often kept me from going into orbit.

Mr. Gomez was doing time for domestic violence, stabbing his wife in a fit of jealousy. He was respected by other inmates for "being the man," and for "keeping his woman in line." In the months he served as PSR teaching assistant I never saw or heard a whisper of violence, and wouldn't have known of his crime had he not chosen to tell me. He's Hispanic; I would have guessed drug-related crimes, a stereotype. He made it his personal quest to read all the educational materials I had on hand for the project and the parenting and family courses I taught. He often asked for extra copies of project materials to use with guys back in the cellblocks who had been at MICC before Project Social Responsibility got underway. He said he was working to earn forgiveness from his wife and family, but he didn't belabor the point. He was a dedicated worker, not a whiner.

Mr. Gomez calmed my nerves after tough sessions, straightened the room, cleaned the blackboard, helped the Spanish speaking men get through the program, set up files, kept up with the mounds of paper work, brought me ice water he got from a kitchen connection, decorated the classroom with odd bits of things he or I procured, watered plants, and found containers for flowers I brought from home. He had a certain dignity, an appreciation for niceties that created a pleasant atmosphere in the classroom. I don't know where he found vases inside an old prison, but once he brought them to our room we kept them there, and I tried to keep them filled. It made a difference. Mr. Gomez made a difference. I could rely on a subtle smile, nod, or look in his eyes when the going got rough.

We started Monday morning of PSR week with a session on roles, rules, and individual responsibility. There men sat in state-issued khaki pants and shirts, white T-shirt showing, khaki jacket draped over the back of the chair, khaki watch cap stuffed into a pocket, khaki belt cinched if the pants were too large.

Someone always said, "Roles? We're inmates, that's our role." Generally they said "fucking inmates," and "fucking role," to which I'd raise my eyebrow before saying, "And students," thus provoking the first argument of the day. Not all saw themselves as students, even though they'd signed a Pierce College registration form and wanted the promised certificate of completion and course credits for this mandatory program.

We built a list from there. Son, father, brother, uncle, husband or partner, lover, employee—the list went on. When I said lover, they narrowed their eyes. They wanted to see what I said as much as hear it. They listened when I talked about showing love from a distance. Some scoffed, but they listened. I suspect they hadn't met many women inside the system who talked about emotional intimacy versus phone sex, a staple of prison life. Some blushed. Sometimes I blushed. I'm Scandinavian; it's easy to tell when my face reddens.

In Washington State, all male inmates enter the system at Washington Corrections Center (WCC) in Shelton, an old lumber town now sprouting new shops and restaurants, a nice change for families and friends visiting men housed there. The men go through intensive testing and review for classification before being assigned to the prison where they'll start serving their time. Classification is the point system process that determines an inmate's custody status. They start with points based on their crime, earn points by programming, lose points if they get infractions. Too few points, custody is closed, and the man is sent to an intensive management or close-custody prison with fewer privileges, closer surveillance, and little movement within the facility.

Many of the men who went through PSR started their time with medium custody status for short to mid-range sentences of three to seven years, but there were a fair number on restricted minimum status; their points were high but they still had too much time left to qualify for an honor camp or minimum custody facility placement. They'd been convicted of more serious crimes, had done time at a maximum security institution, and were getting closer to release. Some of them had been around, seen it all, and after verbal expressions of displeasure, employed nonverbal tactics meant to intimidate mere mortals such as teachers. When they couldn't stare me down, they turned and stared out the windows. I left what some presenters considered the safety of the lectern and made my way to their desk-chairs, crouching down if necessary, to make eye contact and start some non-threatening dialogue.

"What do you see out there? Deer browsing just outside the fence? Lucky deer, come and go as they please."

Invariably someone snickered. A snicker beats a sneer every time. I prowled the room, looked at badges, made comments based on DOC numbers, posture, attempts to push desk-chairs through the back wall, or drag them out the door into the hallway. All my antics and delays were designed to give the teeming testosterone time to settle.

Sometimes, to rouse curiosity, gain empathy, or get their eyes off the clock's hands, I related one of my early MICC experiences. "I was in the main corridor waiting to go through Key Control when someone tapped me on the shoulder and said, 'Let me see your badge.' I turned, expecting a security officer, and found a man in civilian clothes, reeking of cigarettes, and glowering. 'I thought so,' he said. 'Yellow badge, bleeding heart, nose-wiping, do-gooder. You ought to go back to teaching kindergarten.' Actually, he said kiddie garden. Then he postured for a group of onlookers. He discounted my worth without knowing me. Just for the record, I don't wipe noses, but Mr. Gomez does keep toilet paper in the classroom for that purpose in case any of us need it."

They generally laughed, and someone almost always said, "Dude in the story's a dumb fuck." I'd agree, ignore language or sometimes frown, and we'd carry on.

Most of the men newer to the system were more cooperative than the old cons. New inmates had just suffered the inertia of jail, and then the restrictions of WCC's Receiving unit where they went through psychological tests and health probes done with army-like sensitivity. They were ready to settle somewhere and make the best they could of a bad situation. Getting settled meant more privileges, including visitation and phone calls, recreation, education, and possibly a job that would let them buy from Store: tobacco and papers when smoking was still permitted inside; candy, chips and soda, and better quality personal hygiene items than those provided by the state.

Rigidity does not succeed in education, parenting, or any viable relationship. We were trying to lay a foundation with the men in PSR to garner their cooperation, a process DOC's case management required. Abandonment, rigidity's opposite, was another problem we needed to counter in PSR to make the program succeed. Prison is a rigid environment where many feel (and frequently have been) abandoned by society at large, and all too often by family and friends who find maintaining a relationship too emotionally taxing.

Imagine someone you love in prison. Imagine a relatively short sentence of sixty months, with one-third off for good behavior. The person will do forty months in a corrections facility. How many of approximately twelve-hundred days will you subject yourself to the stress of prison visiting? How many collect phone calls will you accept? How often will you write a letter?

I've seen the pain, not just the anger, of those locked away. I've shielded crying men from others' eyes. Still, I never forgot my students came to the classroom and program via criminal acts. It was my job to help them learn how to make better choices, not to coddle them.

After the first two hours with a new group, the entire PSR team met to discuss behavior patterns I'd observed, possible problems, what parts of our vast curriculum might be most helpful, what might meet the most resistance. We learned early on that even the toughest old cons were impressed by the number and status of presenters who came to them: associate superintendents, correctional program managers, security captain, lieutenants, sergeants, correctional officers, prison job coordinator, grievance coordinator, disciplinary hearings officer, education director, academic and vocational teachers, education support staff, living unit supervisors and unit counselors, psychiatric social worker, chemical dependency counselor, hospital staff, chapel staff.

They were warmed up to the notion of classroom discussion by the time an associate superintendent came in to talk about the institution's expectations of them. Even the toughest cons admitted they were surprised someone would come down out of the ivory tower, interact with them with respect, listen to them, answer their questions, and try to learn their names. A small thing, you may think, but in education it's often the small thing, the seemingly insignificant moment, that matters the most. In prison the impact is increased two-fold, ten-fold, maybe even a hundred-fold. Inmates have been condemned for their criminal acts. Most of them need reminders, often just simple indications, of their own humanity.

They sat up straighter, but went silent, when the shift lieutenant entered. Those in khaki do not trust those in blue, and Lieutenant

Burton had a tough-guy persona earned by performance of his duties. He'd grown up in the projects of a Pittsburgh suburb, fought in Korea and Vietnam, and worked at McNeil Island when it was still a federal prison. He'd strut across the front of the old classroom, point his finger, spout clichés, and say, "Equal worth as humans does not mean equal power in every situation," a line he'd heard me say and adopted as his own. The men listened and nodded. It was an important concept, and worked better coming from another male—one with power. They needed to see me as a Pierce College instructor, not as the law.

The lieutenant and I started out on a bad note over his finger pointing habit, and his general resentment of the extra work the program caused his officers. He whipped up his arm like he was drawing a gun, pointed his finger, crooked it once, and the pointee came as if lassoed. I'd been advised to get the lieutenant on board our PSR team, get him to drop in at least long enough to show the men we had his support, but aim for making him a regular presenter.

I was in the corridor, the prison's main artery, dashing from a meeting with the associate superintendent to Education, when the lieutenant and I had our set-to. I had a parenting class to teach in five minutes and wanted to grab a few bites of lunch, use the restroom, and find the proper stack of materials to haul to whichever classroom was available. The shift lieutenant's office was across the corridor from the stairs to Education. The corridor officer saw me coming and walked to the stairwell door, key in hand to let me through. She'd be announcing Period Movement in a matter of minutes. Lieutenant Burton strolled into the corridor, pointed at me, crooked his finger, and sauntered back toward his office.

"The lieutenant wants you," the CO said.

"I don't respond to beckoning fingers. I have a name." I knew he could hear me. If I'd addressed him directly, he'd have heard a good deal more.

She frowned, but unlocked the door. "It's not a good idea to ignore the lieutenant."

"Maybe not for you, but I work for Pierce College, not the lieutenant."

I was halfway up the stairs, on the first landing, when I heard him call my name. I turned and glared, and forgot all my resolve not to get into a power struggle. "Do not ever point your finger at me. I consider it demeaning."

He nodded, and laughed a contagious laugh. "Jan, will you please come to my office for a minute?"

I was Jan, he was Lt. Burton. Condescending, now. He held the power. I declined, with what seemed a reasonable excuse.

"I have a two-hour class to teach, and I haven't had lunch."

"It will only take a minute."

I was on the spot. The project needed him, one female officer was watching (and grinning, but he couldn't see her), and several male officers had gathered in the corridor. Where had they been? Had our exchange gone out on their radios? I started back down the steps, vowing I would not continue if he turned his back and left me to follow. He waited, and while he waited he pointed his finger at one of the male officers.

"You, go on up to Education and meet her class so she can eat her lunch."

That's how it's done. The officer reared back, stunned. "Me? Teach her class?"

"Did I say teach her class? Or did I say meet her class? Take attendance. You can handle that, right?"

"Right, LT, right."

Students in our program answered much the same way when the lieutenant spoke to them. He'd give them his lieutenant look. "I'll bet most of you have said, 'Sometimes a man's gotta do what a man's gotta do.' Am I right?" He'd get nods. "Well, it's the same with the system. My officers gotta do what they gotta do. You follow the rules, you'll be okay. They jack you up for something you don't have coming, you let me know. They nail you when you're out of line, don't come whining to me. Take it like a man. Right?"

"Right, LT, right."

Who but a black lieutenant with a tough-guy reputation could have accomplished so much with such a simple speech? His presence on Monday morning told those men MICC security sanctioned the program, but some of the things he said made me cringe. Cringe and grin, too. Something about those men got to him. He agreed to help with the afternoon program. I'm not certain what made him give in and decide to join us, but have long suspected he liked how I dealt with him, and with inmates.

On his Monday morning forays into the classroom he'd say, "This program's mandatory, but that doesn't make it *all* bad. I've been listening to her and I've learned a lot." He'd point at me and then at them. "You listen up, you might get something out of this."

On that note he'd stroll to the classroom door, stop and point at the men. "I'll be back this afternoon."

Most of us on the team gave it our all. We played up the status of presenters from the associate superintendent and shift lieutenant, and other staff who generally weren't seen on the education floor. We reminded those men they would return to their families and communities, where they'd associate with people who'd never seen the inside of a prison, and who had little empathy for offenders.

Wind blew onto the island from Puget Sound, hummed through the concertina wire atop the fences, and set the rhythm for our work. Week after week we performed our Project Social Responsibility dance for a new crowd, a new chain that gathered at the cellhouse sergeant's desk when the intercom crackled to life and a voice announced, "Period movement, period movement."

We perfected our performance over the weeks and months. As one experienced teacher said, we landed on the education floor running and danced as fast as we could.

11

| Chain Day – MICC |

Seeing a person in shackles still makes me shudder and look away. Shackling men together in a chain dehumanizes them. I needed to see men arriving on McNeil Island as a chain to better understand what they went through on their way to the PSR classroom. During the program planning stage and the trial run first session, Pierce College sent a videographer to the island to create a film that would introduce the PSR concept to other prisons in the state. The film opened with Chain Day, the day men transferred to the island from other prisons. In those years, they traveled by bus to Steilacoom, and by the regular McNeil Island ferry on the 8:40 a.m. run. They arrived in orange coveralls, fully chained for their transfer.

The film crew, the MICC associate superintendent overseeing the project, the education director and I waited at the dock for the ferry carrying the new chain. The men had agreed be filmed without their faces appearing in the video.

The event imprinted on my brain just as it was being recorded on film.

The Chain waits until other passengers have disembarked and headed for their work stations or homes. When it's their turn the

Chain moves like a giant orange centipede, down the ramp from the ferry's gaping port-side-door, onto the float; across the float and up the long gangplank onto the dock; along the dock and up the sidewalk, single-file, in perfect step to keep from tripping. Hands cuffed at their waist fronts and connected by chain to the waist back ahead; ankles cuffed, connected, clinking against planks and then cement. Officers with them, fore and aft; officers watching from the towers; officers waiting at R & D. Receiving and Delivery.

The videographer caught the contrast: the beauty of Puget Sound with sunlight reflected back from its surface; the long pier jutting out from the rocky McNeil Island shore, the float and creosote-covered pilings, the ferry cutting a wide swath and making a perfect portside landing. Pristine, snow-clad Mount Rainier in the distance, looming above a black-green forest. Orange coverall-clad men in body chains.

We used the film with PSR groups and in professional gatherings when we presented the program for other institutions' consideration. A couple weeks later I met a chain where the video left off so I could have a complete picture of Chain Day.

Gates and doors open for them, clang shut behind, until they're inside the basement R & D room where processing begins. Receiving and Delivery. Processing. A commodity. Words carry clout.

The men are cold or hot, depending on the weather and the idiosyncrasies of an old building's heating system. Their wrists and ankles are sore; their arms, legs and backs strained; their sweat and breath rancid. They need haircuts. They need the restroom.

An officer produces a key, starts unlocking chains. What does he feel as he frees those individuals from their bondage to all the others? Another officer collects the chains, keeps them from tangling. They clank, produce an odd rhythm. I hear it as discordant plunking on a cheap guitar.

There are brown folding chairs arranged for the men. An officer orders them to sit.

"Man, I need to piss."

A thumb is jerked, indicating a restroom. "Make it quick, we're running late here."

There are twenty-one men in orange coveralls, most rubbing first one wrist and then the other. There are a handful of officers—one sergeant, the rest line-staff. There's me, in a navy-blue tailored suit, skirt below my knees, and navy pumps; my conservative outfit for such an austere occasion. I've been ordered to be here, to see how it works. I'm out of place, worse than a voyeur. I've seen enough, but don't leave. I'm introduced; I nod and smile. I want to close my eyes. My chest is tight with empathy but also with memory of a time I'd come close to acting a fool over being chained. I think about Orwell. In a few days I'll be reading his essay to this group. Will I tell them how I felt at this moment?

Somewhere there are mothers wondering about their sons, and how they're being treated on this day, their transport day from the Washington Corrections Center at Shelton to the McNeil Island Corrections Center.

Somewhere there are victims wondering about their victimizers, and how they're being treated on this day . . .

I think about them, and swallow. It sounds loud, my swallowing.

If the group arriving together each Thursday was referred to as the Chain, then it made sense to me, a humanist, that the men be viewed as links, as individuals, which they surely became again as those chains were unlocked and collected. They were, of course: I/M Doe, J, #123456, C321-2. Inmate John Doe, number 123456, living unit C, room number 321, bed number two, or upper bunk.

Their numbers weren't tattooed on their bodies, just on their psyches.

I've had the chain-list since the day before, and have reviewed the names and numbers. Names tell me nothing; not age, not ethnicity, not criminal background. Numbers tell me more. Much more. In

Washington State the Sentencing Reform Act, enacted July 1, 1984, changed how criminal justice operated, and how time was meted out. The DOC started issuing six-digit numbers beginning with 9. Numbers beginning with 9 indicated new guidelines, no indeterminate sentences based on a judge's experience, sense, or whim. Determinate sentencing follows the grid.

The system ran out of 9 numbers by 1990, and started using 7. Most old guidelines inmates, those sentenced before July 1, 1984, and still in the system or back with violations or new charges, have six-digits beginning with 2. Now and then I saw a 1, and once a 0. Someone's grandfather, in the system longer than forever, waiting to die.

There are also men whose inmate number begins with 6, which tells me they first did time in a Washington State juvenile facility. For some, the system is the only parent they've known.

The chain is seated now. The sergeant grabs a clipboard with the chain list, and calls out their last names and numbers.

"Here, here, here . . ." They've been told how to answer; "Yo," and grunts are not acceptable. Their eyes are on the floor, some voices barely audible.

They're given cell and bed assignments, printed rules and regulations, routine orders about where to report next, where they'll get their ish.

Ish. Their state issued khaki pants and button-front shirts; their underwear and socks, and one red bandana; their watch cap and cheap tennis shoes; a bar of soap, a comb or hair-pick, and a toothbrush. (With the influx of gangs, the institution stopped issuing red bandanas. They have khaki ones now.)

"What about our personal property?" asks an inmate.

"It's on its way," the sergeant says.

"When do we get it?"

"When it gets here."

Their property—the few possessions they've been allowed in

prison—is somewhere else. It never arrives with them. In some cases it never arrives. Period. There are always tort claims for lost or stolen property being filed and investigated. A man takes a good leather jacket to prison, or a cashmere sweater, or just a pair of jeans that fit. Something special to wear on visiting day. It disappears.

"When's it expected?" The question is ignored.

"What about the money on our books? That come with us?"

"Listen up," the sergeant says. "I don't want to repeat any of this. Your property gets here when it gets here. Your money gets on your books when it gets on your books. This is how we do things at McNeil Island. We go through the rules with you, we get you assigned, we get the hospital staff in to answer questions, we get you fed. You do as you're told. You go to gym or yard if your unit's called to go. Otherwise, you stay put. I don't want any of you getting written up before you get started. Is that clear?" He waits for nods. "Tomorrow morning and every morning next week you report to 3/4 cellhouse sergeant at 0830 hours for escort to the education floor for orientation. Unit counselor here will tell you more about that. You'll see more of Ms. Walker in orientation. Anybody decides to get out of orientation by messing up and going to the hole this weekend goes through orientation when he gets back in population. It's mandatory, order of the superintendent. Any questions so far?"

They shake their heads without looking up. It's time for me to leave.

Over my years at McNeil, men told me Chain Day is one of the worst days they experience. Most want to get their state issued gear and bedding, and flop on their bunk. If they're lucky, their cellmates won't hassle them, and they can escape into sleep. More than a few say they've thought about the Big Sleep on Chain Day.

I climbed the stairs from R & D to the main corridor, pushed the button to summon an officer, and waited to be let out of one secure area so I could enter another. Lieutenant Burton happened by and unlocked for me. Or perhaps he'd been there, waiting for this moment.

"What did you think?" he asked, his hazel eyes dancing. I always found those eyes in that brown face intriguing. Whose genes gave him those eyes? He could read what I thought about seeing the chain go through their introduction to the island, and found some delight in my misery. We'd become friends—wary friends, I'd say, neither of us quite certain the other should be trusted. My rational, compassionate arguments butted heads with his rational, tough law and order arguments.

"It's demeaning, demoralizing. I'm depressed."

He unleashed his deep laugh, and one of his clichés. "They didn't get here by singing too loud in the church choir."

"No, but how they got here is a long story, isn't it? One that started early in childhood. They all have a life story; they've all internalized a sense of being bad, no good, worthless . . ."

"Whoa, whoa, whoa, you don't know that."

He was wrong; I did and do know. Studies of criminal behavior show the majority of people who commit the most serious crimes were battered and abused, and internalized self-hatred by the time they were five or six. If they had a balance, even one person who saw worth in them, it might have been enough to keep them from the criminal path. But too often the battered and abused child acts out his anger and hurt at school, and gets in trouble. Teachers and administrators deal with the problem all the time. Too often they can't get the child's family to intervene so they must remove the child from the classroom and possibly from the school.

The Family History and Patterns course I taught helped inmates identify such patterns and pull the loose thread that unraveled their history to the point where they saw how it began. I believe we can use information and knowledge of conditioned behavior patterns to do more to deter crime. I believe this information should enter into every person's critical thinking. My beliefs are not borne of a bleeding heart liberal teacher's do-gooder confusion. My training and expertise are in child and family studies, my experience solid and growing—still growing even now as I write. And I am not alone. Researchers at major universities are writing articles and books citing statistics about the problems children of incarcerated parents face and positing theories about the damage that will be carried forward into the next generation and the next after that.

I saw the patterns in my classrooms: mother and daughter; father and son; mother and two daughters at WCCW and the same woman's son at MICC; men at MICC who named a woman at WCCW and before I could say I didn't know the woman they'd say, "She's my sister," and tell me what they knew about me from talking with her.

Every man on every chain had a story. Most of them would rather spend their prison time in solitary confinement than tell. Things brought to light get into records. When you are incarcerated you don't trust, don't feel, don't tell. You build a wall and hide behind it until you hear your child is in trouble at school or using drugs or stealing cigarettes. Then you know it's time to tear down the wall. But how?

It was my job to help each of them find a way so they could begin preparing for their reentry into society. That was the goal of Project Social Responsibility. All of the men on this chain I watched get unshackled will go back out to their families and communities once they have done their time. They will be our neighbors; their children will be our children and grandchildren's schoolmates and teammates.

In the second decade of the 21st century, over 650,000 ex-offenders are being released from prison each year. They need community support to reintegrate. Those most likely to succeed are those who used their time inside to complete academic and vocational programs, and who reached out to their children to help them stay out of the prison pipeline.

12

| The Chain Unlinked |

Chain lists and daily attendance rosters listed inmates by last name, first initial, DOC number and living unit. DOC personnel took attendance with last name and number as a standard practice, often with annoyance in their tone. As part of my determination to treat inmates like students, I made an effort to put names with faces, and to learn first names, during the first two PSR hours on Monday morning. It took more time than barking out a name and number, but it let me observe them for clues to their group dynamic. Some men liked being asked, and even smiled as they responded. Some got into their "Who wants to know" or "Who cares" attitude. I cared, and moved to stand or kneel by desks of the most reticent until I had eye contact. "I want to know your name."

Every chain developed a group personality, some memorable enough to be discussed for weeks. Though the men came from different prisons and diverse backgrounds, they were representative of the state's prison population as a whole. Men of color are disproportionately represented in prisons across the country, and that was true of every chain arriving at McNeil Island. We grew accustomed to young black males from inner-city gangs, Hispanic men with limited or no English skills, older men—black and white—nearing the end of long sentences, and others who fit none of those definitions making up any given group. Because the program was mandatory by the superintendent's edict, we worked to make the information and material presented meaningful to all.

The smallest chain—only eleven men, not the twenty to twenty-five we usually met—earned the label of "most fragmented." They arrived in the bleakness of winter when flu running rampant in the prison had reduced DOC staff to a minimum. Mr. Gomez was out sick, as was the shift lieutenant.

Eleven unlinked individuals trooped in to the PSR classroom, anger seeping from every pore. Five of them slumped into desk chairs across the back of the room and stretched their legs to block that aisle; two took window-side seats and fixed their gazes on the distance; one sat door-side, fourth row back, head down; one absolute center, hands folded; two front and center, side-by-side, chairs pulled too close.

Had the shift lieutenant been there, he might have said, "Actions speak louder than words. One picture is worth a thousand words." He most certainly would have told them to sit up straight and reminded them they needed to show respect for others if they wished to be treated with respect.

The group included one Hispanic surname, quite obviously one of the two men in the front. He looked very young. I hoped the man beside him spoke Spanish, and was sitting close to help him understand the materials in the packet I'd distributed. When Mr. Gomez was present, he sat with the non-English speaking men and gave them verbal and nonverbal clues to help them follow the instruction. I believe he also offered a measure of comfort in a new and strange setting.

We were having a Pacific Northwest day—cold rain, curling fog. Most of the men wore jackets though their trip from the cellhouse was a dry one. They were buffered against something else. Why hadn't someone called fog-line? (Fog-line halts inmate movement to programs and most workstations, beefs up perimeter checks, and gives teachers a little extra time to prepare lessons, grade papers, use the restroom.)

I took a deep breath, introduced myself, asked the men to answer roll call with their first names. Some did; some grunted to show their disgust with the mandatory program. The Hispanic man, whom I will call Alano Diaz, said, "No hablo inglés," and grinned. "Alano," the man beside him said, and placed a protective hand on Alano's arm. The toucher was perhaps ten years older.

I stared at the hand until it moved. We all knew the rules: no touching. I asked if he spoke Spanish.

He shook his head. "Nope."

I looked at the clock. Eight-forty-five. I'd be alone with this group until 10:30, and again from 12:30 to 2:30. Maybe a plea for help in the 10:30 meeting would bail me out. Maybe not, with so many out sick.

I distributed folders, paper and pencils, the program schedule— all things Mr. Gomez handled. "Our bilingual clerk is on sick call." I said. "I'll do the best I can."

"Sheeiit."

My eyes narrowed and held the speaker's—one of the men at the back. "I wouldn't be surprised, I hear it's a nasty flu." He got the message, gave me a belated grin. It didn't ease the tension in the room.

I turned a desk chair around so it faced them, and sat. "Okay, let's hear it. Tell me what other than the usual prison complaints is bothering you."

The older man of the two seated in front thought Alano should be excused from the group since he couldn't understand a word I was saying. I heard a similar request every week; it opened a door for me.

"I'm not authorized to excuse students. Take it up with the cellhouse sergeant when you go back at 10:30." It wouldn't change anything, but it told them who had authority in the matter. I scanned the room. "Next?"

Most of the others spoke, several at once. They had places to go, things to do, jobs to try for. I nodded, restated their gripes with expletives deleted, a concept I taught in positive parenting classes, empathized with their frustrations, kept my own to myself. They got most of it out. It had been a miserable trip from Shelton, where they'd been held in restricted units too long. An extremely unpleasant officer greeted them on arrival at the island. They were stuck in cells with men who snored all night. And farted.

"We been jerked around since Thursday, and we're tired of it, man."

I nodded again. "I understand, but I'm not the Man, not the person who can do anything about those concerns. I'm a Pierce College instructor. Coordinating this program and teaching some of the sessions is my job, and I'm going to give it my best."

While I spoke Alano tore a piece of notebook paper into quarters. I shook my head at him. The man beside him leaned in close and whispered, "Shh." A gust rattled the windows just then, and men laughed. It had been a loud whisper, and seemed responsible for the window. Laughter helped, but it didn't last.

In the somewhat less strained atmosphere, I introduced the material on roles, and got some discussion going. If the lieutenant had been there he would have said it was like pulling hen's teeth. Alano folded and creased another piece of paper, and another. The quiet man in the middle of the room, the one I'd deemed a loner, finally spoke. His voice was soft, difficult to hear over Alano creasing and tearing notebook paper. My blood pressure rose.

Most of the time I avoided using my position of authority in the classroom; I liked my confrontations to be in discussions of controversial material, but the tearing annoyed me, and it wasn't because notebook paper was so difficult to come by. I collected Alano's torn papers, and set them on the lectern.

Finally, period movement. Men tripped over desks in their haste to get out of the room. Alano went to the lectern, pointed at his papers. I nodded, and he gathered them like they were pictures of his loved ones. The education secretary in charge of supplies, a rather rigid woman with a German accent and a sweet smile, would have a fit if she saw precious notebook paper torn into pieces. She said her budget was inadequate for our needs. I understood her position, and would have written a check on the spot if she or any other person would step into the classroom with me to ease the tension during the next hour.

She, of course, had a deadline to meet. All the education staff, a resourceful bunch, had deadlines to meet or other places to be. I don't know how they knew that chain was so badly fragmented, unless they read it on my face. I went to my office to make a couple phone calls, planning to beg someone on the PSR team for help. No one answered. Word spreads fast. It began spreading back in Shelton before those men ever chained-up for the bus ride. I was on my own.

The old education floor had two long, perpendicular corridors, a security challenge when only one officer was on post, which was the case many mornings. The officers' desk sat in a recessed area near the top of the stairs, about the middle of the main corridor that ran from a large learning-lab classroom on one end, past a standard library, law library and education staff offices, to the staff restroom on the other end. The other corridor had nine classrooms, my office, an inmate restroom, and an alcove that served as a cramped waiting room where students gathered on rainy days.

The window in my office door looked out on the alcove. Alano was there with a pencil and his stack of paper, now folded and torn at one corner to keep it together—a tablet of sorts. The older man who sat beside him in the classroom was there, and several men not from the group. Something was going on, going down. I opened my office door as a warning to break it up, and met wary and smug eyes. All conversation and activity ceased, but the message resonated: you didn't see anything, you don't know anything, you can't do anything about it. The intercom snapped to life, and a voice announced period movement was over. There were shoulder slaps, "see-ya's," as men moved toward classrooms.

The group got seated, I took roll, got a couple more first names, and announced how we'd spend the next hour. Alano unzipped his khaki jacket and shrugged it back on his shoulders, an exaggerated feminine gesture complete with adjusting his chest for effect. Under the jacket he wore a state-issue white T-shirt which had odd protrusions. Two odd and lumpy protrusions. Crumpled paper? Not his torn notebook pieces; they were clutched in his hand.

Much as I hate pointing fingers, I pointed at those lumps. "What are those?" I meant it to be rhetorical, to warn him back into his jacket.

"Chessies," Alano said.

Chessies. All eyes were on me. Someone said, "Lana, call him Lana." Chairs scraped.

That's when I realized the older man beside Alano was acting as his pimp. I should have called both men out to the corridor to warn them that such activities would not be permitted in the classroom. Instead, I focused on Alano. "Get rid of them."

"No hablo inglés."

"Bullshit," I said, and watched his eyebrows move up. I nodded. He had heard that phrase before, and possibly understood more English than he acknowledged. Prison administrators believe immersion in the English speaking prison culture helps non-English speakers learn the language. Most of the Hispanic men sought prison jobs, which they combined with education in English as a Second Language (ESL) classes to improve their skills.

"That's English slang. It means I don't believe you, and even if you don't understand a word I'm saying you know what I mean. Get rid of them." *Chessies.* The word sounded British or Australian, not at all typical prison slang.

Alano reached a hand up under his T-shirt and pulled. Toilet paper came out as streamers. He patted it into mounds alongside his little homemade tablet. I took a closer look. The tablet was his 'little black book.' Names. Assignations, I supposed. The man beside him surely helped record the names during period movement. That's what was going down in the corridor alcove.

"Put the toilet paper in the wastebasket. Put the notebook paper pieces in your jacket pocket and leave them there."

He curled his mouth down, opened his eyes wide, and held out his arms. He'd watched too much television. "No hablo . . ."

"Now." I pointed at the wastebasket, but kept my eyes on the remaining ten men. Well, nine. The one next to Alano was too close to me, and I knew where his interests lay. He would collect some of the pay, most likely items from Store, that Alano received for prostituting himself.

Several of the men uttered pejoratives, pervert and queer being the most polite. They knew the relationship between Alano and the other man, and distanced themselves from it by shoving their chairs to the back or far sides of the room.

"What in addition to homophobia must we overcome to make Social Responsibility bearable this week?" No one answered, so I repeated the question. It used up time. I was too irritated to teach. Irritated at prison staff, not inmate students. Someone on staff back in the blocks knew that Alano was what they called a cellhouse whore; someone should have prepared me for potential repercussions in the classroom.

.   The man in the middle of the room said, "You need to define homophobia." He didn't mean for himself, and he was right about the need.

"Homophobia," I said after drawing in and releasing a deep breath, "is a fear of homosexuality. It's very common in heterosexual males. Homo literally means same, though I know it's used as a slang term here; phobia means fear. Hetero, of course, means other, as in other sex." I wrote the words and meanings on the board. We were still working on roles and rules. "One heterosexual male role is to mate with females for sexual purposes, which includes reproduction of the species."

We had an interesting discussion after that, nine of them and me. The man seated next to Alano busied himself with his folder and papers, and didn't look up, and I chose not to make that an issue. As I taught in parenting classes, ignoring undesirable attention getting behavior when possible often stops the behavior. Once the nine men in the middle and back of the room got started talking, they were quite open about their own sexuality, and managed to get in some bragging. They engaged in sexual intercourse only with women, and avoided sexual congress with other inmates at all costs. Their vocabulary was a little dicier, but they meant the same thing.

While the discussion progressed, I noticed Alano and the man next to him doodling or drawing pictures on the back of the program schedule, and on their folders. I glanced at their sketches just long enough to realize they depicted specific sex acts. I needed aspirin. At the very least I needed aspirin.

During the next period movement, before our team meeting, I told the education floor officer about Alano, and asked him to check before the afternoon session to be certain he didn't again have "chessies" inside his T-shirt.

"Shim, you mean?" the officer said. "Check the shim? He's a shim, he wants to take it in the butt that's his problem, not mine. Let him stuff his shirt."

"Not in my classroom." I watched his face, a nice burnished copper face under silver curls. He was a retired military man, and would soon retire again, from Corrections. I'd known him as a gentleman who complimented women on their clothes and hair. Mine was silver-white, lighter than his. He called me an ash blonde, and generally treated me with respect. I wasn't ready for "take it in the butt," or his lack of concern for what I considered a predicament.

Education floor correctional officers regularly looked in on classes through the corridor windows to observe inmates' behaviors. That officer kept a close eye on the program classroom where the men were new to the island, and occasionally stepped in to let his presence be known. It dawned on me that his comment had to do with his own homophobia.

Two days later, when I reached the education floor, he announced, "Shim's in Seg on a Major, a 504." His laugh thundered down the hall.

Seg. Aka the hole. Serious Infraction 504: Engaging in sexual acts with others with the exception of spouses during approved extended family visits.

Had the cellhouse officers waited for Alano to make his move so they could infract him? Of course they had. Until they caught him in the act they couldn't stop it. In truth they could never stop it, but they had to make their point now and then.

Word circulated that he'd been a problem in the system for a long time. As per instructions I wrote a report about the entire incident and my reaction to it. In retrospect, I would not confront such an act in front of a group, but instead move the confrontation to the corridor outside the classroom, though the windows along the room's corridor wall wouldn't have provided much privacy. I still would have told the man to remove the protrusions from his shirt, and the rest of the class would have observed. That classroom in that early 1900s building didn't offer many choices. I couldn't leave a class unattended, there wasn't an officer in that corridor, there were no intercoms or phones or buzzers of any sort in the room, and I'd chosen not to wear a body alarm while teaching. Some teachers wore or carried one; others, like me, found they interfered with the rapport we wanted to develop. (More than one woman teacher unknowingly set off her body alarm and brought first responders thundering up the stairs to the education floor.)

Mandatory programs and court ordered classes always present problems for attendees and teachers or facilitators. I did my best to make PSR and all the classes I taught interesting and worth students' time. On the final day of PSR, the education counselor came in to the classroom to help men register for classes, a relatively easy task. By then most of them knew what coursework they needed to meet DOC requirements, what jobs were available, and what vocational programs were open to them. They left with a certificate of completion and an appointment to meet with their personal counselor/case manager. They said thanks, almost to a man, and see you soon. Most would be on the education floor, enrolled in classes ranging from adult basic education to college level credit.

My ever growing list of notes and thoughts about the program were part of our PSR team's ongoing discussions. I noted what worked even with the group that included Alano, and what struck me as unrealistic for chains with widely differing educational backgrounds. We had addressed diverse levels of understanding at length in the weeks of planning PSR, but it came up again every week in our Monday morning meeting. We always circled back to the issue of teaching Critical Thinking, and what we should expect to see in inmates' behavior patterns as a result of presenting materials and demonstrating critical thinking in our interaction with them as a group and individuals. I explained my interaction with Alano to the team, said that I'd mishandled the situation and that I'd admitted as much to the men in the group. The men respected me for that and accepted it as a lesson. They left the program to start their serious work of doing time and planning ahead so they could return to their real world—their families and communities; I prepared for the next week, the next chain, the next challenge.

The Therapeutic Community programs now being used in reentry prisons are based on the belief that lifestyle change occurs within the social context. Offenders work on their behavior and thinking patterns that brought them to prison while also working on the role addictions played in their crimes. During my volunteer days at the women's reentry prison I heard many women participants say sessions left them wrung out. I understood, though not from the same side of the classroom. It is exhausting work for all.

13

| Thinking is Critical |

When inmates sought me out to talk about their crimes, I often asked, "How do you feel about that now?" Some of them came up with an answer that showed remorse; others shrugged, unable to find words. Either way, they were starting to think about what they'd done and that opened a door that would lead to opening the gate to freedom. But it was just a start.

Thinking is critical to learning. I incorporated Write to Clarify Thinking activities in the parenting and family courses at WCCW, and used it in similar classes at MICC. I used prompts to help students focus on issues pertinent to their lives. Hundreds of students wrote at least a sentence and sometimes several pages responding to the statement, "Blaming others for where you are at the moment (prison) keeps you a victim," with a choice to agree or disagree. I also found that having students make memory lists by years or by age helped them look back. They could think about one year at a time as a means of pinpointing what was going on in their lives when they started getting into trouble. That dovetailed with the reparenting work discussed in Chapter 8. I searched for methods or tricks that would help them think and that would that fit their learning level.

The adult prison population nationwide had just started the steep mass-incarceration climb when we launched PSR, with many new arrivals testing below fourth-grade reading level. They needed Adult Basic Education (ABE) classes where correctional educators developed Individual Education Programs (IEPs) to meet their needs. Once their reading comprehension improved, their ability to reason also improved.

Critical thinking, which we incorporated into PSR, is a concept that requires reasoning skills for problem solving, and pushes students to rethink choices they made. We considered that a necessary step toward planning for release from prison and reentry into society. We needed a teaching method that would meet educational levels from ABE level to college-educated, and we needed to deliver it during the jam-packed PSR week.

Picture the typical PSR classroom of twenty-four adult males. Eight were African American; two or three were Hispanic; occasionally one was Asian, Pacific Islander, or Native American; the rest white. A large percentage of the African Americans were biracial but considered themselves black. Every group had at least one man with some college education and one at ABE level. We knew the complexity going into the program. Tom, our education director, believed he had the ideal answer for moving those groups toward critical thinking: present them with a story to ponder. Give them all a copy of the story, but read it aloud, so they could hear the words and the reader's voice inflections. He also touted his ideal story—George Orwell's "Shooting an Elephant." He'd studied the essay in depth and used it when he taught high school. English literature anthologies include it for examples of narration and description.

The essay, first published in 1936, was set in Burma (now Myanmar) during the 1920s when that country was under British Commonwealth rule. The essay's major themes include imperialism, social status, personal conscience, choices and consequences.

Tom saw Orwell's discomfort and ensuing behavior in a place strange to him as comparable to inmates' unease when plunged into the prison environment. We would draw the parallel and facilitate a discussion about other choices Orwell might have made. The men would practice critical thinking before they attended the class with that title on the second day of PSR. Though some of our team members argued the essay was beyond our students' reach, Tom won out, insisting that I would remain with the group during the session. The men would trust me by then, the fourth hour of that first day in the PSR classroom. He would read and lead the discussion; I would be there to define unfamiliar words for them to set the scene.

He and I plowed ahead as a tag-team, urging the men to think about the reason for Orwell's decision to shoot the elephant. When Tom's director duties called him to meetings, many off-island, I handled the presentation alone. In truth the men accepted me more readily than Tom, who was more officious.

"Shooting an Elephant," relates an experience Orwell had while in service with the imperial police in Burma. Those familiar with Orwell's *Animal Farm*, and *Nineteen Eighty-four* know his incensed attitude toward repressive government, imperialism, and despots. He was nineteen or twenty at the time he left English university to serve in Burma rather than complete his education, and he found himself loathed and ridiculed by the Burmese. He opens the essay by stating he was hated by large numbers of people, the only time in his life he was important enough for that to happen.

For our purposes we started with the essay's third paragraph where Orwell moves from describing his dislike of imperialism (he calls it an evil thing) and of the country's population, to narrating the event, which he calls a tiny incident in itself. An elephant has gone "must," broken its chain, escaped its handler, and is ravaging the marketplace. It has already destroyed a bamboo hut, killed a cow, overturned a rubbish van and "inflicted violences upon it." As a police officer, he is called on to do something about the elephant, and sets out on a pony to see what is happening.

The men generally liked the elephant being influenced by an attack of "must," which we defined for them as rut, a word they knew. They could identify with a male being a little out of control under such circumstances. There would be some chest beating, a high five here and there, a little bragging. I'd grin at them; I'd come to expect that reaction. Then they asked exactly what violences were inflicted on the rubbish van. The bamboo hut and dead cow were adequately explained and of less interest to them.

In the next paragraph, Orwell describes the area where the elephant has been seen and the discovery of a man trampled to death, his arms crucified and his back skinned. Some of the men found that quite to their liking; others saw it as racist, since Orwell calls the dead man a black Dravidian (Indian) coolie. We learned, in time, to prepare them properly for the coolie's ethnicity, and to teach a little geography and history before reading the story.

Orwell paints a picture of the place, the squalor, the crowd of two thousand or so that continues growing. The power of the crowd seeking excitement convinces Orwell he will have to shoot the elephant. He doesn't want to for several reasons, none of which have to do with killing an animal. The elephant has a greater worth alive than dead. Killing it is akin to destroying a valuable piece of machinery, but not killing it will leave him looking a fool. That is what he cannot permit. He shoots the elephant. It is a disastrous shot, as are the subsequent ones; the elephant takes half-an-hour to die and then is stripped to the bones for its meat.

Orwell shot the forward part of the elephant's massive head, thinking the brain would be there. He later learned he should have aimed for the ear hole. In preparing to use the essay, I made a trip to Tacoma's Point Defiance Zoo to study the elephants' anatomy and demeanor. I needed to see their heads in profile and to gauge the distance between their eyes and ears, to understand Orwell's dilemma.

Orwell violated his personal values to protect his worth in the eyes of a crowd he despised. He did what the crowd expected someone in his role as British officer to do, and in the act lost rather than protected his sense of self-worth. Orwell wrote that in such acts, in his case becoming the oppressor against his better judgment, a man destroys his own freedom. I considered the story's most telling line to be, "He wears a mask, and his face grows to fit it." In fact that, and the essay's closing where he admits his motive—he shot the elephant "solely to avoid looking a fool"—did trigger thinking and discussion with many of the men. Some drifted off into quiet thought, which we honored by not pushing them to talk.

When it worked best, inmates drew the parallel we intended: Correctional officers were sometimes pushed to behave certain ways due to the badges they wore, the expectations heaped on them. Many inmates had been "acting out" for attention, position, a sense of power, for much of their lives. They complained about "the man" jerking them around; they didn't believe that getting negative attention satisfied a need within their psyches and drove them to continue acting out. I'd watch their eyes as awareness settled, notice little frowns furrow foreheads, or heads lower so no one could see too far into their own recognition: they had hurt others, and in the act hurt themselves.

The stage was set for Tuesday's critical thinking session, so pertinent to personal crime-reexamination. We were working toward our goal, and helping our students prepare for their future choices. In the process we introduced the value of literature in learning, and possibly inspired some men to read something other than *Playboy* or *Hustler* at the prison library.

But some of the time getting to the lesson's objective was a lot like rowing upstream with broken oars.

In the early weeks of PSR one man sobbed so hard my teaching-assistant had to procure an additional roll of toilet paper from the men's restroom—an infractionable offense if he was caught. We generally acquired our supply when the janitorial closet was open, and kept an extra roll of the rough tissue locked in a file cabinet for the next time we needed it.

The sobbing man caught me off guard as he gulped and asked, "Why did the elephant have to die?" Tears streamed from his eyes, mucous from his nose.

"Don't pay him no mind," another man said. "He's crazy."

He may have been. Many inmates do have mental problems and would be better served in mental facilities. It was also common for a man to make such an announcement. Craziness went with the territory, and no one seemed offended when someone pointed it out. I felt duty bound to offer the distraught man comfort, a difficult task to accomplish with just words. Touch, even a brief encounter of my fingers and his skin, could convey the wrong message. I used my ever-present but just-under-the-surface mothering skills and watched those teary eyes beg for more. He would have huddled in my arms if I'd opened them.

Now and then a man in the group thought the story was a warning: they'd be shot, literally or figuratively, if they got out of line. I heard lengthy, rather logical diatribes on the unfairness of infractions and sanctions for things they likened to an elephant tipping over a rubbish van—things such as wasting food or supplies, stealing a piece of toast from Mainline (prison dining hall), smoking where prohibited. (Smoking has since been banned at all Washington correctional facilities.)

One week a man compared the elephant's shooting to a crime scene, and continued extolling the glory of blood and gore when I said, "Stop!" I wound my way through the classroom tangle to stand in front of him. He kept on, lost in another place, an ugly place. I smothered his words with my own. "Stop. No more. The end. You will not continue with your story. Do you hear me? Stop now." It was one of the most graphic tales I heard during my tenure, and I listened to or overheard many, some exaggerations and fantasies. Inmates, like disturbed veterans of war, tend to borrow others' experiences and embroider on them for status within the system.

"Huh?" the man said when he felt me standing there. He struggled to get his eyes in focus.

Now and then men remembered hunting trips for deer, elk, bear, squirrels if they were from Missouri, crocodiles if they were from Louisiana. They were fifth-graders at camp, out-telling the last tall tale, getting in a little chest pounding.

Fortunately I liked men in general, had been reared by a father who hunted, and reared sons of my own.

No matter how well our discussion went, it always ended with one or two men upset over the elephant's death. They were still talking about it the next day, and many came by my classroom weeks and months later to mention the dead elephant, stripped to the bones for its meat. Soon the new chain, who heard about the story from cellmates during their free weekend before PSR, asked about the elephant first thing Monday morning.

By the time the intercom announced period movement to end PSR's first full day, and Mr. Gomez straightened the classroom, I felt like I'd wrestled an elephant. I'd spent four hours interacting with the new chain, and one hour in a meeting about them. To the best of my knowledge, I was a pioneer. There were Department of Corrections personnel who had been in the same room with a group of inmates monitoring tests and distributing information for long stretches, but interaction was minimal. I was a guide on uncharted terrain, still scoffed at by naysayers, occasionally heralded by Project Social Responsibility team members. My empathy for Orwell's Burma experience deepened with each presentation of his essay.

In a sense, I became part of each chain. I was stuck with them and they with me. Once the week ended, we could all get on with what we were in prison to do, which for me was teaching parenting and family classes, and dealing with the next chain, and the next, reading them Orwell's account of shooting that poor randy elephant.

14

| Guys Doing Time |

Tom, the education director, had been right about Orwell's essay working with most of the population who were "Just a bunch of guys" that would appreciate a guy story. Time dedicated to critical thinking skills in PSR wasn't expected to result in dramatic alterations in inmate behavior or thought patterns. Presenting something for discussion, in this case the possibility of self-control and thinking through choices, was the key. When combined with the PSR communication component and the information on family history and patterns, it opened a door to a higher degree of self-reflection over day-to-day choices and a less judgmental view of institutional authority in general.

We set the stage the hour before reading and discussing "Shooting an Elephant" in a serious review of traditional male roles and how societal changes impacted expectations placed on men, especially in their relationships with women. Lieutenant Burton agreed to participate in the presentation if someone developed curriculum and a lesson plan for him to use. I wrote it, explained what we wanted and needed from him, coaxed and coached. He never used it. I doubt he ever looked at it.

In the shift lieutenant we got the traditional male we needed: a rigid, obstinate, inveterate officer. He followed my lead as I introduced specific societal changes. At times I felt like the straight person in a stand-up comedy act. I provided the material; the lieutenant provided the levity. When we got into male sex role conditioning, a major area of my master's thesis research some years back, the lieutenant bloomed. Jungian therapist and author Jean Shinoda Bolen would call him an Ares Man, an archetypal warrior, dancer, and lover. By dancer she meant a physical rather than mental man. The lieutenant couldn't be bothered with preparing the materials we presented, or even writing on the board. While I lectured and wrote, he moved about the room interrupting me, expanding on a notion I put forth, a sociological fact, a bit of history. Ares men are reactive, and lust for battle. Pity the inmate who wanted to argue with the lieutenant, unless the man hooked his father instinct, another Ares trait personified in the lieutenant by how he handled the officers who answered to him. He issued orders with that pointing finger and clipped words, then carried their personal crises around as a pre-ulcer and high blood pressure.

A shift lieutenant runs security-side of a prison while he's on duty. Every sergeant and corrections officer on every post is his responsibility, every inmate his charge, every employee and visitor on prison property his concern. The lieutenant took his job seriously. Now and then he'd complain, in the privacy of my office, that things were easier when he didn't meet every inmate face-to-face, when they were just names and numbers. It got harder to order a man to Ad Seg when it was someone he'd met in PSR.

But he stuck with the program. Together the lieutenant and I painted a picture of how sex-roles changed with history beginning in the early twentieth century. While I wrote key words on the board—*the Great Depression, WWII, Korea, Civil Rights Movement, Vietnam, Desert Storm*—the lieutenant and students talked about how men saw themselves during those times. But when we moved from those tangible moments in history to sociological change, the lieutenant said, "That's her department." I'd write *Advent of Television*, or *Sexual Revolution*, or *Increasing Divorce, Drug Abuse, Spousal*

Abuse, Child Abuse, Increasing Crime, and ask how they impacted male sex roles.

"You answer her," the lieutenant said, and if no one did he'd point his finger at a man and say, "You, that's an order, you answer now."

For as often as he repeated it was "my department," he warmed to the task of teaching and interrupted me often. He didn't agree with all of my views, and sometimes pointed his finger and called me opinionated. I'd narrow my eyes, point back and tell him to look at himself. He'd laugh. The guys loved it.

When the intercom snapped to life and a voice announced, "Period movement, period movement," the ten-minute break provided each hour on the half-hour during the program day, there were always men who groaned. They didn't want it to end. When I look back on those sessions I suspect some of those men thought they'd found a set of parents—a firm traditional father and an informed liberated mother. Others thought they'd stumbled into a road show, a diversion from the boredom of prison. I remember it as exhausting, but oddly successful. At the very least we gave them material for thought, and having them think about life events and choices is what we coveted in that program.

The lieutenant left the floor laughing. If I was lucky I managed to use the restroom and grab a drink of water before the next hour, the one when Orwell's elephant entered the room. I'm continually amazed at the power of metaphors.

I mentioned Jean Shinoda Bolen, the Jungian analyst whose book, *Gods in Everyman,* became part of my work with classes at McNeil Island. I'd been granted the right to use her earlier book, *Goddesses in Everywoman,* as a text for Family History and Patterns one quarter at WCCW. The women resonated to Jung's universal archetypes, and wrote lists of psychological difficulties they wanted to overcome and strengths they wanted to build. Though the course was a resounding success, use of the book was permitted only one quarter. Subsequent quarters I wove material from it with several other works to create a synchronistic offering designed for female students. It was easy to substitute Bolen's *Everyman* work as part of a similar course for male students who were ready to rethink their criminal behavior.

Writing about Bolen brings another book to mind—one written by Richard Heller, an author in my community. His story, told in the novel *Blueprints*, shows readers how archetypes inform our lives. Heller's protagonist personifies a Hephaestus man, an archetypal rejected son who earns his way in life as a craftsman: farrier, sculptor and writer. The author remains dedicated to horses, especially those he shod and those he saved when their hooves seemed damaged beyond repair. He's comfortable in that world and growing more comfortable outside it as other male archetypes develop in his psyche. That's part of the purpose of critical thinking and reasoning. You can think and learn and grow. That concept circles back to and connects with the reparenting work cited in an earlier chapter.

I had a break from the PSR program on Tuesday when a basic skills teacher and a vocational instructor joined forces to help the group apply critical thinking to current issues and their coursework. They were followed by housing unit officers and counselors, a disciplinary hearings officer and a social worker to focus on conflict resolution and communication skills. I rejoined the men on Wednesday to discuss family history and patterns, parenting rights and responsibilities, and preparing to return to their families and communities. When time permitted a Correctional Unit Supervisor stepped in to discuss specifics of making the best use of inside visiting, and to explain the timeline in preparing for their release from the facility. The fourth hour of that day was devoted to cultural differences in families, with the English as a Second Language (ESL) instructor or a DOC Spanish-speaking counselor facilitating. After the three intense hours I'd spent, I felt ready for a break, but there was another class to teach in another classroom.

Some PSR groups were glad to have me back on Wednesday mornings, anxious to see what I'd throw at them (their term) and who I'd drag in (also their term) to help make my points. Those who were dads wanted some of the handouts they'd heard about back in the blocks, their name for the cellhouse. "Those papers that say we have parenting rights," a man would say, giving me the opening to answer "And responsibilities." They wanted specifics about how to communicate with a toddler, a ten-year-old, a teen. They asked about parenting stepchildren, a new girlfriend's kids (many incarcerated men found new girlfriends while they were locked up), their own kids who had a new stepdad. They came prepared for the discipline versus punishment argument, some extolling the virtues of spanking to keep kids in line, others calling those men assholes. They told their stories, some openly for all to hear, others privately during break or later in my office.

One man, Adam, had an uncommon last name that led me to suspect his father might be someone I knew from my high school years. Adam mentioned his hometown as he told a story about falling out of a tree in his childhood, suffering a serious fractured leg, and being beaten by his father for climbing the tree. His mother had to wait until the following day to get him to a hospital for treatment. While he spoke, Adam rubbed his leg above his knee. I asked if he still suffered pain there. He moved his hand to his chest and said, "No, not in my leg. Here, in my heart."

Adam had a short sentence during which he earned his GED and began college level classes. His mother, also someone I remembered from my high school years, came to the island prison for an awards ceremony shortly before Adam's release. He introduced me to his mother as his parenting and family teacher. She said she'd heard a lot about me from Adam, then narrowed her eyes, said she recognized me and mentioned my maiden name. She even remembered my mother who'd been a popular substitute teacher in our school system. We had an odd reunion in an odd place—the visiting room in that old prison compound. She and Adam's dad were long since divorced, she'd worried about Adam's behaviors through his teens, she believed prison made a difference in his life. She thanked me profusely for my work with incarcerated men. Tears spilled from her eyes and ran down her face. I choked up, too. She'd been one of the pretty and popular cheerleaders who married one of the handsome, popular guys. It saddened me to know how their story played out.

Of course I hadn't told Adam that I recognized his last name, but his mother told him at that event. She sent me a note through Pierce College after Adam's release to say he was in college, doing well, making new friends. One of the major stumbling blocks in post prison reunification is avoiding old relationships that may include former crime partners, drinking or drug buddies, emotionally toxic family members often found in the families of the incarcerated, and old haunts or hangouts in small towns and hoods. Many of the young men coming inside had never strayed far from an inner city area where they'd learned criminal behavior from somewhat older men and taught it, in turn, to those somewhat younger.

Teaching guys doing time the rights and responsibilities of parents in prison always included the information on how to tell children the truth about prison, but delivered with caveats: Tell the truth, but no gory details; tell the truth, but don't reveal sex crimes inside the prison fence; tell the simple truth. As I listened to myself while watching their faces, I heard the dissonance: truth is rarely simple.

Our culture values truth. My edition of Bartlett's *Familiar Quotations* refers to 220 "truth" quotes, and another 26 about "truths." Children are encouraged, or ordered, by parents and other adults to tell the truth. Witnesses in court raise their right hands and swear to tell the truth, the whole truth, and nothing but the truth. Still, we read or hear news accounts of persons lying under oath.

My mother accused me of embroidering the truth to improve a story, which I do when I want to entertain or make a point. Yet, as I write this, I avoid some truths about former students' crimes because their inclusion would serve only as gratuitous shock, when my purpose is to examine the worth of an unusual career and show how those doing time can return to society to lead productive lives.

When I said, "Tell the simple truth," to a group of PSR inmates, thought-wheels whirred. Which truth? The one they denied, diluted, plea-bargained down to the least possible prison time? The one they still can't face themselves? That truth?

I dropped "simple," a poor qualifier, which left the value-weighted word "truth." The concept worked well with students enrolled in Positive Parenting, which included a unit on dealing with children who lie, cheat or steal. Those students, enrolled in a class to learn parenting techniques, could filter the information through their parent role, not their criminal behavior role. I needed a different group approach for PSR, and went back to the basics.

I broke an adult rule (or law). Prison is my consequence. It's not your fault.

When I said "It's your responsibility to tell your children where you are, and why," to a new PSR group during the Parenting and Family session, the anxiety level in the room shot up. I felt it, smelled it, like a fetid odor carried on a changing wind. I heard and saw it: chairs scraped; eyes turned away.

The explanation looks good on paper or the blackboard, but it doesn't roll off the tongue with ease for several reasons. First it requires the parent to take responsibility right up front. "I broke an adult rule." That doesn't fit the advice parents who are also convicted felons receive from defense attorneys.

I'd give my little lecture on telling the truth, and hear, "Wait a minute; I'm not copping to anything."

And, "Consequence? Who the hell talks like that?"

"Me," I said. "My children, who learned my tricks, and suggested consequences when they knew they had to face them. My students, who get beyond those value-weighted words 'good' and 'bad,' as in, 'That's a good girl,' or 'You're a bad boy.'"

Bad boy, hah! They'd been called worse than that. Most of those men had grown up with abusive, derogatory language, often delivered with a physical exclamation point—a swat, slap, arm-jerk, or worse, and were so unaccustomed to appropriate verbal discipline they sneered at my three sentences. They'd used parenting methods their parents used on them, methods "necessary" to keep children in line.

"And it succeeded with you in your childhood?" I asked. "You complain about punitive treatment by correctional officers and the system, and yet you justify the same actions by parents?"

It got their attention. Of course I explained it's human nature to defend parents and practices that were the norm in our childhood. They needed to consider alternatives, learn or relearn appropriate disciplinary methods, and choose for themselves. I knew inmate students, almost to a person, suffered horrible guilt for something they'd said or done to a child. They needed to forgive themselves and move on; they needed to work on strengthening their parent-child relationships.

Some children knew the truth about prison because the parent was arrested in front of them, or the crime occurred in their presence. Some knew because they were victims, as in cases of child abuse or child sexual abuse. Even in those cases, the child needed to hear the parent say those three things:

I broke an adult rule. Prison (jail) is my consequence. It's not your fault.

Many male felons considered it easier to tell a child, "I did something bad," than to say, "I broke an adult rule." Stimulating discussions led to most of them finding a "good" way to explain their crime and incarceration to their children. In the end I was less concerned about the wording than the communication.

A successful discussion, especially one where students could argue a bit, and hear me concede they were the ones who knew best how to talk to their children, got them thinking and learning. I wanted to provide information and suggestions, not an absolute solution. And I liked the energy of those arguments. It created a healthy learning atmosphere for all of us. It led to my next favorite statement:

"Separate deeds from doers. 'I did something bad,' not, 'I am bad.'"

They liked that. "Hey, Mom, I'm an okay dude, I just did something bad."

I soon learned the men in PSR who beat their chests the hardest for all their tough-guy misdeeds and clung most tenaciously to the convict code were the same ones who stopped me in the corridor to ask questions, or sent me kites, an inmate-to-staff form, to request a private meeting. They wanted their children, nieces and nephews, parents, other relatives or a special friend to see them as persons, not just criminals, but couldn't risk showing their need in class. I understood, and told them so.

During one PSR session a biker with huge tattooed biceps (he'd had to open the seams of his state-issued T-shirt sleeves to accommodate them), came up at period movement and shoved a blank piece of paper at me.

"Write that stuff down. The explanation stuff. Not the 'It's not your fault' part. I got that okay. The rest of it. The 'deeds and doers' stuff. I'm a doer, you know what I'm saying, but I got a couple kids out there and I don't want them to end up in prison."

"Sure, Mr. Johnson," I said, and smiled up at him. On first role call he'd told me to call him Mad Man. I'd given him my left-eyebrow-raised look, and settled for Mr. Johnson. His DOC number indicated he'd been around the system for some time, and had an image to maintain. He had long hair, an unkempt beard, and dark-circled, hard eyes. He stood too close, but I wouldn't back up. Maybe he, like me, was myopic.

"I've got other materials I can give you, if you're interested."

He looked at me with such mistrust it made holding my pen steady enough to write the deeds and doers stuff, as he called it, a serious challenge. But write I did.

"Do you want other materials?" I asked, as I handed back his paper.

"You know something, you've got a nice smile."

"Thank you," I said, and kept smiling, though I wanted to put space between us. When you teach, you go with what works.

"What ages are your children?" I asked, staying in teacher-mode.

"One's eleven, one's almost fifteen."

His eyes softened. Or maybe that was magical thinking on my part. "Would you like me to photo-copy some information about explanations for pre-teens and teens?"

"Yeah, but don't make it a big deal. Just hand it to me, okay?"

"Okay, if you promise me one thing."

He pulled his head back, but kept his feet planted. "Yeah? What?"

"When you tell your children about doing time, be honest about how sad it has made you."

It took him ten seconds to answer. A coppery taste formed in my mouth. Dry and coppery.

"Yeah, okay, you say so, I'll tell 'em." He took the paper and lumbered out the door. The remainder of the week he stayed in the classroom through period movement when I was there, which told me he wanted to talk. An inmate forgoing a break was a sign something was going on. I went to him, sat in the desk-chair next to him, initiated conversations with him. All who observed, and many did, saw me make the move, not him. He taught me some truths about bikers' lives. I urged him not to romanticize the life to his children, especially not the criminal expectations placed on certain biker gangs to earn pins some wear on their leather jackets. He gave me one nod. I don't know if he rode with an outlaw biker gang, or rode alone as a latter day cowboy. It didn't matter. He wanted to do something right for his children.

"Kids know I'm in prison," he said. "Me and my old lady are straight up about that. I'm sending her them papers you gave me. She's doing her job, she's the mom. I talk to the kids on the phone."

"Keep calling them. It helps them know you, and you them. It's more important than most people realize." We both smiled. He liked hearing he was doing something right. I sensed he could read the items I'd photocopied but struggled with comprehension, a common problem with incarcerated students who had damaged their brains with drugs. My colleagues who taught basic skills talked of teaching the same math or English concepts over and over. A student seemed to grasp it during the lesson, but would forget it by the next day. I looked at Mr. Johnson's eyes and tried to read what he needed from me, and took a stab at his concerns.

"Children in their pre-teens and teens tend to get caught up in two major worries about parents. Some fear they won't live up to their parents' successes. Some worry they will repeat their parents' mistakes. Keep telling your children you trust them to make better choices than you made."

He nodded again and handed me his pencil. "Write that down."

I wrote and talked, trying to cram it all in. "Keep explanations simple. Simple works better for all of us. Simple and honest. And tell them every time you make any progress in any area in prison. If you work, tell them what you're learning and doing on the job. If you attend school, send them some of your assignments. If you enjoy music, write or talk on the phone about what you like. Try to learn what TV programs they watch so you can discuss them. And ask your children what they think about current shows, movies, music, even political matters."

He kept nodding. His eyes changed; something internal was changing. A teacher who sees such change, especially in an inmate student who is a little intimidating, feels thanked and rewarded. I never saw him after PSR week, but I would bet he kept doing all he could to help his children cope with his incarceration. After all, he was a doer.

15

| Plea Bargains – A Reality Check |

The officer who said I was so serious was right. I grew up with a strong work ethic at my core and wore it like a mantle. My parents worked hard, without complaint, and I tried to do the same. I pushed inmates to find worth at the center of their beings, to lift themselves from prison malaise and personal moral decline to make time work for them. I believe Mr. Johnson had been doing that before he came through PSR, and that he took away something from the program that helped him continue doing his time and taking more responsibility as a dad parenting from a distance. He'd committed a crime; he was doing his time, working in prison industries and sending money home.

It became clear to our PSR team that we needed to help men deconstruct their criminal behavior by helping them understand criminal law and sentencing guidelines. I'd done that with the women, but many of the young men at McNeil Island had some gang related issues that the women didn't.

As Dewayne, a black man who spoke from experience, said, "Real time stops when you enter prison, and doing time begins." He represented inmates during the original Project Social Responsibility planning stage, and remained an activist for black inmates' rights throughout his incarceration. He was a law library clerk who worked with white and Hispanic men with the same professional attitude, but he really worried about the young black men. He could cite statistics about the imbalance of blacks incarcerated across the country. He told first hand stories of how young black men are treated on the streets of America. I hear him now as this country is reeling from the deaths of unarmed black men at the hands of uniformed policemen. I picture him nodding when prominent black men tell stories of cautioning their sons about potential confrontations with persons in positions of authority, and how they should handle such events.

Dewayne was an articulate man who referred to other black men as brothers and who knew black history well enough to teach it. He understood sentencing practices, and though he never worked as my TA, he mentored me in the sense he let me see what I read in the law through an inmate's eyes. He spent his work week in the prison law library, and became a walking, talking resource. Now and then, when he could break away from his law clerk job, he spoke to a PSR group about doing time.

"You've got to fit time into the frame," he said. "First, you need to know how much time you're sentenced to do, and how much you can get off for good behavior. Earned time, the system calls it. If you have a long sentence you need to get into the law library to start working on an appeal. Even if an appeal isn't going to happen, you want to get a look at the law, make sure your time fits your crime."

Men nodded as he spoke, and I made notes so I could better help another man, another classroom full of men. I'd heard it before, from my female students, from the beginning, but hearing it isn't living it.

"How many you here, especially you brothers, met your public defender five minutes before you went into court?" Dewayne asked. Hands shot up. "How many you agreed with whatever he said?" The same hands waved.

"Hell," Dewayne said, looking at me, "at least half these guys don't even know what crime they copped to."

He spoke from experience. He'd been anxious to get out of an overcrowded county jail cell where he slept on a mat on the floor, breathed in bad breath and body odors, and listened to men cry out in their sleep. Prison, he'd heard, was a walk in the park compared to county jail.

"When my public defender ran it down for me, the case the prosecutor had against me and what I could plea to, I said, 'Bring it on, man, let's just get it over with.' I knew the bus ride was coming. At that point I figured the sooner I got started, the sooner I'd get done. Reality set in some time later, when I got to the island and saw the old cellhouse. Maybe I should have done the jury thing."

Most men and women in prison have given up their right to a jury trial, accepted plea bargains, and settled in to a prison cell or room. They're advised, and know in a secret corner of their minds, that truths they want to keep buried tend to come out in jury trials and may result in a much longer sentence. But once inside, they start to wonder if an expensive criminal lawyer could have done better, if a jury would have been sympathetic to their plight. I believe most plea bargains are indeed bargains for the offender, which is why the court uses them. It speeds up the process, imposes less time on the offender than a jury trial might, and clears the docket. For most of them, there's no money on hand for a criminal attorney and no real property to bond for use as payment.

One young Tacoma man learned the hard way. He was given an eleven-year sentence in a plea deal, far too much time, he thought, for what he'd done. He withdrew his original guilty plea and opted for a trial. His family had some prominence and funds to hire an attorney known for helping young men through the trial process.

The jury handed down a 100-year prison term.

Under the plea he could have earned one-third off the eleven years, done a little over seven years, and been out of prison before his thirtieth birthday. The case remained in the local news for several months while the attorney filed and was granted an opportunity for a more reasonable sentence.

Dewayne believes accepting the plea bargain he was offered was a wise choice in his own case, given his crime. We distributed copies of the state criminal code's sentencing grid and seriousness levels. He tapped a spot on the grid, told the men to find it. Some needed help; it's an overwhelming document. My TA and I circled the room to make certain all were with Dewayne.

"Here's where the judge sentenced me. Seriousness Level ten, X on the grid, Offender Score two, which means I'd had two prior convictions. You see, time increases for every conviction. Legislature's tightening up on us. My sentence range is sixty-two to eighty-two months. I got seventy-two months, right in the middle. Six years to those of you don't know how to break it down.

"Now, if I look at the crimes in Seriousness Level ten, nothing fits what I did. My public defender got creative, made my assault beef into a kidnap because I dragged the guy out of the bar before I beat the shit out of him. My original charge is up here at twelve. XII on the grid. Assault 1. With my Offender Score, I could be doing as much as 147 months. Go figure."

In his telling, now several years after the event, Dewayne's was a crime of passion. Some dude was messing with his woman and Dewayne went looking for him, found him in a nightclub, dragged him out of the crowd to a parking lot, assaulted and seriously injured him.

"*Your* woman," I said. "Do you still see women as property of men?"

Some men hooted and made comments of approval. Of course women were their property. Others watched me with wary eyes. Dewayne rocked his hand. "Not so much. I'm doing seventy-two months over that . . . woman," (I gave him points for not saying bitch) "and she's way out of the picture. Waaaayyy out."

Men nodded, or slumped lower in the old desk-chairs; some muttered pejoratives, and looked away from my raised left eyebrow. Dewayne taught them a real life lesson much more powerful than anything that comes from a textbook.

Even after working in prisons for eighteen years and

volunteering inside for several more, after listening to countless men and women describe their lives inside, I do not understand the reality of doing time, of being confined to a prison cell, of always looking out through chain link fences topped with razor wire. For some young men, it's almost a rite of passage.

Young black males who came through Project Social Responsibility said, "You be black in this here society, you be goin' down." They said it with anger edged with pride. They fit a norm, albeit a negative one. (Bureau of Justice statistics, in Racial Disparities data, state that 1 in 3 black men will likely be imprisoned in their lifetime. Compare that to 1 in 9 Hispanic men and 1 in 17 white men. Further, they show that blacks make up over 33 percent of the nation's prison population, but only 13.2 percent of the U.S. census count.)

I asked those men how it made them feel, and challenged them to write essays about their perception that young black men get fingered first, almost without a police investigation taking place. "Write about your feelings, your mothers' worries and warnings." Now and then one did. It made thought-provoking reading.

Unfortunately, many I urged to write couldn't—literally could not write because they couldn't spell words or construct sentences or even describe or identify what constituted a paragraph. At any given time a large percentage of the prison population nationwide tests at a reading comprehension level that classifies them as illiterate. Not just inner-city blacks; not just men and women for whom English is a second language and who may be illiterate in their native tongue. Adult Basic Education (ABE) classrooms inside prisons have a proportionate number of nonminority students who suffer the same dilemma.

As I saw more and more seemingly illiterate young men came through PSR, I began asking if they understood their sentences. What part of the criminal justice system made sense to them? They'd been arrested, booked, taken to arraignment where the charges against them were read aloud. If they were lucky, someone might tell them the time connected with the charges. They had the right to have their pre-sentence investigation report read to them, if they couldn't read it themselves, but most didn't. They pretended they could read, and signed on the line provided just above their typed name. They were streetwise men, able to recognize their names in print, and to sign in cursive of a sort, usually a joined-printing. They got by.

How often did I hear, "I didn't do nothin', I was just hangin' with my homies when some shit went down," before I figured it out? Many of those young inner-city males were sentenced for anticipatory offenses. Most of them had rap sheets; they weren't innocent bystanders hauled off the streets without cause, but in some cases they were in the wrong place at the wrong time. A corrections officer on the education floor referred to them as street rats.

"City cops made another sweep, dumped the residue in the prison dumpster." Guys, usually young, caught up doing a rip and run or five-finger shopping, shoving matches, territory protection, and not much of anything beyond hanging out where they're not welcome.

They talked about their "public pretender," their assigned counsel who may have met with them for less than ten minutes before going into the courtroom to stand before a judge. Don't blame the public defenders—most of them are overworked, and barely have time to read the charging papers before representing their client.

For my part, I tried to help them understand what happened when they were "just hangin' with their homies." We read together the explanatory paragraph for anticipatory offenses in the sentencing grid of the criminal code.

> For persons convicted of the anticipatory offenses of criminal attempt, solicitation, or conspiracy under chapter 9A.28 RCW, the presumptive sentence is determined by locating the sentencing grid sentence range defined by the

appropriate offender score and the seriousness level of the completed crime, and multiplying by 75 percent.

Some said, "Huh?" At least they were honest about not understanding. Most said, "Shit," which meant the same thing. If they were interested, I'd show them the sentencing grid, the number of months for a given crime—one they asked about with all the innocence they could muster—and do the math on the board.

"Take a 48 months sentence as an example," I'd say while doing the problem on the board. "Multiply by 75 percent, and you get 36 months."

Math! Who can do math? That decimal thing was out there, man. They could do street deals in their heads, but not math with pencil and paper. I once considered math-anxiety a female disorder. Not so; most of those streetwise men drew back when I started multiplying by 75 percent. In most cases, I referred them to their primary counselors for specific information about their sentences. And in all cases I urged (and sometimes ordered) them to register for basic education classes. Those patient ABE teachers and their TAs helped those men increase their skills, which I suspect many put to good use back on the streets where they would continue to find it difficult to get decent jobs.

DOC primary counselors picked up where public defenders left off, explained to inmates how they got the time they were doing. But counselors are not trained in the law, or adult basic education skills for that matter. Try explaining the previous criminal code paragraph, or any other legalese, to those whose comprehension level tests below fourth grade and who have trust issues and walls higher than fences around the prison compound, and protective barbs sharper than concertina razor wire.

Over the years, even after Project Social Responsibility was modified and renamed, and I was free of most of its responsibilities, I maintained my reputation as a safe person to ask tough questions about almost anything. Men came to me with all manner of questions, many of them legal. If we couldn't sort out the answer with the help of my copies of legislative or administrative codes, I sent them to the prison law library to ask an inmate clerk.

I've heard all the snide comments about jailhouse lawyers who spend their time and our tax-dollars looking for loopholes in the law, and read news stories about frivolous lawsuits coming out of prisons to clog court dockets, but I appreciated those law library clerks. They knew how to read and use case law as well as the criminal code (legislative law) and prison disciplinary rules (administrative law), and they helped me help students. Awareness and understanding, I believe, helps all of us cope better with consequences for our behavior.

Now and then I heard inmates say that jailhouse lawyers, just like those in the free world, weren't cheap. Prison is a moneyless society, but services come with a price. A jar of instant coffee, a couple packs of tobacco and cigarette papers (before smoking was banned), candy bars, sodas, other things sold at inmate store. A man once asked me if he could have the purple pen I used to grade papers. (I never used red ink for grading; my students associated it with failure.) He said someone in the law library would help him with his case in trade for my purple pen. He threw a little tantrum when I suggested he just buy a pen at Store, and pay with that. Pens at Store had only blue or black ink. Other colors were considered contraband, and could lead to an infraction.

I learned early on in my prison teaching career, long before transferring to MICC, to keep pens and pencils in my possession at all times. As I mentioned in the preface, I wore mine over my right ear. Its visibility taunted inmates, one officer told me. I should keep it in my pocket. I said the remark sounded sexist; all pockets are not created equal. He left the issue alone after that.

I went to the law library clerk who'd allegedly asked for my purple pen, to see if the tantrum-throwing student could get the help he needed in some other way.

"You're not giving up your pen, am I right?" the clerk said. I shook my head. He shrugged. "It was worth a try, but here's the straight take on the bro. It's a waste of time and paper for him to appeal. He'd better stick with school . . . maybe a vocational program . . . otherwise he'll be rippin' and runnin' and doin' life on the installment plan. Even at the low end of a hundred bucks per day you taxpayers spend on each inmate, I'd bet he's going to cost you a million bucks. You can take that to the bank."

16

| Coping with Consequences |

Here's another thing I could take to the bank—I would be teaching discipline versus punishment to every PSR group, every parenting and family class, and every individual male offender who found his way into an Open Door session for as long as I remained at MICC. I spoke of consequences, a word male offenders didn't like. They preferred punishment; they knew punishment firsthand. I unraveled that with students in programs, classes, Open Door, and informal discussions in prison corridors, and came to the same conclusion every time. Punishment is inflicted on a person by an outside force; it's beyond personal control and it permits the punished to blame others for the circumstances in which they find themselves. Consequence implies personal choice led to the circumstance. That's heavy, man.

As a parent-educator I urged students to *discipline* their children rather than punish them, a fine distinction, considering each verb is included in the other's list of synonyms. I'm repeating here that discipline, by my definition, is meant to teach, train, or correct. Students at MICC saw discipline as other-inflicted. They went to disciplinary hearings where an officer read the infraction written against them and issued a decision. They might lose earned time or good time, or be given a sanction, a word defined in Webster's dictionary as that which induces observance of law. The prison system hopes sanctions teach. Inmates see sanctions as punishment.

In Washington State, all prison discipline is defined under the state administrative code section for the Department of Corrections. General infractions include unauthorized possession of stamps, theft of food, abusive language, refusing to obey an order, smoking and possession of tobacco products, and unexcused absence from any assignment. They're not too far removed from misbehaviors parents cope with daily. Comparing prison infractions, disciplinary hearings and sanctions to parenting helped me teach that negative consequences result from misbehavior.

The sanctions imposed for such infractions range from a reprimand and warning, which become part of the offender's record, at the low end, to confinement to cell or room with exceptions (generally school or work assignments), with up to 120 hours of extra work duty at the upper end. They're similar to what a frustrated parent might choose as a consequence for a child's misbehavior. They're far more reasonable than the serious abuse many students had experienced at the hands of a parent when they were caught with a forbidden item, when they sassed or cussed or refused to do as told, when they were caught smoking or skipping school.

Serious or major infractions range from serious misdemeanors through criminal felonies under state law and result in more serious consequences, just as more serious misbehavior within the family requires more stringent measures. The most serious must be remanded to local police departments. Those that can be handled within the prison may result in removal from open population to Ad Seg, reduction of custody status with loss of privileges and possible transfer to another facility, and time added to a sentence.

Whether they called incarceration their consequence or punishment, there were many men who saw being sent to prison as easier to handle than explaining prison and their crime to their children. One man I'll call Luke said, "Prison as a consequence is easy. I did the crime, this is my consequence. Telling my little girl what I did is the hard part."

His crime couldn't be argued away or made more acceptable by substituting another word. It was truth time; time to explain the adult rule or law he broke. Time to talk about choices and actions, and the consequences that reach beyond prison into families of victims and victimizers. Choices that change their lives forever. Luke's four-year-old daughter knew he was in prison, and she wanted to know why.

"Why can't you come home, Daddy? What rule did you break?"

Luke took every course I taught, and talked openly from the time he came through Project Social Responsibility about his father-role and his worries. Luke was in his late twenties when he was moved to McNeil Island, and had done several years for murder. He had recently married a childhood sweetheart who had a daughter by a man who left before the child was born. To the child, Luke was Daddy, the only daddy she knew, and she wanted him to come home. She was bright, inquisitive, and a tad impatient. She didn't like the early morning trip to catch the bus that transported visitors to the MICC boat, the boat ride itself, or the long walk on the island. Luke said she whined at visiting, and continually asked why he had to stay behind when she and Mommy left.

Luke's blonde good looks made staff ask, "What's he doing here?" He was athletic, well-groomed, personable, polite to staff and inmates, and an academic high-achiever. He followed prison rules without complaining, picked teachers' brains, and delighted the librarians in his quest for good literature. What could he possibly be doing in prison?

The answer is Luke was doing much the same thing Mr. Johnson, the biker, was doing: learning to cope with a long sentence for committing a serious felony.

For its part, DOC supports and permits inmate visits with family members and friends from the community because it fosters family unity, makes inmates more manageable, and eases their transition back to society. All visitors must be approved in advance, be on the inmate's visitor list, and abide by the institutions' policies. Like most prisons, McNeil Island had a designated visiting room and specific visiting hours.

Though DOC and individual prisons work to make the process dignified and orderly, there are always problems and complaints from inmates and visitors. Luke's daughter wasn't unusual. To visit MICC, visitors registered at the DOC bus depot located on the grounds of a state hospital approximately two miles from the mainland ferry dock. There they boarded buses for transport to the waterfront, walked from bus to ferry, and waited in line for a personal check-in which included a trip through a metal detector. Most women visitors carried clear plastic purses or clutches so an officer could easily see the items they were bringing inside. They needed one piece of picture identification. They could bring in limited specific personal hygiene items for themselves and their children and cash for vending machines or to buy chits.

Visiting hours at MICC were 9:30 a.m. to 2:30 p.m. five days a week, with most visits on weekends and holidays. Registration at the visitor parking area began at 7:20 a.m., the boat departed at 8:40, and arrived at McNeil Island at 9:00. The walk to the visiting area and check-in there consumed most of the half-hour until visiting officially started.

Think about Luke's young daughter's day and you will understand why she whined. Her mother wanted to check in at visitor parking before 8:00 to assure making the 8:40 boat, so they left their Tacoma home before 7:30. By the time the child saw her daddy, she'd spent two hours traveling and waiting, looking up at men and women in uniform, and listening to their sometimes impatient comments or commands. At lunchtime, her daddy and other inmates were served a sack lunch; she and her mother, and other visitors, had to buy food from vending machines. (Inmates were not to give their food to their visitors, but most I knew did, and many officers let it go. Now and then, possibly to make a point, an inmate was infracted.)

Inmates tended to get caught up in their own preparations for and expectations of visits, and forgot what their visitors had to endure just to get to the visiting room. Some inmates didn't like my reminders of the ease of their morning on visiting day. Their breakfast was prepared; all they had to do was walk from their living unit to the dining hall. The rest of the morning was theirs to fill as they wished until they heard their name called to walk to visiting. Now and then one would ask, "Whose side you on?" I always answered, "The visitors' side, especially the children's."

Luke appreciated all that his wife and daughter went through to visit, but his daughter's whining was becoming a major problem. He practiced positive parenting suggestions which included reminding his daughter to use her regular voice, and ignoring annoying behavior when he could. He knew he needed to do more. He needed to answer her questions about why he had to live in prison, and not at home. Though he was reluctant, he tried the simple truth approach I taught. When he said he'd broken an adult rule and prison was his consequence, his daughter said, "Say you're sorry, Daddy. Say you're way way way sorry, and you won't ever do it again. Then you can come home."

Luke found me first thing on a Monday morning after his Saturday visit. "Okay, Teach, now what?"

We'd had discussions in class about explanations using proper crime classifications, being matter-of-fact, and avoiding all gory details. We'd even practiced some answers. Luke had tried saying 'murder,' gave up, tried 'homicide,' and found it too unrealistic for a child. He said no way was the M or even the H word going to pass his lips. Why, he asked, should children have to learn such words?

Why indeed? Most children don't need to learn them, but they hear them somewhere. Inmates' children often overhear them, or are mocked with them.

Luke sent home class assignments so his wife could study the material along with him. They talked about discipline and problem solving on the phone. His wife started using "time out" on their daughter, always explaining it was a consequence and what misbehavior earned it. Soon that precocious child asked, "How long does my daddy have to stay in Time Out?" He knew he had to do something more to help her cope with his incarceration, and asked me if I'd listen to the story of his crime to help him find a reasonable explanation. I already knew Luke's crime involved homicide and agreed, teeth clenched, to hear the details.

Luke grew up in a small town. His parents divorced about the time he started high school, his dad moved to another state, and his mom started dating. Luke admitted he felt abandoned, though he hadn't used that word at the time. He said he got caught up in some rebellious behavior, but soon learned his mother's threats to send him to his dad were just that—empty threats. His dad settled into a new life, and soon called only on Luke's birthday and major holidays.

Luke started roaming at night with a group of kids who had similar broken-family backgrounds. They formed a gang, though it wasn't as sophisticated as inner-city gangs, and had no affiliation beyond the city limits of their farm community. Their gang was "into finding adults who would buy them beer and smokes." Now and then they did a little five-finger shopping, stealing chewing tobacco, candy bars, sodas, and now and then they got caught and had to work off the value of what they stole. Luke's mom knew he was getting into trouble, and warned him again and again she'd send him to his dad, though they both knew his dad didn't want him. In retrospect, Luke said he wished someone had imposed a more stringent consequence.

"Here's how we'd work it," Luke said. "We'd get our hands on some money, some of it guilt or payoff money from our moms or their so-called boyfriends so we could eat out and catch a movie. Instead we'd pool resources and find a guy willing to pick up beer or cheap wine . . . whatever, long as we had the price plus a little profit for the buyer. There were older guys around who got their own six-packs from profits they made buying for underage guys. We'd drink fast, and go looking for a fight. Any fight would do. We were all angry at the world. I'm not blaming my mom and dad, but I know it wasn't a good scene for any of us. Dad's gone, mom's dating and sometimes having dates sleep over." He studied the desktop for a time. "I know, from experience, how important both dads and moms are to kids."

One night, shortly after his graduation from high school, Luke and some of his buddies picked a fight with Mexicans who migrated to the area for farm work. Both sides got into name-calling, pushing, rather typical Saturday night stuff. "We rumbled, man. Fought over some guy's girlfriend. Battered each other with empty bottles and sticks and rocks. In the end we were all losers. Bruised and cut from broken glass. Guys on both sides needed stitches and casts. And one of their guys was dead, though we didn't even know that until the cops got there and got most of us rounded up. One kid on our side said I'd delivered the deathblow. Maybe I did, maybe I didn't. Either way, here I am. I was the oldest one on our side. Just turned nineteen. I'd been warned by cops more than once to clean up my act. In hindsight, I'd say the cops should have locked me up sooner. The kid who gave me up was only fourteen. He went to juvie. He's out now, having a life. No way am I telling any of that to my little girl."

A muscle at the corner of one eye twitched. Luke wanted to cry.

I agreed he should find another way to tell her the story. As she grew she'd need to hear specifics, but at four she needed a simpler explanation. I watched Luke struggle with his emotions and reminded him, gently as I could, children of inmates often look up old police reports when they reach maturity. His head shot up. He hadn't thought of that.

"Let's try reducing the story you told me to its basic elements. Something a four-year-old can understand, but without painting the same kind of scene. Something like this: 'When I was nineteen-years-old, my friends and I got into a fight with some other kids. People got hurt. One boy died. When there's a death, the prison sentence is very long."

Luke thought. The eye muscle twitched. "I wouldn't have to say the M word."

"I think you will have to say it, eventually, if you were convicted of murder—or even of manslaughter."

"Murder two," he said. "I got just under fifteen years; I qualify for earned time and work release." (Sentencing laws at the time of Luke's crime permitted him to earn one-third off his sentence and to do the last several months in a camp. Those laws have since become much more restrictive.)

The weight of it, the reality of his sentence and telling his daughter the truth, suddenly seemed too much for Luke. He dropped his head and hid his face behind his hands. "Oh, God, how can I tell her anything? I don't know, I don't know." We were in my office, with the door closed, but a large window permitted officers and others to look in. He had his back to the window, but remained aware of it. He didn't want to be seen or heard crying.

After a time I asked Luke what his wife wanted him to do. They were working together to parent, and her need and opinion were an integral part of his decision.

"She wants our daughter to know the truth, but she wants me to do the hard part. She says I have to tell, and then she'll take it from there."

"What do you want to happen?"

Luke looked up, and a little grin softened his face. "I want you to come to visiting. I want you to handle it. You can make it all better."

"We all want a mother, at times. Responsibility isn't easy."

A primordial groan came up from Luke's depths, as he realized he'd be explaining his crime to his daughter and future children through all their developmental stages. I'd seen it happen with other inmate parents as they reexamined their choices through the eyes of those they loved and hurt. For me it was heart wrenching to witness such pain, and to come to terms with the whole picture. In Luke's case, another family, a transient family far from their homeland, had to cope with a senseless, preventable death.

Luke wrote out and practiced what he would say to his daughter. Thinking about it made him sick to his stomach. He reported he'd thrown up a couple times. He ran the track when he could get to yard, and said running helped. Maybe the endorphins flooding his brain let him forget the task he had ahead, and the pain he'd left behind.

Luke must have been the first man on the education floor the Monday morning after he told his daughter about his crime. "Here's how it worked. She was sitting on my lap, and I told her I had a sad story to tell her, and it was a hard one for me to tell. Then I said it like we practiced. The fight, and people got hurt, and one person died. And she pulled away and gave me a look that broke my heart, and she said, 'No, Daddy.' I said, 'Yes, that is what happened,' and I started to cry. She put her arms around my neck, and she said, 'It's okay, Daddy, don't cry. I still love you, and Mommy loves you. But it's very bad to fight. Is that why they won't let you come home?'"

Tears came to Luke's eyes while he talked. Still he felt pleased with the visit, relieved he'd opened the door to honest discussions of his crime and incarceration. He told his daughter how old she'd be when he finally got to go home. If all went well, if changing laws for violent crime didn't change his time, he'd be placed in a lower-custody institution in two years. His daughter would be in school by then. His wife and daughter had moved from Walla Walla to Tacoma, over 250 miles, when he was transferred, and he envisioned them always moving to be near him, but that wasn't realistic. His wife had a job she liked, a church group that supported her, a place in her community. His daughter attended preschool and had friends.

Luke was working on a college degree, and had a growing interest in human behavior. He knew telling a four-year-old child about his crime was just one step on a long climb; a simple explanation for a four-year-old wouldn't suffice as she approached adolescence and developed mature thinking and reasoning skills. He started to look at his family patterns, how his parents treated him during a traumatic time in their own lives, how he handled what felt like abandonment when his father moved. Though they had made some poor choices, his parents continued to provide for his physical needs. Luke ignored offers of support from within his high school and community; he had chosen behaviors he knew to be wrong. He hopes someday he can help steer at least one child away from the line he stepped over.

The consequences of Kenneth's crime, second degree child abuse, will live with him in a more immediate way than those of many who were sentenced to far more time. Assault of a child in the second degree assumes the act was intentional and the bodily harm greater than transient physical pain or minor temporary marks. Kenneth had "lost it" with his infant son, and violently shaken the baby to stop his "out-of-control" crying.

His first-born son suffered brain damage from shaken-baby syndrome.

Kenneth was sentenced to three years and court ordered parenting classes. I first met him in Project Social Responsibility, where he stood out because of his height and his impatience to get started fulfilling the court order. He said he would be permitted supervised visits with his son as soon as he enrolled in a parenting class. A Child Protective Services case worker would accompany his wife and child to the MICC visiting room for special visits. (Two mid-week days were reserved for professional rather than personal visits. Legal, social services, and community-placement interviews were among those classified as professional.) He was anxious to start learning. I had to stop him from talking openly about his crime, especially in PSR. Child abusers are often victimized in prison.

Kenneth and his wife married young. She was pregnant—not an unusual circumstance. Neither his parents nor hers were thrilled about the marriage; both had wanted their children to complete college first. Kenneth was a high school All-American athlete. His wife, a pretty, soft-spoken woman, had admired his athletic ability, but didn't participate in sports herself. Both were white and called themselves working middle class. She had an uncomfortable pregnancy, and then a fussy baby. The caseworker told me neither set of new grandparents was much help to the young couple.

Kenneth said, "I did it. I shook my son, and hurt him, and I want to spend my life making it up to him. I just want to do my time and get out and take care of him."

"How will you do that?" I asked.

"Take care of him forever. Do things for him forever."

"How does that help him grow and develop? How will he develop the ability to cope with the learning disabilities the psychologists project? How will he learn to be, and do, and think?"

Kenneth's head hung, and I had a lump in my throat. My challenge was to teach him the realities of parenting a child who would struggle with learning, with structure and identity, with sexuality and responsibility.

In addition to PSR, I taught six parenting or family related college level courses, which were rotated over a four quarter year. Some were five credit classes. I couldn't teach every class every quarter and manage all my PSR responsibilities, but Kenneth wanted them all at once. He was determined to learn and succeed. No wonder he'd made All-American. Students like Kenneth can consume a teacher. I had to slow him down, convince him he needed to take one or two classes at a time. Even with one year off his three-year sentence for earned early release, and credit for jail time served, he could fit in all six classes as they were offered.

I joined Kenneth, his wife and son, and the caseworker at their special visits on two occasions, and I stayed in touch with the caseworker by phone. She held high hopes for the child's continued progress because the marriage remained strong in spite of the remarkable odds against it. Kenneth and his wife drew on their faith, and accepted support from a church family. She and the child attended special parent/child classes in the community and he had a former employer who would find a place for him when he got out.

Kenneth made a horrible mistake, but he wasn't a horrible person. For him prison served a purpose; it was his penance. He needed to do time to grow beyond the quagmire of guilt to the purposefulness of responsibility. Rather than get bogged down in shame and suffering, he used guilt as a springboard to learning. I knew he would never quit suffering and believed others would benefit from all he'd learned. He vowed to become active in helping parents and children when he was released, and had started a community project, with the support of his wife and church, while he was still inside.

Not all of those I taught, especially not all who went through PSR, chose to tell their children the truth about their crimes. Some didn't have the chance; the children heard it elsewhere, or the courts terminated parental rights, which ended the parent-child relationship. Some, especially those who had committed heinous crimes while drugged-out, simply could not find a way to explain what they didn't understand. For those, I suggested saying to their children, "I can't talk about it; I can only say it's not your fault, and I'm very sorry." In many of those cases, the children were, or had been, in therapy because of the crime, and had responsible adults helping them cope with the consequences of their birth-parents' choices.

But not all who came through PSR chose to listen and made that clear from the first time I called role. One young black man said, "I's a miss-oh-guy-ness, I don't be answerin' to no woman."

"Missile Guy?" someone said, which gave me the extra second I needed.

"Misogynist?" I wrote the word on the board and suggested he learn to pronounce it if he intended to hide behind it. He became one of my followers, though he remained an annoyance for that PSR group. As we wrapped up on Friday, another man in the group, an old con, waited to tell me he admired me for the work I did. "I have to hand it to you," he said, "the stuff you tell these guys, the way you handle them. You've got balls."

He meant it as a compliment. I thanked him and watched him go, thinking, *"Balls," said the queen—"if I had them I'd be king."*

17

| Family Matters |

The Washington State Department of Corrections supports inmates' connections to their families. Their website has one section devoted to "Family and Friends." The following is a quote under the header, "The Family Role:"

> DOC acknowledges the vital role families play in an inmate's life and the reentry process. We provide programming that is culturally relevant, gender responsive and informative. It is our intention to identify the challenges faced by the families impacted by incarceration, and to provide support and services relative to family needs. These services include parenting classes, assistance with reunification and referrals to other entities providing social services and support.

By Friday of PSR week the men had all the basic information necessary to work with their assigned primary counselor and the case management team on personal goal setting and preparing for release. Their goals included family matters. They received appointments and were told that failing to appear would lead to an infraction. They needed to sign off on their plans for the four core areas of PSR's overarching program: education, employment, family relationships, and personal awareness. Education staff registered them for classes, unit supervisors assisted with employment applications and reviewed their physical and mental health issues. They still needed to state what they would do about family relationships.

The time had come for each man to talk with his case management team about his family, including what support he might get from them. Those men who were serious about planning for reentry had made notes from our Wednesday sessions, including how to use a genogram (a pictorial family tree) to look at traits and influences from their family of origin. Genograms are used by genealogists, family therapists and medical personnel to create a picture of a client's family background.

In some PSR groups I demonstrated the genogram using my family as a way to spark thinking about family history and patterns, what family members would be supportive during reentry, and what family members might be problems. Inmates with chemical dependency issues often come from families with similar problems, and should plan to stay away from those family members during their transition back to the real world.

In an early PSR session a man who told me he was doing life spent most of his time looking out the window. He'd said he liked being on the island in Puget Sound better than in the old pen in Walla Walla. I didn't expect him to pay much attention to the genogram, so he surprised me by speaking up.

"You young guys, you ought to pay attention to the lady here. She's on to something. Any of you got a family out there, you owe them better than doing time. You still got a chance, you do right by them. On the other hand, if they keep booze under the sink or beer in the fridge, you better steer clear."

The weight of his words settled on those men. I watched for a time, thanked the man and said, "Your message may be the only one anybody here will remember as the months go by."

There were some nods in that group, but no one chose to talk about family matters or show much interest in the genogram handout. I sensed the wisest course with them would be personal disclosure. I grabbed a piece of chalk and turned to the blackboard.

"My dad and mother," I said, drawing the square and circle that represented male and female on the genogram, "their marriage line, and their siblings." My dad was the youngest of thirteen children; my mother had four brothers, one sister and one half-sister. The length of the sibling lines caught their attention.

The men looked at their handout explaining the symbols.

"Your parents both had a lot of brothers and sisters."

I put an X in Dad's square and Mom's circle, and their birth and death dates below.

"They're dead?" one of the men by the window asked. He sounded alarmed, but that could have been projection on my part.

Another, who'd been writing, said, "Not really old. Sixty-six and sixty-five."

"My dad died of a massive heart attack while landing a salmon during a fishing derby. His catch won a hundred silver dollars. My mother, who wanted nothing to do with those heavy coins, or the money in any other form, died of a heart attack nine months later while helping dress my nephew, who was then three-years-old."

All their eyes left mine to look out the window or at their handouts. They weren't about to let the emotional reality of parents' deaths get too close to their own locked down feelings.

I went along the board X-ing out all but one of my dad's siblings, saying, "heart attack, heart attack, heart attack . . . this living uncle had cardiac bypass surgery, this aunt and this one had cancer, this aunt died in her teens . . ."

From behind me I heard, "Lot of heart attacks."

"Yes, a serious pattern of heart disease in Dad's family." We talked then of lifestyle and diet, of the hard physical work my dad and his brothers did, and the hearty meals they ate. Those incarcerated men I saw as students advised me to be careful, given my history. That pleased me. Still, they didn't disclose anything about their families, nor did I ask them for personal information. Two men were writing, possibly creating their own genogram, possibly doodling rather than looking up. I moved to my mother's side of the genogram, and started the X thing again. Five of the seven were dead at that time.

"Some serious alcohol problems on this side of my family," I said, chalk still busy. "My mother's father died when she was a child, before her youngest brother was born. I don't know much about my grandfather, but an older cousin who is the daughter of this aunt here (I pointed to my mother's half-sister) believed he drank heavily and got violent when he was drunk."

I let them study the whole picture of my parents' generation, let them think about problems I'd mentioned, both common in families of men who go to prison: alcohol and violence. They looked up at the board, looked down at their handout of symbols, looked back. One man said, "The way you drew the half-sister . . . was she the man's child, and not the woman's?"

"Right," I said. Finally, I had a little interaction, and at least one man paying attention enough to discern what the genogram told them.

"Her mother die? The mother of your half-aunt or whatever she is to you?"

"We thought so, until my mother died and we found some old papers of Grandma's among Mom's things. One of the papers was my grandfather's divorce decree. My mother's youngest brother almost had a stroke over that news. My grandfather's divorce was one of those family secrets . . . the kind of thing children aren't told. Every family has some secrets. This one wasn't so awfully bad, but it upset my mother's youngest brother. He had created an idealistic image of the father he never knew. Their father, my grandfather, had been divorced, not widowed, and the child that was their half-sister stayed with him. Divorce didn't fit his picture."

One man nodded, then another. I added symbols for my generation and my children's. I wrote 'M' for migraine headaches by the symbols for my mother and both my sisters, and mentioned that our children had occasional headache problems, too, but not as severe.

"Migraine headaches are a pattern I've identified in my family. They began with my mother. I'm working in spite of one right now, not as bad as hers were. Perhaps telling you what I believe is the origin of the pattern will help my headache ease. Perhaps it will help you understand the innate power of family history and patterns."

Their eyes changed, they leaned forward, and they listened with interest to the story of my maternal grandfather's death.

My mother was seven when her dad died, suddenly she'd been told, of an asthma attack. He died at home; she knew nothing more. She had no idea where she was at the time, possibly high in the limbs of a madrona tree where she went with her books to hide and read. She loved books, and read beyond her age.

That's all she knew, and all my sisters and I knew until after her death when I learned from her older sister that Mom had been there in the same room and witnessed her father's death. She suppressed the event, a lifelong suppression for her. Was it trying to peck its way through her subconscious shell every time she had a migraine? Were those migraines, nearly sixty years of them, related to the heart problems that caused her death?

Why did her sister, my Aunt Stella, tell me this story so graphically some ten years or more after Mom died?

"He died. What difference does it make how he died? He died, and we managed, and here we are," Aunt Stella said in her rather gruff matter-of-fact way.

Yes, here we are. My two sisters and I are still impacted by the death of a Grandfather we never knew, due to the trauma it inflicted on our mother who suffered debilitating headaches the rest of her life. They came on when stress built up, and sent her to bed in a dark room for two or three days at a time a couple times a month.

Mom's dad died in his home on Puget Sound, north of Bremerton, in the house he'd built at the turn of the century for his wife. At the time of his death he worked in Seattle as a carpenter, and commuted by auto ferry to spend weekends with his pregnant wife and their children: sons sixteen, thirteen, and four; daughters ten and seven.

I imagine my grandfather choking, unable to breathe, and panic settling over the household. They're all there, though the four-year-old was napping in a bedroom. Was the north wind howling down the Sound as it often did? Was rain blowing in under the roof of the big front porch? Was my grandfather drunk, or in a rage at a child?

What caused *this* asthma attack? What made it worse than others? My aunt doesn't know. She remembers a wheezing sound; she knew her mother was worried. She remembers her older brothers bolted from the house at their mother's orders, spoken in Swedish. They ran to the beach, dragged the rowboat to the water. Stella watched them row away, side-by-side on the middle seat, their strength doubled. Then they were out of view, her dad was slumped in a chair, and her mother was boiling water to make steam to help with the breathing.

"Where was my mother?" I ask.

Aunt Stella shrugs. "Under the kitchen table, with a book maybe. Or out in the barn sneaking food to a kitten she'd saved from drowning. Who knows?"

There's a long spell of time when calm prevails in the house at the edge of the Sound, though my aunt knows her dad isn't doing well. But she's only ten, and not completely aware it isn't just another weekend day when her father's home for a time. In her old age she remembers her father as a wonderful man, and is certain he never spanked her, though he may have spanked my mother who seemed determined to avoid chores. Aunt Stella says my mother always got out of helping in the house. Where, I wonder, did Mom develop her outstanding cooking skills?

"Your dad taught her," says my aunt. I don't protest. My dad could cook.

The boys and the rowboat return with a passenger, a doctor from the naval torpedo station at Keyport, over four miles away. My aunt remembers some scurrying after the doctor came on the scene, and possibly more boiled water. Her father is stretched out on a daybed in the living room. The room is hot, crowded, but quiet. The doctor is in charge now. She thinks her mother assisted him, and she has a clear memory of my mother, now in the living room, standing by the door that opens onto stairs up to bedrooms.

There's an odd noise, then a gasp, a shout, a moan, and a child's scream. My mother's. My aunt recalls the scream and describes seeing blood.

"Then all hell broke loose," my aunt says. "The boys and the doctor ran for the rowboat, and rowed off to get more help. Mom sent me up the hill to a neighbor's to get linens. Your mom was screaming and screaming, and banging the stair door against her head. Screaming and banging, and the boys and the doctor going off, and my mother just rubbing and twisting her hands. I remember I didn't run when she sent me out. It was a steep hill."

The navy doctor had tried to perform a tracheotomy. My aunt didn't know if the knife slipped, or if the doctor wasn't practiced in that procedure, but in his attempt to open the trachea he cut the jugular vein.

I told snippets of the story to PSR groups when it seemed appropriate, and only mentioned that my mother's migraines seemed associated to her father's death when a group engaged in discussions they generated.

How should her father's death have been explained to my

mother when she was seven? I'd suggest something like this:

"Your dad had a history of serious asthma problems. He had a very bad attack. A doctor came to the house and performed a surgery. It's a dangerous surgery. Your dad died. You were there, and you were very scared. I'm sure you remember the blood. Seeing blood frightens children."

Once a simple, straightforward explanation has been made, the child should be encouraged to ask questions and express feelings. Traumatic events need to be discussed again and again, and even written about.

That was the history, the secret that I believe was the psychological cause of stress-related migraine headaches. I further believe that my sisters and I learned a pattern of not talking about stress, or not learning positive ways to reduce stress, and experienced similar headaches. Once we had identified the pattern and its origins, we talked openly about stressors in our lives. It helped, though it wasn't a cure. Migraines are complex. We also learned to be stoic from our Scandinavian parents, for good or ill, and that remains with me to this day.

Some therapists call family secrets a conspiracy of silence. Someone doing, or having done, time in prison is often a family secret. Thus, my mother's story, or more accurately my story of learning the truth she never knew, relates to inmates in an orientation or family program. They need to find ways to help their children and other family members hear and cope with the truth of their criminal behaviors, and the resulting incarceration. They need to search for and examine patterns that influenced and conditioned them so they can help their children avoid them.

That is a responsibility of parenting. Building trust in students was a responsibility of teaching. No two PSR groups heard the same stories told the same way, but they heard something that helped cement my reputation for understanding that bad things happen in families. They arrived in PSR, many of them angry, and left, as they said, with food for thought. Some of them reported back that they'd gotten square with their families, or started writing their own history, or had something on paper with their case management team. Some were progressing with their prison psychiatrist, or speaking up in a chemical dependency group.

Some came to me with their stories. That's part of teaching troubled students in any setting. Some of those who wanted to tell their stories were sex offenders. That was another challenge.

| Sex Offenders Inside |

I did not become inured to criminal acts because I taught criminals. Some of them told me stories that gave me sleepless nights or haunting dreams. I didn't dump what they told me on anyone else. The only way I could reconcile the crime with the person was to remind myself that I was a good teacher of the subjects I handled and of steps my students could follow in changing their behaviors. They each had a good therapist to help them with the whole picture of their lives and crimes. I did not argue any individual's innocence, or get on soapboxes on their collective behalf. I did like some students more than others. Any forthright teacher at any level would admit as much.

One of my favorite students killed a man who molested his two stepdaughters. He was sentenced to prison for Murder One.

Another man I enjoyed having as a student and classroom assistant is now out and rebuilding his life. He had to register in his community as a sex offender for attempted adult rape.

My fondness for them had nothing to do with their criminal acts. I liked them for all their other characteristics and traits. Both were honest about their lives before prison, worked hard to grow beyond what put them there, and expressed sorrow for the pain they had inflicted on their victims, the victim's family and their own families and friends as well.

One of these men is an accomplished fine artist whose work is shown and sold in galleries. The other is an artisan with wood. I own and treasure one item created by each. (Sales of items crafted by inmates is handled by prison staff.)

Both are intelligent, educated, and accomplished in other areas. Both worked as Teaching Assistants in Adult Basic Education classrooms, and took every college level, personal awareness, and vocational class they were permitted by legislative mandate during their incarceration. They spent time in my classroom both as students and as volunteer assistants when my workload overwhelmed me.

At the time they committed their crimes, both were abusing alcohol and other drugs. I offer that as information, not excuse. It is a common factor in the commission of many crimes. At least one former Catholic priest who sexually abused young boys admitted to alcohol addiction, and suggested in an interview that other priests guilty of child sexual abuse also were alcoholics.

Why did I care? For two reasons. First, understanding human nature and motivation is important to me. Even after working with untold numbers of adults who sexually abused children, I still struggle to understand. Second, almost all sex offenders return to their families, or start a new one. That reality needs to be considered when we make decisions about them and all other offenders. They came from families and have families. Recent studies examining problems faced by children of incarcerated parents have identified problems with depression, learning ability and shame. Social programs need to focus on serving the children's needs rather than severing their relationships with their parents.

Whether committed by male or female, child sexual abuse garners the most severe emotional response from the taxpaying public. We hate it. We are sickened by it. We want such offenders removed from our society. We ignore their need for education and guidance, their own background as victims, their shame and suffering. We want them locked up forever.

But that doesn't happen. I repeat, almost all sex offenders return to their families, or start a new family. They need help if they are to learn to cope with their offenses inside the fence and back outside in our communities.

It may help to hear the story of the loner from the homophobic PSR group. He was the man who said I needed to define that word. When he told me a chapter of his story, he merely scratched the surface. It took at least a year and several classes with me before he related the whole story. I'd sensed he was a child sex offender on our first meeting, when he sat alone, when he told me I needed to define homophobia. I suppose now I could say those were clues, but in reality I think it went deeper. To my growing despair, I found I could spot them in a group of offenders. There was an air about them. Remorse? Shame? Possibly, but if those feelings did exist they were underlined by more telling factors. Those men didn't fit parameters of prison-wise older offenders or streetwise younger ones. Most were well-groomed, had high verbal skills, and once held successful positions in their communities.

They were "typical guys next door" in Middle America.

Ron, the loner and first sex offender to confide in me, said without preamble, "You couldn't help your mother with the problems that developed in her family, but you've helped me. I'm a sex offender. My stepdaughter's my victim. I've been worrying about keeping that a secret here, and I haven't given much thought to her . . . the rest of my family . . . how they're all hurt . . . what they need to do. I see, now, the danger in secrets."

I remember feeling prickly things climbing my spine and slithering down my arms and thinking, Dear God, do not reveal your crime in this place, that's not what I meant. I remember saying, "There are professionals here who will help you with your burden. You do know, of course, not to discuss your crime with other inmates."

A sensitive response on my part? Not at all. I did make good eye contact with him and must have had a look of empathy on my face, because he met my gaze and tried to smile. His eyes were wet. I think mine must have been hard.

"No," he said. "Oh no, I don't intend to admit to anything beyond problems with alcohol and an estranged marriage. Guys tend to think domestic violence when they hear your marriage is on the rocks, and I let that ride. It's just that I found a new way to think about some things, and I want to thank you. You've already helped me."

It's always nice to be thanked. Maybe Ron's sense of clarifying his thinking was just that, but I wasn't certain what Ron expected of me and didn't want to hear specifics of his case. In his defense, he wasn't trying to dump his worries on me; he was simply thanking me, and stating the nature of his offense. He'd started doing what I'd urged the men to do: search for and examine patterns that influenced and conditioned them so they could help their children avoid them.

The Washington State Criminal Code specifies sixteen classifications of crimes in the chapter titled "Sex Offenses." They range from rape in the first degree and rape of a child in the first degree to custodial sexual misconduct. They do not include incest offenses, prostitution, or patronizing a juvenile prostitute. Those are classified in chapters titled "Family Offenses," "Indecent Exposure and Prostitution," and "Bribery and Corrupt Influences."

I may have missed other classifications; I'm not trained in the law.

All have the same classification in the prison convict code— Rapo.

Scum, the worst of the worst, fair prey for prison rapists. Especially if they committed child rape or molestation, which makes them "baby rapos" or "baby fuckers."

In other inmates' eyes, Ron was all the above.

During my tenure at the women's prison a woman dubbed a baby fucker was raped vaginally and anally with a mop handle to "teach her a lesson." Does that make sense? They hate the crime, so they do the same thing.

Ron knew he would be subjected to such treatment if the general population learned details of his crime. He was handsome, rather slight of build, an easy mark.

Another among my female students doing time for sex offenses was a woman in her middle years who had several grandchildren. She was called a baby fucker because her husband had sexually abused their daughters, and she had known about it but hadn't stopped him. She wanted to enroll in parenting classes and participate in the parent-cooperative preschool program meeting inside the fence. Other inmates banded against her and she accepted it as her lot in life, much as she'd accepted the abuse she also suffered at her ex-husband's hands. She remained in ABE courses and longed for an opportunity to learn more about positive parenting, child development, family history and patterns. When I first met her, she made an X beside the signature line on her school enrollment forms. She couldn't write, or even print, her own name. During her incarceration, she earned ABE certificates for learning to read and write, and for math; she was there long enough to get her GED.

Her daughters visited her over the years, and were ready to welcome her home to her role as mother and grandmother when she was released. They forgave her, though not their father. Her earliest parent-education was accomplished by completing worksheets as she learned to read and write, and met with me one-on-one. She never got past the inmate barrier blocking her from parenting class and preschool lab participation. That's the strength of the convict code, even in a small women's prison.

At MICC the PSR team believed confronting inmate attitude included getting men to examine their view of sex offenders. We needed to push them to rethink the rapo label, and to speak out against acts of violence done in the name of cellhouse law. That became part of my presentation, much as it was in parenting or family history and patterns classes. Men needed accurate information about sex offenders and offenses, and I had completed special training in that field. Because discussion stirred up such anger, I kept my presentation academic, beginning with legal issues, statistics, and definitions, and heavily focused on pedophiles and child molesters.

According to the administrative staff, over half of all male offenders then at MICC had references to attempted adult rape in their presentence investigation reports, but they had not been charged with a sex crime. Their accusers were generally women with whom they had personal ties. Some accusations were seen as statements made in the heat of an argument, others as "piling on" or "getting revenge." Some primary counselors said it went with the territory—the women had criminal backgrounds, too, but the accusations had to be noted.

Psychologists, sociologists and criminologists define a pedophile as a person who sees the relationship with the child as romantic, grooms the victim for sexual encounters, and uses charm and threats to keep the encounters "our secret." Pedophiles usually abuse the same victim again and again over an extended period of time. They may have multiple victims, often siblings or friends in a community group, but they tend to abuse far fewer children than child molesters do.

Child molesters, by contrast, tend to have multiple victims, chosen at random. Molesters rarely victimize a child more than once. A prosecutor told me it was not uncommon for a molester to have one hundred or more victims a year. A child molester is the unknown "bad man" lurking in the alley or more often the playground.

There is no known "cure" for pedophiles or child molesters, though behavior modification is used with some who fit an "amenable to treatment" profile and who agree to the tenets of treatment. The majority of their victims are female.

I gave groups time to digest the information, and didn't interrupt the diatribe that followed. The sexual scandal that reached into the Catholic priesthood, and that is being addressed by the current Pope, is part of sex offender dialogue. Most of the offending priests were labeled serial pedophiles, and most of their victims were young boys. As you might guess, those homophobic MICC students considered men who sexually abused boys worse than rapos and baby fuckers, and unworthy of life, even in prison.

Where does Ron fit into this picture? Where does his offense register on the criminal justice scale? On the emotional barometer? I'm going to relate Ron's story because it is similar to the stories of so many men I taught at MICC, and because he and most of the others have returned to society and have not reoffended.

Ron took several classes from me, worked for a time as a TA on the education floor, and met regularly with a DOC psychiatrist. He had been charged with and found guilty of child rape in the second degree, defined in the state statute as "sexual intercourse with another who is at least twelve years old but less than fourteen years old and not married to the perpetrator and the perpetrator is at least thirty-six months older than the victim." The age specifications in the offense are critical; pedophiles and child molesters almost always select much younger victims.

He was sentenced to seventy-six months, the mid-range for a first offense in that classification for an offender with no prior criminal record. Had he been charged with incest in the first degree, a crime with similar parameters but classified as a family offense, he could have been sentenced to as little as a year and a day. (The year and a day sentence, or twelve to fourteen months, sends a man to prison rather than just to county jail.) Prosecuting attorneys and the criminal justice system decide case-by-case whether to charge an offender with a sex offense or a family offense.

Ron felt he'd been unfairly treated by the prosecutor, and believed with professional help he would be able to stay with his family and heal the wounds. He wanted his wife and all the children to have counseling, which they were getting by the time I met him. He hoped their counselor would encourage his wife to remain in the marriage and bring the children who weren't his victims to visit. His wife had been having an affair, which was the reason Ron used for becoming involved with his stepdaughter; he saw it as getting back at his wife for the hurt she'd caused him.

He was also a late-stage alcoholic at the time. He'd had a couple DUI's (driving under the influence) convictions, though no jail time for them. He was a successful blue-collar worker with a good income, a nice home, children who succeeded in school and extracurricular activities, and he and his family were respected members of a church. And then his wife went out and had an affair.

Ron had a knack for downplaying his crime, the sexual abuse of his stepdaughter, to focus on other factors of his life that showed him to be a victim. He'd been through treatment programs for alcoholism and quoted literature that declared alcoholism a disease. He had a disease, his wife went out and had an affair, and he found solace elsewhere.

It took Ron a long time to look back at his family of origin and identify the patterns he'd followed. Rather than work to understand the origins of the pattern, he wanted to skip ahead and get his family of procreation to understand. But he needed to go back. Ron's dad was an alcoholic and was physically abusive. His mother drank, but only socially. I always pointed out use of qualifiers such as "only." Inmate students often used qualifiers when they talked about their lives and family issues.

Finally, when it became clear Ron's wife wouldn't bring the children to visit, and in fact was filing for divorce, he started telling the rest of the story. The pattern emerged. His mother had sexually abused him. She saw him as her little man. Her husband was often away from home, or home but passed out. Ron was a victim of sexual abuse and a child of alcoholics. He started drinking young to ease the pain of the things his mother did to him. He once tried to talk to his grandfather about his mother and was beaten and called a liar.

There's the pattern. Abuse begets abuse begets abuse until someone stops it. Ron knew he needed to face his own role as victim in his family of origin, do his work to find resolution, and then help his family of procreation. He needed to expose the secret and break the pattern; he needed to free his children. He just didn't know how to begin.

His children's counselor helped them, but children heal faster when they know the sexually abusive father understands the harm he's caused, and has a sense of why he committed the abuse. They also must hear the abuser say it was not their fault. They needed their dad's permission to talk and heal, and enough history to know he'd entered adulthood, marriage, and fatherhood as a wounded human who brought his pain, his family secret, to the new family.

Ron needed to quit being a victim—part of his pattern—so his children could get healthy. He needed to quit blaming others because it was keeping him a victim. He needed to grieve for the hurt done him, and I urged him to do so. But my role as parent educator was to teach parents what children need and how to help them achieve those needs.

I liked Ron and willingly listened to him when he wanted to talk about his life, but I also expected him to work with a therapist. He was a good student, grasped concepts including family system theory, and continued to reach out to his children. Their relationships mended. His stepdaughter was able to confront him, with her counselor's help, and then to forgive him. Ron, with his therapist's help, worked through the grieving process to the point where he could start planning for his future goals and responsibilities.

Ron's mother was still alive. She continued to be his biggest stumbling block. He couldn't get her to admit she'd ever done anything to hurt him, or any of her children. She was the perfect martyr—the wife of an abusive, alcoholic man and the mother devoted to her children—and the only thanks she got in her older years was a bunch of messed-up kids. She had complaints about all of her children, but of course Ron disappointed her the most. It's not easy to have a son in prison for a sex crime: the whole world reads about it in the paper. (Ron said it never made the news, so far as he knew. He lived in the greater Seattle area, where most crimes don't get newspaper space.) Like him, Ron's mother was a victim who used blame as a shield.

It should come as no surprise that the grandfather who beat

Ron and called him a liar had sexually abused Ron's mother through most of her adolescence. Did the abuse go back farther? If so, that information is buried with Ron's grandfather.

That is one family's pattern of a dirty little secret: sex abuse. In some families it takes incarceration to break the pattern. Families whose incarcerated member learns enough to help the rest of them are fortunate.

When Ron left prison, he registered as a sex offender with the police department in the community where he settled, but no one posted negative flyers about him. The likelihood he will reoffend is very low.

Over the years I met and worked with several dozen men with stories so similar to Ron's they seemed to be reruns. They were nice-looking, well-groomed men, most of them white, who had grown up in financially stable families; attended good schools; married relatively young; established themselves in successful careers; attended church at least somewhat regularly; and drank socially at parties with friends or after work with buddies. They had nice-looking wives who also worked outside the home. Most wives had a child by a previous relationship, not always a marriage. Somewhere along the line, as the marriage faltered, the drinking got heavier, and the man slipped into serious alcoholism. He functioned in the workplace well enough to stay employed. He functioned less well at home.

Those inmates were neither child molesters nor true pedophiles. They were generally responsible men who sought education and counseling. Many worked as teaching assistants in basic education programs, where they helped students with math, reading, and English course work. In time many of them went on to prison industries jobs and sent money home to their families. Some had wives and children who visited; some were able to remain in touch with their children only by mail and occasional telephone calls. Completing parent-education courses was part of their case management plan, and often part of a court order. Those men were sex offenders.

They were sex offenders who would return to their families. They would register as sex offenders with their local police departments, report to their community corrections officers, seek and find jobs, and reintegrate into society. One of the most important things I taught them was how to explain their crime and incarceration to their children: how to unravel secrets and tell their children the truth. Telling the truth wasn't easy for them, and teaching them how wasn't easy for me, but I kept at it for their children.

I worked with them without judging them, pushing them to learn all they could about parenting before they returned home. I taught all the men who came to me, whether they enrolled in a course or sent a kite to the education floor because they thought I might be able to help them with a problem or get them some information. I taught them right up to the time that parent education was eliminated from the curriculum by the legislature.

Long before the legislature declared parent education at McNeil Island a frill that could be handled by volunteers, there were detractors who maligned me for the tax dollars spent to educate Ron and others with similar crimes. I said to them, "Would you rather they not be educated?" I say it still and urge them to research the issue. They need to think it through away from the emotions that arise on both sides.

About the time I was preparing for an early retirement due to the drastic cuts in correctional education in Washington and most other states, a DOC unit supervisor at McNeil Island told the education director and me that he wanted a special course developed for men who had sexually abused a minor child. He said the course should be called "parenting for sex offenders," and every man who came to MICC with that in his criminal record should be forced to register for the class. I was shaking my head NO before I had a chance to reply. The education director's face registered shock. Neither of us knew what prompted that man to broach such a suggestion at that time. We all knew the ramifications for such offenders. Neither the community college nor the prison hierarchy would have permitted a course so titled.

In Washington, sex offenders who are deemed likely to reoffend, or who refuse to participate in programs designed specifically for such offenders, are remanded to a special commitment center, currently housed at what was the annex honor camp on McNeil Island. Sex offenders who are amenable to treatment, and who will return to their communities and families, should be encouraged to participate in parent education courses. It's in the best interest of the children.

19

| Teachable Moments |

Though I often wondered about specific events in the lives of my students, I didn't ask. So how did I come to know so much about so many? They told me, some more than I wanted to know. They trusted me, even when they didn't like the messages I delivered to them individually and collectively.

One man who'd become so institutionalized he no longer wanted to leave prison told me I reminded him of his mother. He didn't mean it as a compliment, and may have enrolled in courses I taught so he could point out errors in my curriculum and beliefs. He started with Behavior Management, the class designed to help inmate parents reparent themselves while learning how to parent their children. But Richard had no children. He just wanted to reparent himself because his mother had done such a poor job. It was her fault he was back in prison, and at McNeil Island rather than Washington State Reformatory at Monroe (now the Monroe Correctional Complex), the institution that paroled him to his mother.

A standard life sentence at the time Richard entered prison was twenty years, with one-third off for good behavior, or thirteen-four in prison vernacular. He'd been a respected member of the Lifers'

Club at the Reformatory. Men sentenced to life often came together in prison clubs or groups to make sense of doing time. They created items in hobby shops to give as gifts to other inmates' children, and helped new inmates adjust to the reality of prison. Richard did well with the structure and familiarity of that environment.

"See, at the Reformatory I've got my time down and nobody hassles me. I do my thing with other lifers, and I get respect because I've got time in. Then I go home, and my mother expects me to get a job before I even figure out the bus route. She's all the time on my case. She figures she's working to provide the home and the food, she's been sending me money through the years, and she wants me to take a job. Any job. Finally, I couldn't stand the nagging so I went out and did a job. Robbed a bank, work I knew how to do."

Richard's classmates watched for my reaction, saw my left eyebrow climb, and climb more, before I spoke. What words did I choose? I don't recall, but I know they centered on the comfort of blaming others for poor choices. I wrote, 'Blaming others keeps you a victim,' in huge letters on the dusty chalkboard. I may have added exclamation points, though I tend to avoid such punctuation. Like his mother, and not incidentally the parole board, I would expect him to get a job on release and found his excuse about bus routes weak.

It took most of the quarter for Richard to realize his mother, a divorced woman in her sixties who'd had all the responsibilities of rearing two sons, was tired. She'd struggled with the reality of Richard's earlier crime, visited him in prison, sent him money, permitted him to parole to her. She'd lived alone for several years and then suddenly had a grown man in her home; one who wanted to take time adjusting to the real world, have good home-cooked meals and an allowance, so to speak, so he could buy a few things he needed. When Richard realized he had pulled his mother back into a developmental stage she completed twenty or more years earlier because he returned to his own interrupted adolescence, he began to understand. In our last conversation, before he managed a transfer back to the Reformatory, Richard said he hoped his mother lived long enough so he could get back out before she died.

I still think about him and wonder if she had the same hope, or if she feared it would be a rerun of the bad times she'd known with him. She'd been doing time, too.

The message—blaming others for your choices keeps you a victim—blossomed on blackboards, erasable white boards, small posters, assignments, and activity sheets throughout my tenure. Blaming parents seemed more prevalent among incarcerated men than women, though some of what I term parent-blame was levied against government, society, the system. I saw those entities as equal in the eyes of the blamer, and their complaints as adolescent railing against authority. To my knowledge, no scientific study supports my premise that female felons more readily accept responsibility for their choices than do male felons, but the theory fits my understanding of sex differences and maturation rates.

Brad was another man who took parenting classes even though he wasn't a father. He soaked up information, wrote essays as he learned and helped students who struggled with spelling, grammar and sentence structure. One night, when class ended, he dropped a note on my desk with three words in big letters: No Self Esteem.

We'd just completed a unit on building self-esteem in children through encouragement and proper discipline, during which he grew increasingly quiet. In his self-evaluation, at the end of the quarter, Brad wrote an essay about a boy whose mother was a drug addict and prostitute. To me it was an ugly story of a boy who often went out into the night streets to wander while his mother worked; to Brad it was a revelation. He had needed time in prison to separate himself from his mother, and to find a sense of self-worth. He learned far more than positive parenting concepts; he learned he had an inquiring mind, could do well in academic and vocational subjects, could help those with less developed skills, and had a right to grow up as an individual without the stigma he'd accepted. He served his relatively short sentence and made it in the real world.

I often think of those two men as opposite ends of the men-doing-time continuum. Both were white males. Richard blamed a mother, who had likely fulfilled her role (at least well-enough), for his long-term incarceration, yet he seemed to like his life inside. Brad chose to grow beyond the unpleasant life he endured with his mother and to establish himself as a responsible citizen. In between were hundreds of men who felt guilt and shame for the hurt they caused their victims and their own families, and some who continued to blame society's rules for their incarceration. Most found ways to do their time, and grew up a little whether they set out to do so or not.

For several months Lonnie, an African American (he preferred that to black) man who had done much of his sentence in an intensive management unit at another prison, came to the alcove outside my office every morning during one of the ten minute period movements. I often joined him and asked how he was doing. He always answered, "Same ol', same ol'." He was enrolled in basic skills in a learning lab, where he was gradually improving his reading skills and learning early math. He came to talk to me about his family, or his perception of them. Though he never said an unkind word about a family member, he did say, "Life hurts." He had been locked up since about age nine, and had liked intensive management at the Washington Corrections Center in Shelton, where he was alone, better than being at MICC, where he was housed in a cell with nine other men. Intensive management is a maximum security placement for offenders who are security risks or who need treatment for mental disorders.

When a psychological update suggested Lonnie's mental state showed he needed to return to intensive management, he came to tell me goodbye, and thanked me for teaching him about families and parenting on his own. He said it was the most he'd ever talked to a woman. I hadn't realized he saw our ten-minute sessions as a class and made a note to remember: we don't always know when we're teaching.

Curt, another black man, dropped by my office regularly to check out my outfit of the day. I made most of my clothes in those days (tailored wool or linen suits and dresses, silk or fine cotton blouses) and we discussed padding stitches on the underside of jacket lapels and collars to give them a proper roll, easing in sleeves, quality linings. He knew fabrics, fashion, how to create a wardrobe that stayed in style. He was a massive man who worked out with weights to stay in shape and kept his head shaved for effect. As he said, no one messed with him. He'd been a tailor's apprentice in Seattle, sold drugs on the side, gotten caught. He wanted to go back to tailoring and suspected he would give up some of the buffing-up when he got out. Suits don't fit well over such massive chests and biceps, and he wanted to model some of his own creations. He asked me not to tell anyone about his tailoring career. To other inmates, drug dealing was acceptable, an interest in textiles and design marginal if it went beyond looking good in your threads, and tailoring was just woman's work with a fancy name.

Curt was transferred from McNeil Island to a work camp without fences, a step up, a step closer to release. He was anxious to go, even though it meant working for the Department of Natural Resources (DNR) planting or thinning trees. Not all men wanted to transfer to work camps, especially camps in remote forested areas. Curt went, determined to go through the process, though he'd never lived outside an inner city area. His attitude and willingness to do what it took to get beyond prison made him more likely to stay out once released. He was an articulate man who demonstrated appropriate respect for authority figures, worked as the teaching assistant for the math teacher and treated all the men who came to the education floor as students. He tutored back in the blocks to help men prepare for tests (and, in a sense, for life). He was their go-to guy. He's one of the many former felons who did his time, reintegrated into society, and didn't make the evening news or get any newspaper ink.

Most men I worked with knew when a transfer was pending. All inmates had regular six-month or annual reviews with their counselor/case managers. When time to move on neared, they watched the Daily Transfer Sheet and let their anxiety interfere with school or work performance. Now and then men received an education or job hold so they could remain at an institution, but as the prison population increased, holds decreased. The system moved numbers and crime classifications, not men. Empty beds filled with men who had earned enough points for less restrictive settings, men who lost points and were being disciplined, men a staff member wanted moved. Male inmates are always on the move. Many overcrowded jail and prison systems refer to some inmates as "on the bus," on the move until a bed opens.

The Daily Transfer Sheet, distributed to all areas of the institution, included a list of men leaving MICC and their destinations, a list of men moved to or from Ad Seg, cell or living unit changes, job assignments and changes, and Lay-ins and Call-outs. Lay-ins are used for illness and cell-confinement; Call-outs for movement to an area not generally open to an inmate. I started holding Open Door sessions at MICC to avoid the whole process of Call-outs for men who needed assistance with Office of Support Enforcement paperwork, or with letters to court or other agencies about their children.

One man who heard I wrote "good letters" asked for help with his correspondence with a superior court judge in a rural county. Paul, a young white man, wanted to explain his plans to care for his son, who was living with an older female relative. A dependency hearing regarding the child's placement loomed. Paul feared the state would soon file for termination of his parental rights by reason of his incarceration and disappearance of the boy's mother. The current caregiver, Paul's aunt, was in poor health.

Paul arrived at MICC mid-quarter, registered for a parenting class, caught up, and read text materials for other parenting and family courses not being taught that quarter. I helped him with his correspondence, and wrote a letter to the court stating what coursework he had completed. I'd written similar letters for women for years, and found the men wanted and needed them, too. Paul was the first man I taught who filed to gain primary custody of a child whose mother was out of the picture.

Though state law requires that parents only be represented, not present, at dependency hearings, someone at MICC thought Paul and his son deserved a chance. He was escorted to his county's court, where he stated his case. He received custody of his son, and to his surprise a ten-day early release from prison. Ten days may not sound like much, but it means a superior court judge and the Department of Corrections saw worth in him as a person and as a father. He had completed a treatment program for his drug-related crime, and said he'd learned his lesson. He'd nearly lost his child.

Word got around that Paul got custody and ten-day early release. There was some general grumbling that he wouldn't have gotten either were he black and from Seattle, but a black Seattle man disproved that sometime later.

John enrolled in parenting classes when he was returned to McNeil Island for a work release violation. He was angry and belligerent, and wanted to make me his enemy by comparing his tough life as a black male to my easy one as a white female. John needed to show the state a satisfactory completion of a parenting course. He was in class by court mandate at a time when my patience-quotient had been seriously taxed, and I was having trouble meeting all the needs of all the men who found their way to my classroom and Open Door. He wanted to argue, or possibly to beat me down with words. He needed me more than I needed him, but he refused to acknowledge that until the state filed for termination of his parent-child relationship to free his son for adoption.

When John first went to prison, his mother took his son into her home. The boy's mother, a drug abuser on the run from the law, abandoned him shortly after his birth. While John was at work release in Seattle, his family left a car close enough to his job so he could drive to his mother's home for visits with his son. He fit it into his schedule and didn't get caught. Father and son grew in their attachment. It worked right up to the time John's mother died of a heart attack, and the state stepped in to take John's son.

"The state snatched my son from my people and put him in a

foster home with Caucasian parents," John said. He made Caucasian into a dirty word. "I went crazy, got terminated, got sent back inside, to this here island."

I explained how child dependency laws worked. When John's mother, an approved foster care provider, died suddenly, the child had to be moved to another approved home. A member of John's family, who wanted to keep the boy, didn't qualify. Unfortunately, the state often has too few African American foster families.

Once John decided to learn parenting concepts, he aced three separate classes, not because he was bright (which he was), but because he loved his son. I helped him write letters to his son's caseworker and the court, a big step for him.

"I'll help you, but I won't write for you," I said, and asked him what he'd learned.

"That I'm responsible for most of my son's problems." That was not an easy thing for him to accept, but he did. It felt like a blackout shade snapped open and let in the light. His son was acting out, running away from foster care, and using abusive language. John wrote, in part, "I have learned those behaviors occur when a child is angry and hurt, and he is likely angry at me and his mom. I believe I am the person who can best help him cope with his problems and feelings. At age eight, I know he would be difficult to place for adoption."

In the letter, John admitted he sold drugs, stated he completed a chemical dependency program, and listed the vocational certificates and college credits he had earned. The petition for termination of his parental rights was filed. I was subpoenaed to court as his parenting teacher.

The state's attorneys couldn't attack John's performance or grades, so they dwelled on his attitude. I described it as cocky in the beginning, but dedicated once we agreed which one of us was the teacher. They asked if I knew about his blatant violation of work release rules, and permitted only a Yes or No answer. Before dismissing me, the judge asked if I had any further comments. He must have seen comments trying to jump out of my mouth.

"I don't approve of inmates on work release violating rules, even when the rules impede personal growth, and told John as much. He acknowledged it was a poor choice, but said he wanted to spend time with his son and swore to me he will keep the boy out of crime and in school right on through college."

John's parental rights were not terminated, and he was granted ten days early release. He liked to say he won his case. I like to think his son won, and so did society. The last time I heard, father and son were making it in the real world. John's day in court worked in the best interests of his child.

During my first few years at MICC, I taught one or two classes a week at the Annex, an honor camp about three miles from the main institution. Most of the men there did hard physical work during the day and took classes at night for specific skill development. I liked working with them and always enjoyed the short drive outside the fence, even though the Pierce College car was so decrepit its headlights sometimes quit mid-journey. Men at the Annex had more freedom of movement than those inside. There were no fences, just general boundaries.

At one time well over half of the inmates at the Annex were young Hispanic men with short sentences for drug-related offenses. Most would be deported to Mexico when they completed their time. They did their assigned work, studied English, and congregated in groups with other young Hispanic men for camaraderie and safety. Most were slight of build, easy marks for prison predators. Rumors of ugly incidents occurring at the Annex abounded, but investigators couldn't get anyone to talk. There are strong bonds among men doing time. Even those not involved in incidents generally won't "snitch-out" those who are. When the Hispanic men decided to settle the score, they used a stick (some reports said baseball bat) to beat an abusive man to death.

Official DOC word said the fight broke out over use of a kiln in the Annex hobby shop. Word among inmates differed; a score had been settled. The version didn't matter. Within hours, all the

Hispanic men at the Annex had been transferred from the island to other institutions, and much of the remaining population moved inside the main institution to Ad Seg. One of my coworkers who taught English as a Second Language lost her entire class. I lost half of mine. A shroud of silence draped the island. Inmates inside and at the Annex simply didn't talk about it, at least not where they could be overheard.

The public never seemed surprised when such prison incidents made the news. They rarely heard or read stories of inmates' successes. They certainly didn't know how many incarcerated men earned academic or vocational diplomas, moved up the employment ladder, made amends with their families, started paying child support or restitution, or sent most of their earnings to mothers who had supported them through their bad times.

Though some officers said men flocked to Education because women were accessible there, inmates said they came to learn. School made life inside seem a bit more normal and it rewarded them with understanding, awareness, certificates-of-completion, and academic credits.

We called one short-lived but rewarding attempt to create a more normal environment FACT: Fathers and Children Together. FACT gave men enrolled in positive parenting classes an opportunity to interact with their children in a child-oriented space away from regular visiting. There had been a similar successful program at the women's prison.

The associate superintendent at that time worked with MICC administrators to find funds for equipment and supplies, hired a professional early childhood educator to work with the fathers and children, and cajoled chaplain and staff for space in the prison chapel meeting room. While qualified fathers and children met for a few hours in what became a child's center, I met across the hall with mothers and caregivers to present the same basic positive parenting materials the fathers used in my classes.

From the beginning it was difficult to get children transported for the weekday program, which took place when caregivers worked and older children were in school. In evaluating the pilot, we recognized it needed to be offered on weekends in conjunction with regular visiting, but in a separate space. There are many successful programs like this in place in prisons nationwide, including one at MICC that remained in place until closure of the facility.

In an odd way, a man I'll call Jerome embodied the determination I saw in many prison fathers to right wrongs done to their children. He struggled to learn positive parenting concepts that differed drastically from his own upbringing. Jerome was on the tall side of average, with ebony skin and searching black eyes. He worked fulltime in the prison kitchen and took parenting classes at night. He spoke about his daughter and son with love and devotion, and remorse for their circumstances. They were in foster care, and part of a special social services program to give them a better chance in life. Their mother had abandoned them; Jerome didn't think she'd return.

Prior to our first FACT session, Jerome often showed up on the education floor dressed in kitchen whites, a white-gauze hairnet over his thick hair, and rubber boots used in the kitchen scullery on his feet. He asked questions about specific situations and told me his son, by age four, demanded to see a search warrant when police came to the door.

"How do you feel about that now, Jerome?" I asked.

He lowered his head. "Ma'am, it was an awful thing to do. I love those children, and I want them to have a chance, so I'm doing all I can to earn their respect."

On the day of our first FACT meeting, I waited with the group teacher and students, including Jerome, for the caregivers and children to be escorted into the prison and brought to the chapel. The men were nervous. They paced, looked at the clock, looked in a mirror, smoothed their hair. CO's radios crackled, and officers exchanged information. Finally word came that the group was headed our way. The men moved to the chapel steps. I waited inside, watching through the window.

Some children skipped along the sidewalk, uphill from the dock; others clutched a woman's hand. All were dressed in what looked like their Sunday best, though we had sent word they would be working with paint and other craft materials. There were no black children among them. I stretched for a better look. My chest hurt where my heart must have stopped beating. Had the dock officer who did the first check-in made a mistake when he called over the official visitor information? Why was Jerome sent to the chapel if his children didn't make the trip?

I moved outside, ready to console Jerome. Children and caregivers climbed the steps. Jerome stood there grinning, arms open, tears in his eyes, as a boy and girl about eight and ten ran to him and clambered into his arms. He was the first of the group to make introductions.

"Ms. Walker, Ma'am, I'd like you to meet my daughter and son."

The other men introduced their children; the escorting officer and chapel CO herded caregivers into our separate room. Delighted children's voices floated on a breeze. Beyond the chain link and concertina wire, sun sparkled on the waters of Puget Sound and the MICC ferry returning to Steilacoom. I followed the caregivers into the room where I'd set up tables, an easel, and stacks of materials. The caseworker who brought Jerome's children was unaware of my surprise, and I didn't mention it. I assumed he was their step-dad, a situation that is common in prison, though I knew even then to beware of assumptions.

When the program ended, an officer escorted caregivers and children to the boat, and Jerome went back to work. The FACT teacher and I cleaned up the rooms and locked away supplies: paints, colored paper, children's scissors, glitter and glue, books, and assorted items you might see in a preschool. She ran for a boat; I returned to the education floor, and my next responsibility. I didn't see Jerome until the next day, when he poked his head into my classroom just as men were leaving for period movement. He smiled at me, looked down at his wet rubber boots, back at me with tears in his eyes, back at his feet.

"Ma'am, could we talk?"

"Of course, Jerome. Tell me about your children. Did they enjoy the program?"

He nodded, shifted his feet. "I'm sorry for the surprise, Ma'am. It's not something I wanted to bring up in class."

Something in his demeanor told me I was wrong about his being stepdad to those two children. "I could see they love you."

"Yes Ma'am."

"Are they adopted?" That would be quite unusual. Black children get adopted into white families, but almost never the opposite.

"No Ma'am, they're my children, born to my wife and me during our marriage."

I'm neither doctor nor scientist, but I knew those children weren't his by blood. I closed the door, got him to sit down, and sat beside him. "Jerome, you don't need to tell me anything. I know all I need to know. You love them, they love you, and a caseworker thinks enough of you to keep you and the children together while you do your time."

"Ma'am . . . Ms. Walker . . . I do want to tell you. See, those two were born to my wife during our marriage, like I said. When they were born, I waited for their skin to take on some color, and for their faces to tell me they were mine. Well, the first didn't come to pass. They stayed white. But those faces told me they were mine all the same. If my wife found her pleasures in some other man's bed, well, that's life. Those children are mine, right enough, and I supported them all the time I was out there, and I send them money off my books every month."

Jerome was blinking back tears, and I was too. I grabbed the role of toilet paper I kept handy for such times, tore off a length for myself and left it close enough for him to use if he chose.

He blew his nose. "I love them more than my life. Love them enough to do this time and go on out of here back to the real world and wash dishes for a living this time if need be. Whoever put those children in my wife's body must have done it for me. Seems I can't do it for myself, somehow. The social worker's okay with that, long as I do right by them. Those agencies never got no word out of my wife, and now she's gone they're not like to hear from her."

We both tore off more squares of toilet paper, and I told Jerome I felt privileged to know him and to have met his children. And then I broke a major prison rule, and a legislated one for that matter: I put my hand on Jerome's and gave it a squeeze.

Every man I met at MICC had a story to tell about life's influences and personal choices. Most of them, like Jerome, do their time and return to our communities. I saw them as men, students, sons, brothers, husbands, fathers. They were men doing time, and then they were men who had done time, and finally they were men.

20

| The Power of Writing |

I believe in the power of story and writing their stories gave students another way to think about their lives. I made writing an expectation, indeed a requirement, of every course I taught, from term papers for college-credit courses to Writing to Clarify Thinking as part of every assignment for parenting and family courses. I'd done so with women students, some of whom struggled for a time to find an opening, then wrote vignettes or volumes about their lives. Men deserved an equal opportunity to look inside themselves.

"Write," I'd say to male students, and see blank stares or frowns.

"Write? Write what?"

"Write down what you're feeling right now."

Heads reared back. Chairs scraped. "Feelings?"

I'd walk around the room, look at blank papers, squiggles and doodles and use the quote attributed to sports writer Red Smith. "Writing is easy . . . just open a vein."

Early in my McNeil Island days, an education director decided to take advantage of my determination to get men to write and assigned me a preparatory-level English course. We called it

Writer's Workshop; men who considered themselves writers and chose to enroll called it Creative Writing; men assigned the course by the education counselor called it Hell.

Some men who chose the course saw themselves as authors waiting to be discovered, others used writing to fill time and sort life, and thought they might have something to say. Whether skilled enough to be published, or mediocre at best, all benefitted by working to learn the craft of writing. Somewhere along the learning curve they made self-discoveries that taught them more than most curricula ever could. One good writer who was reluctant to submit his work, wrote in the Farewell Book students later created for me, "I'm grateful for . . . your writing class. For me, it was so much more than merely putting words down on paper. I put part of *me* down on paper, and there were those who listened."

Self-awareness. There, in a thimble, was what I hoped to accomplish with all the Writing to Clarify Thinking and Writer's Workshop assignments I cajoled, charmed, and threatened students into writing.

Most of the correctional officers I knew, including Lieutenant Burton, scoffed at my belief in any inmate's ability to grow through self-awareness, but I hold the belief as truth.

Eddie, a career criminal who robbed banks with some degree of success, committed burglaries when opportunity permitted, and managed two innovative prison escapes, asked me to critique his life story, written as fiction. He was in his late fifties or early sixties, had some talent and prior training, and a few poems published by small (he said obscure) presses. I made several written comments on his work, but I saved what I saw as the most important character revelation for when we talked. As a boy, Eddie had gone into a church during a wedding, stolen money from the purse which the bride had left in her dressing room, and then cut a chunk out of the wedding cake that waited in the church basement.

"Tell me about the nine-year-old boy cutting into a wedding cake and taking off with a piece," I said. He frowned for a moment, then shrugged as if to suggest it wasn't a big deal. I don't think he saw it as very important, certainly not as clever as some of his heists, or his escape from a southern state's prison. He talked without telling me what I wanted to know, so I told him theories about young boys who steal, which suggest, regardless of object, the boy is trying to steal love.

"Nah," Eddie said, though he did agree with me about symbolism of stealing from a bride on her wedding day, and specifically of stealing a piece of wedding cake topped with a bride and groom, thereby ruining the centerpiece of the new couple's reception. He listened to me and read literature about children who steal. He admitted that no other explanation of stealing seemed to fit. There was no peer pressure involved, no test of skill, no real rush from the deed; he had clearly known it was wrong at the time, and he even felt a little ashamed afterward.

"Why, then?" I asked.

Several weeks later, Eddie told me I was right: he was trying to steal love. During those weeks he wrote a long poem about that event and reduced it to a haiku. I preferred the long poem. It showed the anger and sadness hidden behind the swagger.

Does it matter? Absolutely. Eddie helped other inmates deal with their time. He may be helping other writers even now due to his long sentence. His own increased awareness may help them think about what they're writing. I hope he reached the point where he could admit that he was helping.

Collin was another talented writer who needed little more than steering away from clichés, participle phrases, and adverbs. He wrote with pathos, though some of his stories were too brutally descriptive for my taste. He'd been born in Northern Ireland and had watched his dad and other relatives die in the streets. He came to the United States in his early teens when his mother remarried and moved here. From all accounts, his criminal behavior, which included weapons theft and the torture of a person who betrayed him, reflected the horrors of his early childhood and his view that any means serves the end. He was righting wrongs done his family and all Irish Catholics; he was avenging his dad's death, expunging the memory of a boy of six seeing guns pointed at the father's head, hearing them fire, watching the father's head disappear, the father die. I suspect writing saved his sanity and would not be surprised to see his work in print one day, though he will likely die in prison. He was moved from McNeil Island to another prison for trying to escape. An inmate he'd trusted snitched on him. It wasn't his first experience with being fingered.

Therein lies the making of a good story. I hope Collin writes it rather than acts on it. Snitches are never safe.

Sam, the man whose farewell note I quoted, wrote poetry that met the criteria literature professors teach, but he hid most of it, or sent it out to someone he could trust would keep it locked away for him. He also wrote prose, including an outstanding morality short story. I encouraged him to submit his work for publication. He tried once, without success. Perhaps he will try again and one day share his talent with the world. His personal story unnerved me a bit, but Sam needed to write it and he needed others to hear it.

Many men wrote heartfelt poetry. I read all they brought me and encouraged them to write more. Many also wrote fictional accounts of their crimes, and demeaned law enforcement and correctional officers, prison staff, and almost anyone in positions of authority. I told each writing class that I would not read such writing and they wouldn't receive credit for it. Nor would I read pornographic writing, or anything depicting physical or sexual abuse beyond stating what they'd suffered from a parent or caregiver.

Over the years two men asked to drop my writing class because I didn't permit freedom of expression. I signed withdrawal forms for both. One came back later, said he'd grown up, gotten most of his "dark stuff" out of his system, and wanted to work on his skills.

Dan, a man who liked to write editorials about discrepancies in the criminal justice system, also wrote about a motorcycle he found in an old barn and bought from the farmer for a fraction of its value. The bike had belonged to the farmer's son, a Vietnam War casualty, and the farmer saw something he liked in Dan. He wrote with passion about the bike and his first ride, his first real taste of freedom after being released from jail. It was a spiritual story, and a story of spirits, for some unseen force saved Dan from death in a blind turn on a steep grade. He pondered the event and his insatiable appetite for drugs. His parents and sister, a supportive and pleasant family, came to an island graduation program. They said Dan seemed to need time in prison to slow his brain down from thrill seeking. Dan said they had him on heavy meds inside and credited those "ding biscuits" for letting him get his thoughts down on paper.

Clive used his skills to write the curriculum for a specialty course in computer technology. Credit for the writing went to the instructor who hired him as a teaching assistant. Clive's own story revealed a man who'd had some success as a minor league baseball player, but who didn't know how to act in social gatherings. He'd emulated others, escaped from his fears with heroin, and ultimately found his way to prison, where he earned a college degree from an extended learning program offered by the University of Washington. He paid for all courses beyond those offered by the community college at the time.

Men wrote about fathers who abused them with fists or weapons; fathers who abused them in the name of religion, and fathers who set the pattern of criminal behavior and expected their sons to follow suit. Men wrote about children lost to them because the mothers disappeared. They wrote about "messing up" at work release facilities they hated so they could return to the womb of medium security prison. One light-skinned black man wrote about racism until he discovered his own racist attitude kept getting him in trouble. Then he wrote about his black father, a man unknown to him, and how he felt about a man who abandoned a woman and child. He was very bright and had much to offer others with similar experiences, but responded to encouragement with grunts until, just once, a little grin escaped. One man wrote a story about coveting the bread in a sandwich he saw me eating one registration day. The bread had hazelnuts and whole grains, and was quite good. I was grabbing bites mid-afternoon of a thirteen-hour workday without time for a lunch break, trying to be discreet, checking registration forms while I ate. The men had been to Mainline, where they were served a large meal. My classroom served as a place to wait.

"Did the bread look like it would be worth giving up crime, and drugs, forever and all eternity?" I asked.

"Could be," Doug said.

I hope it was worth it, just as I hope all the men who authored stories about their sorrows and losses, their regrets and shame, have found their way back to society. As I said to Lieutenant Burton one Chain Day, every inmate has a story. Writing frees the spirit and reveals the soul, even for those who will never again live outside the fence.

| Inmates and Victims |

Should inmates and victims come face-to-face inside prisons? Does listening to victims' stories help inmates rethink their behavior and do the work required to make better choices? Victim Awareness courses gained popularity along with "tough on crime" legislation, and are still part of the curriculum in some facilities. I was tasked with facilitating Victim Awareness at MICC and found the tenets of the course conflicted with my work in PSR and parent/family education.

A local group of crime victims and their families had come together to make their voices heard and their suffering known to the Department of Corrections. The group developed a course with cooperation of the department, with an end goal of gaining rights for victims that were similar to the rights of criminals. They united on the strength of shared grief and anger, and grew to become an important component of the DOC's work to make offenders accountable for their crimes.

"Criminals," the victims' group argued, "have the right to an attorney at taxpayer expense if they can't afford their own. They have the right to remain silent when arrested, the right to plead not guilty when charged, the right to a trial by a jury of their peers.

What about their victims? What rights do they have?"

Victims, their families and friends, and entire communities, were incensed by the ease with which several offenders had walked away from work release and committed abhorrent atrocities, the same atrocities that motivated MICC to design and implement Project Social Responsibility. The victims' group argued the crimes could have been foreseen; the offenders' records, they believed, indicated those men were not good candidates for release. One had threatened revenge against witnesses in his earlier crime, and acted on it, killing two adults and an eight-year-old girl. He was sentenced to death; the sentence has since been carried out, but as the victims' group said, it doesn't give them back their loved ones. They wanted criminals to know how it feels to be victimized; they wanted criminals to stop committing crimes. And they wanted specific information about individual felons.

They campaigned for classified information about their victimizers' treatment and progress during incarceration, and advance notice when those men or women were transferred from one institution to another, especially from maximum or medium security prisons to minimum security camps, pre- or work release, or community corrections/parole status. They wanted permission to attend classification hearings, and to have their voices heard by those making the decisions about felons who had victimized them, their families, their communities.

And they wanted financial compensation for the expenses incurred for physical and psychological injuries. "Consider a crime scene where offender and victim are both injured, and need medical attention," the group's leader said. "On arrest, the offender's injuries must be tended at taxpayer expense. Arresting officers are responsible for seeing to the offender's transport to a medical facility. Though officers may also call for transport and attention for the victim, taxpayers do not pick up those costs. The victim does."

Crime victims often say they want those who offended against them or their families to remain incarcerated forever, an understandable but unrealistic wish. About 95 percent of all convicted felons eventually leave prison. Rather than standing helpless in the shadow of justice and sentencing laws, the local victims' group started working with DOC and community college personnel to design an education program. The program challenges offenders to empathize with crime victims, and identifies intervention strategies to reduce chances of reoffending.

I attended a quarter-long Victim Awareness class at a pre-release facility before facilitating one at McNeil Island. I made it through two quarters of ten sessions each before petitioning a then new education director to be relieved of that responsibility. I admired the victims' group efforts and the program they helped bring to prison, but the classes were beyond the pale for me. Victims came into the prison classroom with their stories and stark video accounts of egregious crimes. The victims who gave their time in the Tacoma area included survivors of child abuse, child sexual abuse, and rape; a sibling and a spouse of a rape victim; parents of murdered children; the mother of a Tacoma boy sexually mutilated by a man who had walked away from work release; the director of a local victims' group, and representatives from the Sexual Assault Crisis Center and Mothers Against Drunk Driving.

Two of the victims' group members were politically motivated, practiced in speaking out against crime and punishment and, in my opinion, hell-bent on making audiences squirm. Other victims were uncomfortable in that old prison classroom, and struggled to relate their stories. Though they'd spoken at prerelease facilities, they didn't seem prepared for the boat ride to McNeil Island or the long walk to Control, where they had to sign in a second time. An unseen force operated the electronic gates that opened for their entry and clicked shut behind them. I met them at the boat and walked with them, explaining the procedure. We were being watched by cameras. I introduced them to education staff and the officers who would walk by the classroom to glance through the corridor windows every ten minutes or so.

Some members of the victims' group came to the island only

once. They cited the time the trip required and the inconvenience of an afternoon rather than evening event as their reasons for not returning. I believe they found it difficult to let their pain go, to heal, when they had to repeat their stories again and again, watch the video again and again, face men again and again who had committed crimes similar to those they'd suffered.

One of my colleagues dubbed the class Guilt 101.

Early Victim Awareness classes were indeed heavy on guilt and blame without what I saw as an adequate balance of opportunity for offenders to change. Victims spoke to them and showed them depressing videos without providing adequate preparation for discussion. The first students were handpicked by classification staff who considered them amenable to the coursework. I read those students' records for insight to their own backgrounds. My classroom role consisted of distributing assignments, collecting completed work and reading it, writing weekly reports for classification staff and meeting with each student to help him keep the information in perspective so he could find ways to use it for his own work toward growth and development.

Facilitating a program differs from teaching a class, and in truth I am a teacher. I did not find facilitating rewarding. In fact, I found it depressing and dreaded having to sit through the sessions.

As part of the course objectives, inmate students were asked to identify and list five feelings they had about their victim(s) and five ways their behaviors affected victims' lives. Unfortunately, those men hadn't been trained to recognize and identify feelings and hadn't given much thought to the aftermath of their acts. They got caught up in intellectualizing the events. They spoke in terms of thoughts, evident in comments such as, "I feel that it was wrong of me." When I asked where in their body they felt evidence of the wrong, they said, "Huh?" Getting to remorse takes work. The men selected for the group had not been through Project Social Responsibility, so they lacked awareness in basics we covered there. One man said he felt it was wrong of the victim to try to stop him; it was just a burglary, which turned into homicide because the victim came home and got in the way.

Identifying personal patterns of behavior related to the commission of their crimes was another objective of the program. Again, due to a lack of background in human behavior or whole system theory, the men struggled with the concept. They were being pushed to cope with too much at once. To their credit, most of them tried to understand it all: concepts and theories, victims' personal pain and reactions, their own and their families' and friends' despair. One man became very depressed as the sessions went on, and one got more and more angry.

Perhaps Trevor, the angry man, wasn't a good candidate for the program in spite of the case management team's assessment of his readiness. About mid-way through the quarter, he jumped to his feet while a victim was speaking. His desk chair spun into the aisle. His feet tangled with the desk feet and slowed his progress toward the speaker, a man whose son had been killed by a drunk driver. I can only guess what Trevor intended.

He later told me he considered the man a pompous ass, a father who couldn't let go. I knew enough about Trevor's case to understand the old feelings the speaker had triggered, but that did neither of us any good. Of course, the incident had to be reported, written up, and investigated.

Trevor, who was also enrolled in another course I taught, went to Ad Seg. The unit at MICC fit the euphemistic title "The Hole." It was an underground maze of small cells off corridors that could have been dug by a subterranean animal. Focused security lights created eerie shadows. Electric fans circulated exhaled breath and melancholy. I went there with Trevor's assignments and to monitor a final test. I asked why security staff couldn't observe him take the test. It wasn't their job. Officers posted there weren't nose-wipers. How had I forgotten?

As a result of Trevor's behavior, Lieutenant Burton decreed that a blue uniform (correctional-officer) attend the remaining Victim Awareness classes, a disaster for our program's goals. Victims were there to speak to offenders, but their eyes settled too often on the officer. Offenders tempered their questions and responses to fit standards of the convict code. Though I argued, even begged, for the officer's removal, the lieutenant's order stood.

Throughout the quarter I worried about Chayton, the Victim Awareness student who showed signs of depression. His feeling statements, completed at each session's end, first worried and then alarmed me. After one particularly graphic presentation, he wrote comments I decided should be seen by the unit counselor who selected him for the program. My decision upset Chayton, who asked why I'd gotten the authorities involved. My concern for his wellbeing rocked him. I was a teacher, a white woman with an education; he was an Indian, looked down on by teachers and whites all his life. So he believed. We talked about what led to his perception. In time, we talked about other matters, including Native American brotherhood, and how to embrace spiritual beliefs while doing time. The system didn't make it easy, though the DOC did permit volunteer spiritual leaders to meet with the men.

Like most Native American men at MICC, Chayton had a medicine pouch in his cell, stored as required in a shoebox. His was wrapped in a state-issued red bandana, a feather attached, its quill bound with leather and heavy thread. With the influx of Bloods and Crips gang members into the prison, all red bandanas had to be sent out or destroyed. They were replaced by khaki bandanas.

I don't know what happened next, though I suspect Chayton had no one to accept the package with his medicine pouch, and possibly inadequate funds to mail it. He didn't tell me anything.

Lieutenant Burton came to my office one afternoon with a brown lunch bag clutched in his hand. He stuffed the bag into my briefcase, told me not to look at it until I was off the island, not to ask him a question, and not to mention it to anyone, ever. The brown bag contained Chayton's medicine bag and totem. I still keep them in the brown bag for its symbol of simplicity, and have them stored to return one day to Chayton, should he contact me, or to maintain as they are if he doesn't.

What I don't know, the missing middle of the story, is what transpired between Chayton and the lieutenant. Neither ever told me, but whatever did happen impacted my relationship with both men. I respected Chayton for the humanity and spirituality I saw in him, and the lieutenant and I became better friends. (The lieutenant did grant me permission, after he retired, to write about the event.)

I was relieved of the task of facilitating Victim Awareness after two quarters. In time, it was taught without bringing victims to the classroom. Many of the victims burned out. They wanted to enlighten and confront inmates, and further their own cause, but it took a horrendous toll. They needed to make peace in other ways and eventually helped effect legislative changes regarding crime victims.

In 1999 Washington State passed the Offender Accountability Act, which focused resources on offenders most likely to reoffend and cause harm to their victims and communities. The act also strengthened reparation and restitution obligations of sentenced felons. Inmates' earnings and monies sent in are held in a trust account. They draw on their accounts for Store, recreation user fees, education that isn't part of the basic program, health care co-payments, and communication including postage, email services, and newly installed video visiting kiosks that are similar to Skype. Their funds are also drawn on by state law for their legal financial obligations (20%), child support (20%), DOC cost of incarceration (20%), mandatory savings (10%) and the crime victims' compensation fund (5%).

Like most states, Washington's DOC has a Victim Services division. Victims may enroll to receive information about when an offender is moved within the system, when he or she is scheduled for release, and to report unwanted behaviors such as any attempted communication from the offender. It's not a perfect system.

22

| Parenting From a Distance |

Parenting responsibility, like crime debt, does not end at the prison gate. Unless terminated by law, inmate parents have rights and obligations to their children. Parenting from a distance is an emotional commitment they make to do all they can for their children without criticizing or attacking the primary caregiver.

Through my early years in correctional education, I collected information and developed curriculum to address concerns specific to inmate parents to help them maintain a positive connection with their children. The concept became a pilot course at WCCW, with the accompanying book, *Parenting From a Distance: Your Rights and Responsibilities*. It is now in its third edition.

I liked teaching Parenting From a Distance at least as much as I disliked facilitating Victim Awareness, yet they are bound by similarities. Both ask convicted felons to look beyond themselves, think about what they have done to hurt others, and choose to make amends. But the parenting program focused on positive actions incarcerated parents could take to help their children, while the victim program seemed to keep them stuck in guilt and shame.

When crimes parents commit send them to jail or prison, their children become victims. Inmate parents have a right and responsibility to explain their crime and incarceration to their children. I consider it one of the most important tasks of their distant-parenting role. They consider it the most difficult. Stories in a previous chapter show moms and dads struggling to say, "I broke a law, and prison is my consequence."

Children separated from parents create their own ideas of the truth from comments they hear when adults in their lives don't give them clear, honest answers. They develop fears and anxieties, and they need loving encouragement to go on with their lives while the incarcerated parent does time.

Preschool age children see themselves as the center of the universe, which means they tend to feel responsible for the separation and worry about what will happen to them when a parent leaves. "What did I do bad to make him (or her) go away? Who will love me? Who will be my mommy or my daddy? Will Santa Claus still find me on Christmas Eve? Will daddy or mommy know me when they see me?"

Grade school children are saddened by separation from parents and need to express those feelings, learn it's okay to cry, and learn how sad feelings lead to angry actions. In this stage of development, they are learning to think about rules and values, and they are developing internal controls.

Teens fear they will make the same mistakes their incarcerated parents made. They need help seeing themselves as individuals separate from their parents and peers. They need permission to express their feelings about prison and how it impacted their lives. Teens may also reenact the criminal behaviors of a parent as a defense mechanism if they're being ridiculed.

All children at every age and stage of development need to know the incarcerated parent is okay. Communication with inmate parents alleviates many anxieties and fears caused by the unknown, and by movies and TV shows depicting the horrors of jail and prison. While I taught at the women's prison, an inmate's son hitchhiked from Florida to see her. Of course he was denied admittance: he wasn't on her approved visiting list. He was one of many children who set out to find a parent lost to the system.

The young son of another incarcerated woman began acting out in dangerous ways, once setting a fire at a group home. He wanted the police to put him in prison with his mother. Without communication with her, he had no understanding of the system. He'd never heard of "juvie."

Parenting From a Distance explored those truths, and taught simple things: telephone etiquette, preparing ahead for phone conversations, writing letters to children, making cassette tapes for them, celebrating birthdays and holidays from a distance, selecting TV programs children and parents could watch separately and talk or write letters about later.

It taught complex things too: answering difficult questions about crimes and prison, handling financial concerns, including financial support children might expect from the incarcerated parent; preparing for reuniting and problems both children and parents encounter during those transitions, and learning about laws impacting children and families.

Students read dependency laws and codes that affect children and families and learned to cooperate with their children's primary caregivers, especially regarding visiting. In time they begged for copies of information on realistic expectations of visits inside the fence and how children often act out afterward. Children might fuss and cry; revert to earlier developmental stages (thumb sucking, wetting or soiling, tantrum throwing); and withdraw into sadness. That's normal. Almost all children readjusted within a day or two, but not all caregivers were willing to cope with the behavior, and some used it as a reason to avoid taking children to prison visits.

Men enrolled in Parenting From a Distance discussed conflicts they encountered with their children's mothers at visits and about coming to visit. "We have to work harder to help them understand what we're learning," one said. "We messed up, we're in prison, but we've probably learned more about positive parenting and children's needs than they'll ever have time to hear. They're busy doing the hard job. They're parenting every day."

He was right . . . they had learned more theory than most of their children's mothers or caregivers. I reminded them it's easier to come up with solutions for parenting struggles when the children aren't there fussing, misbehaving, and demanding immediate attention. One night an agitated student told the class he'd just had another fight with his old lady. "She's having a rough time with our son, so I was trying to give her some advice, and she hung up on me."

After his classmates commiserated, in male-inmate language, I asked what advice he'd given.

"I told her she's handling him all wrong, she needs to learn a few things."

"She's mothering an eight-year-old boy by herself, and you told her she's doing it wrong?"

"Yeah, because she is."

"Let me see," I said. "What analogy can I use to span the sex differences here? I think telling a woman she's parenting wrong would be akin to telling a man he's making love wrong."

Groans followed, but they were "aha" groans. Point taken. The story, without the student's name, became part of future lectures. Teachers learn so much from students. I learned they needed more than concepts . . . they needed help in sharing the concepts with those involved with their children.

One concept of Parenting From a Distance that developed in the beginning with female offenders had to do with them learning about where their children lived, went to school, and played or hung-out. They could provide similar information about their prison home. Women drew pictures of their living-unit rooms, complete with measurements from wall to wall, so children could get a mental picture of the space where their moms slept, wrote letters, listened to music, and did homework. One day a living unit supervisor stormed into my classroom, paper clutched in his hand, veins bulging in his neck.

"What the hell is this?" He saw escape plans in the making. Room floor plans were not to be mailed out.

A simple floor plan that showed a bed, a desk, and a chair didn't look like an escape plan to me, but I conceded. Instead, we used descriptive words to describe their rooms. My students, all determined women, continued sending out floor plans, though they didn't admit that in class. The mailroom officer let them go out, and the women liked drawing them. Some did elevations to show the room's bulletin board where children's pictures could be posted.

The incident reminded me to teach every parental right and responsibility with cautions attached. Students made things for their children as part of their course work, and I made certain the items were cleared for mailing. Since we had assorted fabric and notions available at the women's prison, students made soft craft items such as small pillow covers or stuffed animals without the stuffing (it could contain contraband), fabric books for infants and very young children, and other small items. They worked with paper to create cards, picture frames, and refrigerator art with colored paper, pens, pencils, glitter, rubber art stamps, ink pads, stencils, and coloring book designs to help create their art. They added talent and love.

The first time I taught Parenting From a Distance to dads, I expected them to have less interest in the lab part of the class than moms showed and was shocked to find they were at least equally enthusiastic about creating items to send to their children. Men not enrolled in parenting classes came begging for materials too. Those who qualified for hobby-shop at MICC could get art supplies sent in if they had money to pay for them. Most didn't; they just wanted one design from a coloring book. I never learned to turn away such requests. The education office personnel reminded me I did too much photocopying for my course descriptions, and they were right. Much of it wasn't for my students, and some of it likely violated copyright laws. *Precious Moments* kids, Disney characters, and alphabet motifs were popular. I hope sharing a few trademarked designs with incarcerated dads will be forgiven.

Men traced the designs onto cards they created or onto blank 3x5 puzzles I found at craft stores, then colored them with the care a fine artist gives to a canvas. One man, whose daughter refused to respond to his letters, heard she showed off her puzzle and cards to a friend of his, and bragged about her dad making them. She wasn't ready to forgive him enough to write, but she cherished the things he sent her.

Now and then a man brought prison designs to class to share. If I deemed them inappropriate for children, they could not be used in the classroom. (Prison designs are heavy on barbed wire, roses and hearts dripping blood, heavy metal, gang graffiti, and tattoo shop drawings.)

Men also painted with watercolors on assorted quality paper, and left their work in the classroom to dry, so at times it was difficult to find a surface for the next class to do academic work. Teaching assistants knew those creations were valued and protected them. Preschools often hang wet artwork on clotheslines, but such lines weren't permitted in prison. We had to find other surfaces, including the floor and desk in my shared office when we ran out of classroom space.

I kept a supply of large envelopes to send out big items, but most men made their own envelopes for cards and puzzles. They traced around patterns teaching assistants made from file folders they procured, generally from the paper recycling bin, and sometimes an unattended desk. Clean file folders made good cardstock because felt pen ink didn't run or bleed on them.

Creative inmates turned bits and pieces of wastebasket scraps into art objects. Foil from candy bars and other snacks were wrapped around paper cut to make picture frames. Paper of all sorts was folded and woven into coasters or mats. Or torn and arranged in collages or designs. Affirmations and sayings I distributed or wrote on the board were copied onto construction paper scraps and used as bookmarks. Some went home to children or mothers, others stayed inside for personal use. As the flowers I brought to the classroom faded, men asked for them, or collected those already tossed. They pressed them to send out with a letter, or drew around the petals and leaves to create "the real look."

I remember those men, with bulging biceps, tattoos, shaved heads and one braided beard coloring their cards or puzzles, following each other's advice for using glitter; separating lace doilies to make valentines for children, mom, and girlfriends. And wrapping their huge fingers around the blunt-point children's scissors I kept locked in the classroom supply cupboard.

Men knew Open Door and parenting lab were privileges, and protected them. Now and then I heard about altercations when supplies gone missing turned up in the wrong hands. (Carbon paper used to transfer designs onto cards and puzzles disappeared at a rapid rate. Inmates used it for tattooing, an infractionable offense.) I didn't condone physical repercussions for lost supplies, and developed a mantra: stolen items ultimately get to children; let it go. I accepted supply theft as part of teaching inside the fence, though it always upset me to open a cupboard and discover items missing. After an especially large loss my TA told me that chatter back in the living unit implicated a part-time teacher who allegedly "borrowed" from my supply cupboard for his class.

"They're doing crafts in his class?" That seemed odd.

"No, he gives things out as rewards when students do well."

I confronted the teacher, explained that the items were purchased with my program budget (and many by me, though I didn't always admit how much personal money I spent; it was a violation of prison rules). He said he hadn't taken anything, but he protested too much. I moved more costly supplies, especially the highly desired puzzles, from the classroom cupboard to my office file cabinet. I'd long since learned not to leave snacks in desk drawers or the staff refrigerator and to carry my purple pen home each night.

A change took place within those men as they created simple items for their children . . . an awareness of their connection to humanity, perhaps. I saw a difference, felt it like a welcome breeze, yet cannot prove it mattered. Even one of the by-the-book officers who worked on the education floor conceded as much. What did he, a trained officer, see during his frequent passes by the classroom? Men sitting around tables covered with simple art and craft supplies. Men intent on a project. Men helping one another. If he had listened in, as I did, he would have heard them talking with pride and love about their children. He'd have heard sorrows at hurts they'd inflicted, and joys at connections they'd made.

When I gained permission to hold Open Door sessions, men came for craft projects and left with valuable academic information. We never did just crafts during those hours. Men who came seeking help with a legal letter often left with a simple card to send a child. While men worked on projects at the classroom tables, I helped individuals complete paper work for the Office of Support Enforcement (OSE) so their children received the legal connection needed to ensure future child support. Low-income parents (all of my students legally qualified as such) were required by law to pay a minimum twenty-five dollars per month per child. By registering with OSE, men accepted their obligation, and contributed what they could toward their accruing debt. Without registering, the OSE would assume the parent's income was much higher. Their debt then accrued at the higher rate. Men I'd never seen, many of them non-English speaking, came to Open Door sessions for help with their OSE papers and personal letters to courts and agencies to whom they'd been asked to respond. I kept standard letters on disk, typed in individual names and DOC numbers, and printed out their letters while they waited. It took only a few minutes to lift their burden of concern. Many men, not just non-English speakers, didn't know where to sign a business letter, so I learned to hand them a pen and point to the signature space.

Open Door complicated matters for the education floor's officers, who must know absolutely who is on the floor each hour. The added names of men who came for Open Door meant more work, especially if they stayed through Period Movement to spend another hour eavesdropping on a lecture, or getting help writing to a loved one. Their names, DOC numbers, and living unit information had to be added to each hour's class roster. I often got too busy helping men with individual needs, helping the group collectively, and watching in wonder to remember those additions. Thankfully my TAs made the proper notes and posted them for the officers.

Parenting students also had permission to record cassette tapes for their children. The institution sold tapes at Store and had absolute rules about what could be mailed out. Men read stories on tape, talked to their children, asked questions, and sometimes added music. One man got an angry note from his child because he asked questions, but didn't pause for her to answer. Another man's mother called me to ask if her son could record a new tape: she'd "accidentally" run over the one her nine-year-old grandson played every time they were in the car. "I couldn't stand hearing it one more time," she said, "and now I'm sorry. I didn't understand how much it meant to the boy just to hear his dad's voice."

One Open Door day a young man sent by the education counselor to enroll in a writing class I taught whined and moaned while he waited. Some men were in the classroom working on projects for their children. I could feel them watching him. When I finished a task and turned to him, he tossed a form at me and said, "I don't needs none of you's ejication, I gots me a job on the outs, I is a hit man."

While I looked at him, eyebrow raised, the other men looked at me.

"How does your mama feel about you being a hit man?" I asked.

The man's head and arms jerked back like he'd been slugged. "What you be knowin' 'bout my mama?"

"She didn't rear you to shoot people. She's been worried sick about you for a long time now. She's relieved you're in prison because it's safer than being on those streets. She wants you to learn something in here so you can get a real job when you get out."

"How you be knowin' all that?"

"I get messages directly from my own parents who died over twenty years ago." I watched him frown. "Little messages from them come through all the time."

"How they be doin' that?"

"By what they taught me about the worth of learning and knowledge. By all they instilled in me. Education is a privilege, denied in many parts of the world. You're a lucky man: your crimes brought you to prison where education is offered to you. All you have to do is get out of bed and go to a classroom."

The man sat down. "What you gonna make me do in this here class you be wantin' to push on me?"

"I'm not going to make you do anything. I'm going to assign writing exercises. You may choose to do them or deal with the consequences."

He said, "Shit, man," and looked around the room for support.

One of my regulars said, "Clean up your mouth, man. We work on things for our children in this classroom, and we don't use potty words."

Statements I made in class (I called it bathroom language) often came back from a student's mouth. Luckily the student who spoke up was older, bigger, built like a linebacker, and of the same ethnicity as the "hit man."

More and more men like the "hit man" arrived at MICC; more and more found their way to classes I taught. All my parenting and family classes had to be rewritten to reach ever-lower reading and comprehension levels, and I was assigned more basic skills courses. I taught parenting in them, too.

Through the years, students often thanked me for developing and teaching the distance-parenting concept by bringing me flowers and verse. Their flowers were drawings sketched onto whatever paper they had; their verse paeans of thanks for recognizing worth in them, increasing their understanding of children's needs, and helping them reach out to their family members. Many said I not only taught them, I also parented them.

That happens when one teaches parenting. How could it not?

23

| Going Back Out |

Educational services inside Washington State prisons are contracted through the State Board of Community and Technical Colleges or private organizations that provide chemical dependency counseling or other specific services. I was a contract employee through Tacoma Community College when I taught at the women's prison and through Pierce College at McNeil Island. My badge color indicated my contract status. The back of the badge stated my official title. My transfer to MICC required a new badge. The officer who took my photo typed "parienting" teacher on the badge back. He shrugged when I pointed out the typo, looked at me and shook his head.

"Parenting teacher. For a bunch of screwed-up cons. Locking 'em up's best thing ever happened to their kids." He shoved the badge in a plastic sleeve, laminated it, punched a hole in the top, inserted a clip, and handed it to me. I wore that *parienting* teacher badge for seven years. Toward the end of my tenure, changes in prison policies and young inmates' attitude were wearing me down.

"Burnout," a colleague said. He felt it, too, though he couldn't resign until he found a new position. I had been hoping to find more time to write and made the leap into early retirement.

Though burnout served as a catchword, it went deeper than that. I'd ridden the incoming tide of innovative programming until it crashed against the bulkhead of philosophical and political turmoil. Legislators used the "tough on crime" premise to raise capital funds for building new prisons and modernizing existing ones due to the demands made by mass incarceration. New electronically controlled housing units and a new inmate services complex were built on McNeil Island in 1994 to meet growing needs. Another new building housed an updated visiting room and vocational training facility with provisions for computer science and repair. Those of us who taught on the island were moving into new classrooms at the same time that the legislature was arguing about slashing prison budgets to eliminate some of our classes.

That was just part of the conundrum. The media focused on the news of TVs being removed from prison housing and weight lifting from men's prisons, though neither actually happened. Televisions remained in dayrooms where all inmates in the unit could use them, and personal sets could be purchased by inmates through Store if they had funds in their accounts. There were some crime classification restrictions for working out with weights and a recreational fee is now applied to use them, but the weights remained. There was news of college courses being cut but the true impact of prison education budget slashing didn't get much press. Basic education courses, GED preparation and testing and specific vocational training remained intact. Video courses gained popularity; some eliminated the need for teachers.

An odd sadness lingered over the island when the old cellhouse came down once the new living units were occupied. Lieutenant Burton, along with several other longtime officers, said the ghosts from the old blocks were seeking new quarters. They weren't kidding and didn't consider it a superstition. Too many old federal cons had died in the blocks.

One cell, once occupied by Charles Manson before the Tate/LaBianca murders, had allegedly been closed from the time he left the island after his first stint in prison. There were rumors of a pentagram etched into that cell's floor. Nine-hundred cell house mattresses were burned (or so I was told), and more ghosts were seen dancing in the flames.

There had been several staff changes prior to moving education from the historic building where we'd conducted the PSR program and other classes. Superintendent Callahan, who had signed off on the program, had retired. Associate Superintendent Alice Payne was called to DOC headquarters where she worked her way up to an associate director position. Education Director Tom Rabak left to take a new position in an alternative high school program. He hoped to help teens struggling to meet educational requirements find success. He especially wanted them to avoid prison.

The new education director refused to participate in PSR. When we moved education into our new quarters, that director negotiated with the new superintendent to cut the program from a 20-hour week to one six-hour day. I met with the PSR group for one hour to provide a thumbnail sketch of preparation for the family relationships objectives of case management.

In truth, I didn't mind that change. I'd kept copious notes about PSR and prepared a printable manual that MICC could distribute to interested correctional educators. Tom Rabak and I had an article about the program published in *The Journal of Correctional Education*, and we'd presented the concept at a national Correctional Education Association Conference. The family component of DOC case management remained intact. Men found their way to classes they needed, and to Open Door sessions.

At that time, I still taught six courses that met college social services or mental health criteria and provided transferable credits for qualified students. They included Chemical Dependency and Family Issues, Family History and Patterns, and Behavior Management. I also taught Parenting From a Distance and Positive Parenting for continuing education credit, and writing classes as part of general education. The classes rotated each quarter to give students ample opportunity to complete their family program goals.

As the legislature enacted the "three strikes" law they also eliminated funding for college level courses inside prisons. Yet another new education director wanted the coursework to remain available as continuing education offerings. Thus, I rewrote most of the material I'd used so it could be read and understood by inmates in basic education classes. I continued teaching writing courses every quarter, and I was expected to emphasize writing in all other classes. No problem there; I'd always encouraged writing.

DOC sponsored chemical dependency programs facilitated by men or women in recovery were available inside prisons. The value of similar classes offered through the education department was questioned. I had completed the same training as the recovering facilitators, but I wasn't in recovery or even an adult child of alcoholics. What I brought to the program was extensive training in and a clear understanding of developmental ages and stages. Addiction interferes with development, especially emotional development. Most recovered addicts who ran programs had missed huge chunks of their adolescence and young adulthood; many started using so young it impacted their preadolescence.

I also had the inmates' respect. They asked for a chemical dependency class to remain part of the education department program. In lieu of the eliminated college transfer course, I was assigned the responsibility of teaching a noncredit substance abuse class. Thirty-four men enrolled, many of them ESL (English as a Second Language) students. The education director divided the class into two sections and rounded up volunteer TAs to help.

The TAs, who had completed several college courses, had to register as students to get into the classroom. I spent my off-hours at the computer rewriting curriculum in short statements with plenty of white space. I may not have walked the walk, but I walked miles in the classroom, talking to each man, helping with comprehension.

One of the DOC contracted chemical dependency facilitators at MICC asked for the original college level curriculum I'd developed and incorporated it into their program. I appreciated being asked.

While working at WCCW a document I wrote turned up with another person named as the author.

More students with attitudes similar to the hit man *("I don't needs none of you's ejication ...")* enrolled in my classes. Too many wanted the letter of completion I wrote for every student in every class, but without doing the work to earn it. Several young men whose case management plan required them to register for classes because of low test scores wanted their teachers, the system, and all of society to give them what they had been denied all these years by "The Man." They were angry and saw all authority figures as obstacles to getting their fair share. I was just another authority figure who didn't know nothin' about nothin' when it came to what was going on out on the streets.

When more mature students told me to give up on the punks, whether they were African American, Hispanic, Asian, Native American or Caucasian, I listened. Those men had come from the streets, too, and made a personal commitment to learn and change while inside so they could live when they got out. I made Choosing to Change a writing and discussion assignment in every class, and I was schooled by the pros—the inmates who would make it outside. They were men of all ethnic backgrounds, men who had lived under bridges and survived on food found in dumpsters, men who had committed serious crimes, and men who had committed long strings of minor felonies, and they all said the same thing—even the best teachers can't teach those who refuse to learn.

Those men became my classroom resources. When they "told it like it is," the young guys listened. Some of them entered the discussion, but they rarely put pencil to paper. They were chronological adults who couldn't write a legible sentence. Some of them couldn't verbalize an understandable one. They'd "been failed" by teachers and kicked out of schools. They scoffed at a TA's suggestion that they'd failed themselves. Many of them were fathers. So what? They'd come up without their fathers in the picture.

During that phase of my career, a state legislator visited the education floor to get a firsthand look at what we were doing. She was a strong proponent of tough on crime laws; she wanted to speak with instructors individually to get a feel for our work. When the legislator got to me she said, "And what do you teach, Dearie?"

"Parenting and ..." She interrupted me before I could say "family," or before I could tell her about the parenting text I'd written specifically for the population.

"Parenting," she said, like it was an expletive. "We can get *volunteers* to teach *parenting.*"

I recall telling her to start rounding them up, though my exact words are lost. She didn't wait to hear my answer; she had another teacher to question. I wasn't the only one addressed as "Dearie," so I chose not to take that personally. I later learned that legislator's son was getting into trouble and eventually did time in prison. She might have benefited from a parenting class.

I left the system a few months later, no longer willing to devote my time and energy to a system that was in such turmoil. As I dumped assorted assignments and worksheets into recycle bins, TAs working on the education floor collected copies they thought they could use back in the living units. I smile at that memory. Those men were inmates who chose to help teach other inmates. My colleagues asked for materials they could use with ABE students. I wrote and bound a 50-page booklet, "We're Still Members of the Family," and gave them copies as my parting gift.

Oddly, the system didn't leave me. I turned to writing fiction, completed one novel and started a second while vignettes from my correctional education career bloomed on my computer screen. I set aside fiction, studied the craft of writing memoir, and found a publisher. That work, *Dancing to the Concertina's Tune: A Prison Teacher's Memoir,* was named a Washington Reads book in the "hidden peoples" category.

My young adult novel, *An Inmate's Daughter,* also won recognition in that category. The story is set in Tacoma and on McNeil Island. It focuses on prisoners' families, family secrets, peer pressure, race awareness, and a father who used his time inside prison to improve his parenting and family relationships.

I believed I'd exorcised the ghosts of my eighteen-year career with those two works. I could forget about the curriculum I'd dumped in a recycling bin or given away to other educators and move on to other topics. About that time, Washington State opened a new reentry prison, Mission Creek Corrections Center for Women (MCCCW), in a community twenty-five miles from my home. The first superintendent at that facility was an acquaintance from my career days. She called to ask me to serve on the community advisory board. We established that association under the umbrella of Rebuilding Families, Incorporated (RFI), a nonprofit that helped women transition from prison through reentry to their communities and reuniting with their families.

I worked with RFI as the liaison for the reentry prison and served as their secretary for several years. The organization's director knew I wasn't interested in serving as an RFI mentor to individual women preparing for release due to the time commitment, so she asked me to help facilitate an education program. My heart skipped a beat when she told me the goals of Preparing for Release. It involved women offenders working with us on two Fridays to study and discuss the material and prepare for meeting with their family members who came inside the Saturday following our Friday gathering. The workshops were intense. Offenders and their family members prepared and signed a realistic contract to follow when the woman returned home.

The program was developed and workbooks written by John and Sylvia Peterson, a couple who were longtime volunteers at MICC. I attended the RFI training session to see what facilitating would entail. It paralleled work I'd done for 18 years. I'd retired, written books about my experiences, agreed to serve on the advisory board for a new reentry prison and remained concerned about how prison impacts children and families. It seemed to be the right time to put my skills back to work inside.

We were able to incorporate parts of my Parenting From a Distance concept into the program. It pleased me to find that women offenders and their family members respected the work I'd done.

24

| Rebuilding Families |

Rebuilding Families, Incorporated, registered in the State of Washington as a nonprofit that trained volunteers to assist female offenders with their transition back into the community and reunification with their families. They provided eligible offenders with mentoring inside prison, picked them up at the gate on release and transported them to the community. RFI contracted with associations that provided clean and sober housing or made apartments available for released offenders, paid first and last months' rent and security deposit and helped equip apartments with furnishings and supplies. They also transported women on work release status to those state managed facilities and provided rolls of quarters for laundry room use.

The day of release included shopping trips and an RFI gift card with a small amount of money to spend on immediate needs. Most women wanted one properly fitted bra. Mentors also took the women to agencies that would be providing medications and to meet their community corrections officer. After helping get the women settled, mentors remained available by phone to answer questions and offer encouragement through the process of getting settled, getting reacquainted with children, and looking for a job.

RFI relied on fund raisers, donations and grant support from the Department of Corrections to provide the services their clients needed. The volunteer who manages the clothing room at WCCW and her church's support group worked under RFI's umbrella for several years. She and her church kept her crew going when our organization retired. They are still collecting, washing, mending, sorting and storing donated clothing and delivering them as needed to a locked room inside the prison grounds. Monetary donations are used to purchase new panties and socks for every departing woman, and a decent travel bag to carry possessions out of prison to the real world. The volunteer and her crew spend several hours one day a week "dressing" women at WCCW.

RFI also sponsored a "Little Bus That Could" program to transport children and their primary caregivers to the women's reentry prison for visitation. Buses and vans collected children at gathering spots across the state. Transportation to those gathering spots was provided by the program. Every child with a primary caregiver willing to help the child participate could visit his or her mother inside the prison in a friendly setting that included indoor and outdoor activities. It took intensive planning and coordination, and was touted by prison staff as an amazing event. The volunteer coordinator and her helpers rode the buses and vans as hosts, oversaw crafts and activities, and combined efforts to create a library of photo albums that bring smiles and tears to the eyes of even the most stoic observer.

In addition to my RFI board position, I served as a facilitator for the Preparing for Release (PFR) program at MCCCW and occasionally at WCCW.

The PFR program, as we conducted it, included four sessions— two with the offenders alone and two with the offenders and their family members working on the problems they knew they would face when the offender moved home. We met with the offenders alone on Fridays and the combined offender and family groups on Saturdays, and gave them one weekend between sessions to think through their work and to visit by phone or in person to talk about some of the issues they identified in their first session. RFI facilitators worked closely with the prison's corrections program manager and primary counselors to review applications for the program and conduct phone interviews with the applicants' family members.

In the first session, two trained facilitators met with the women offenders in a classroom setting where we spent some time becoming comfortable in our respective student/teacher roles. The students were anxious about how the program would go. They would be joined by their family members the next day, and they knew it would be more intense than a normal visit where everyone tried to remain upbeat. They would be communicating with their family members about feelings, fears, and especially expectations. One major concern was how their family members would cope with "90 AA or NA meetings in 90 days," a typical arrangement for releasing offenders whose drug or alcohol abuse contributed to their criminal behavior.

We made long lists of roles the women admitted to playing in their families, some of them not so nice: manipulator, drama queen, thief. Those were balanced with more positive roles that they hoped to resume: supportive daughter, spouse, mother, and all the responsibilities those roles entail. Most of the students were participating in therapeutic community groups where they worked through phases of learning about addictions, facing their own realities, and planning for their futures. They were getting ready to reenter society, and they knew they needed family and community support to make it. They spoke openly in the session about the hurt they'd caused their loved ones. We kept boxes of tissues handy to mop up tears.

Our team of two returned to the prison early Saturday morning to greet family members as they arrived and checked in for entering the closed section of the prison. I worked with Audrey Shaw, RFI Executive Director. She met with the women to work on budget and financial management, and I met with the family members to take them through the information the offenders had covered the day before. We all came together in the prison dining hall for lunch and moved from there to a classroom setting for a long afternoon of preparing to write a Family Reentry Agreement.

After a general discussion, each offender and her family found a space somewhere in the room to talk privately, and to write out their goals on easel paper. Facilitators checked on progress but joined a family group only if asked. I was asked by an offender's fiancé to help them hammer out some issues, and spent over an hour in intense mediation/negotiation with them. Jane said in the open session that she was on her last chance. "I either get it right this time, or I'll end up dead in the gutter."

John said he was ready to walk out of the relationship unless they came to an understanding about her son.

The couple made little progress toward writing a contract during that session, but the man left agreeing that they could hash it out over the phone in the two week interim before our next session. He said he'd be back if they made any progress.

Jane arrived at the third session on Friday, two weeks later, still worried about whether he'd come in the next day and whether they would agree on a reentry plan for her if he did. The group knew her dilemma. Jane received some serious peer counseling in that session. She admitted that the conflict revolved around her son, now over eighteen and in legal trouble. The group told her that she needed to review everything they'd worked on in chemical dependency counseling. She and her fiancé couldn't solve her son's problems or protect him from the consequences of his behavior.

John was there Saturday morning. He said he came prepared to negotiate with Jane and asked me to work with them again. Jane was clearly thrilled to see him, though I don't think she was prepared for him to be so firm about one item on her reentry contract: her son could not live with them in his home. There were tears shed, but Jane and John wrote a contract, a tough one that included specifics about her relationship with her son: no more excuses; no more enabling. She agreed, and signed the contract.

At the end of session four of PFR, the group reconvenes. Each offender posts the contract she made with her family members so all can view it. Each then explains the tenets of the contract. Jane was blotchy-faced when she made her presentation, but she was also honest about her son. She said she'd been part of his problem.

That event occurred in one of the first sessions I helped facilitate. Over the years we met, only one family member dropped out after session two. She was an older woman whose incarcerated daughter was in her forties. The mother said she didn't see any change in her daughter at that first Saturday meeting. She advised the prison staff that her daughter could not release to her. The offender had to make other living arrangements, preferably in a clean and sober group facility.

The family members that came inside for their loved ones continually amazed me. They settled into the program agenda to do their part of the work, and spoke openly and often tearfully of the hurt they'd experienced. One thirty-something daughter of an incarcerated mother had been the primary caregiver for several siblings while her mother did time. She told her mother "I'm through. You drink again, and you're on your own. You won't be welcome in any of our homes."

Another woman's father told his daughter that he loved her and would help her, but he was struggling with a deep sadness. Her child, the grandchild he'd helped another daughter care for, was now with the biological father in a distant state due to a court ruling.

One young woman offender and her husband asked for help with their final contract. She said he had to agree to and sign a statement that if she messed up again (used drugs) he had to kick her out. "You can't let me get away with it. Not even once. No slipping. Call my NA sponsor, or call the cops. Our kids have been through too much with me already."

Her husband signed the contract, which included a statement about the gardening area he had prepared for her. "She loves to get her hands in the dirt," he said. "It's ready for her flowers and her vegetables. I'm ready for one of her home cooked meals. I manage to keep the kids fed, but I don't have the touch she does."

She said she loved cooking and gardening, she loved her husband and their children, and she knew her triggers. That seemed to surprise him. "Write those triggers down on this contract." And she did.

In the last session I helped facilitate, a father and his daughter struggled with the issue of prescription medications kept in the home for other family members. Theirs was a three-generation household that included an infant and a toddler. How could he trust her to leave other family members' meds alone? She had two strikes; a third strike would mean life without the possibility of parole. She was in her mid-twenties. Her father was a professional man who often worked long hours. Her mother had serious health issues. Father and daughter agreed to a contract that stated all prescription medications would be in a locked cabinet with the only key in his possession. He would dispense prescription meds each morning for that day, and the family would do an accounting each evening.

As they were writing their contract, I asked the man about his own health. He had a heart condition. Tears formed in his daughter's eyes. She said, "He can't keep taking care of all of us." She added that statement to their contract, with the notation that she would do all she could to help. He said, "Stay clean, get a job, get a life of your own."

We all knew that she was leaving a structured environment for one rife with unresolved family issues and the presence of medications her mother and sister relied on daily. That combination is considered toxic for releasing offenders who have their own history of addictions.

We retired RFI in 2013. Most of us had reached an age where we wanted to pass the torch to other volunteer organizations. Audrey Shaw did most of the complex work of bringing our nonprofit legally and financially to a close. She assisted the Gig Harbor Rotary Club in the development of an instructional manual for use in teaching a Reentry Employment Training course offered at WCCW and team-taught by Rotarians and inmates. Rotarians say she has been invaluable in sharing her insights with them in the area of mentoring women after their release.

Every prison relies on volunteers in many capacities. Every offender that participates in programs made available by volunteers benefits from the program and the relationships that develop. Every volunteer knows she or he helped make a difference in offenders' lives that leads to them rebuilding their families.

25

| Wrap Up |

Where are we now with prison education programs? I believe they remain places where convicted felons become students, though the classrooms have changed with technological advances. The 2014 GED Exam, the new standard for the country, can be prepared for on electronic tablets available to inmates inside prisons and jails, with the test administered by computer. The concern for correctional educators is the length of time required for preparation and the training teachers need for preparation of new educational materials now covered in the exam.

Lecture/discussion classes and writing exercises were the foundations for all the courses I developed and taught inside. The lecture part of the class included the teacher delivering and clarifying information from professional training and personal development. The discussion part of the class was where individual learning happened.

I believe in that method for coursework inside whether its classical literature, earth science, computer technology, parent education or GED preparation. We know students come to class with different learning styles. We also know that most offenders come to class with serious learning gaps. Discussing issues and ideas generates thinking about how to think and learn, and how to prepare for taking tests.

The Correctional Education Association (CEA) now offers a secure electronic tablet with educational materials for incarcerated students. The tablet, called iPEP (incarcerated Person Education Pad) will bring additional methods and support to correctional education programs for CEA teachers and their students. In addition to academic courses, correctional educators can also purchase Reentry Skills programs and post-secondary education courses.

The Rand Corporation 2014 study, *How Effective Is Correctional Education, and Where Do We Go from Here?*, mentioned earlier in this text, concluded with the following statement:

> *There are more than 2 million incarcerated adults in the United States—more than any industrialized nation. This study has demonstrated that education programs can help adults get back on their feet upon release from prison and may help youth with the juvenile justice system to improve their education and employment prospects. Moreover, our meta-analysis of the literature on incarcerated adults suggest that correctional education programs are highly cost-effective in helping to reduce recidivism and improve postrelease employment outcomes. States will continue to operate in a reduced funding environment for at least the near future. The findings and recommendations we have laid out here are intended to ensure that, moving forward, we understand how best to deliver education and vocational training to assist in achieving positive reentry outcomes.* (Page 90)

I am most pleased to report that parenting programs are available in many federal and state prisons. CEA has a Parenting Special Interest Group that helps correctional educators and other correctional staff develop and support parenting classes inside. The group, in conjunction with Jerry Bednarowski, Wisconsin CEA, publishes a parenting newsletter that updates programs for incarcerated parents and support groups. Contact information for the *Parenting Connection* newsletter is listed in Resources, and is valuable information for all correctional educators.

The Seattle Times recently ran an article about college being back in session in some Washington prisons. The article's author cited the Rand report and noted the private funding foundations that support them, including the Freedom Education Project of Puget Sound (FEPPS) that sends professors from several universities to teach inside WCCW. Another Washington State foundation, University Beyond Bars, offers college level courses at the Monroe Correction Complex. Two eastern Washington prisons received funds for small college programs from Doris Buffett's Sunshine Lady Foundation. (Doris Buffett is Warren Buffett's sister). Other states are also finding private funding for college level courses.

The prison system remains a complex entity. Consider the following statistics and think about the consequences for our society.

There are over 2 million inmates in U.S. federal and state prisons, jails, military facilities, immigration detention centers, civil-commitment centers for the mentally-ill, and juvenile detention facilities.

The cost to taxpayers is estimated at 63-billion dollars for 2012, or somewhere over $30,000 per incarcerated person per year. One source said it had reached 72-billion dollars as 2014 drew to a close.

The U.S. has five percent (5%) of the world population and twenty-five percent (25%) of the world's inmates.

The incarceration rate in the U.S. is 716 of every 100,000 people. Compare that to 475 in Russia, 118 in Canada and 67 in Sweden.

The latest U.S. census shows 13.2% of our citizens are black. They comprise 36.5% of the prison population.

The Sentencing Project and the Bureau of Justice Statistics both estimate that 1 in 3 black men will be imprisoned during their lifetime, 1 in 6 Latino men and 1 in 17 white men.

Fifteen percent of male prisoners are serving time for drug related offenses, 55% for violent crimes, 18% for property crimes, and 11% for public-order offenses including weapon violations, drunk driving, and court offenses including morals and decency charges.

Women fare better, but the number of women being admitted to jails and prisons is increasing at a higher percentage rate than the increase for males. Their incarceration rates by race are 1 in 18 black, 1 in 45 Latina, and 1 in 111 white.

Twenty-five percent of female prisoners are serving time for drug related offenses, 37% for violent crimes, 28% for property crimes, and 9% for public-order offenses.

There are no definitive percentage numbers for inmates who are serving time for technical violations rather than new crimes. Technical violations include missing an appointment with a community corrections officer, driving without a valid license, and a long list of restrictions for those who are out but not free. Sending them back inside at the rate of $30,000 per year for technical violations doesn't make financial sense. Neither does it help them learn. Community service at no pay is an option that some jurisdictions use.

In 2013, the last year for which I have statistics, over 19% of federal inmates and about 7% of state inmates were housed in private prisons. These prisons are for profit corporations who contract with the federal government or states' governments to imprison offenders.

The American Civil Liberties Union document, "Banking on Bondage: Private Prisons and Mass Incarceration," included reports from the two largest private prison companies in America to the Securities and Exchange Commission. Both the Corrections Corporation of America and the GEO Group issued statements under the heading, "Risk Related to Our Business and Industry," that include the following:

The demand for our facilities and services could be adversely affected by the relaxation of enforcement efforts, leniency in conviction or parole standards and sentencing practices or through the decriminalization of certain activities that are currently proscribed by our criminal laws. For instance, any changes with respect to drugs and controlled substances or illegal immigration could affect the number of persons arrested, convicted, and sentenced, thereby potentially reducing demand for correctional facilities to house them. (The ACLU document is listed herein under General Prison Resources)

The Bureau of Justice statistics for 2013 lists nine states with 15% or more of their inmate population housed in private prisons. New Mexico tops the list at 43.6%, followed by Montana at 40%, Idaho at 36.4% and Oklahoma at 25.6%.

Washington State and 18 other states do not house inmates in private prisons at the time of this writing. Another five states house less than one percent of their offenders in them.

California voters passed a proposition to reduce its prisoner count by changing three-strikes laws and otherwise reconsidering offenders' cases. Their 2013 prison population was 135,981, a figure that reached 142% of their prison capacity. Their state population numbers well over 38 million.

Texas, with a population near 26 million had a 2013 prison population of 168,200, 87% of their capacity.

New York, with a population near 19.4 million had a 2013 prison population of just 54,550. I cite New York because they are strong supporters of correctional education programs including college courses that can lead to their inmates receiving college degrees.

Florida has a population nearly equal to New York, but nearly twice as many inmates at 103,028.

There is one more statistic mentioned earlier in this work that I want to state again: Over 2 million children have a parent in prison or jail, and another 7 million have a parent who is or has been under some form of criminal justice supervision.

The National Resource Center on Children and Families of the Incarcerated at Rutgers University states: "Parental incarceration is now recognized as an 'adverse childhood experience' (ACE); it is distinguished from other adverse childhood experiences by the unique combination of trauma, shame, and stigma."

Parenting programs inside prisons are designed to help the children of the incarcerated. In a real sense, the children are doing time, too.

I believe in the power of story and hope this work gave you food for thought. If confinement in prison is meant to rehabilitate, not just to punish, then we need to increase social awareness of the rehabilitation part of that equation. We need an open discussion about what education and job preparedness will be available inside the fence and how it will be delivered. My training was "on the job." Most of the correctional educators I met through the years had similar backgrounds—they'd been teaching in their specific discipline somewhere outside the fence before they went inside.

Writers will tell you that writing is solitary work. Most will also tell you it is deeply satisfying. Along with the power of story, I believe in the power of putting pencil to paper. Write down a thought. Put that thought into a sentence. Add another sentence that builds on the original thought. Include a feeling statement. Read it aloud and listen to your words. Make changes or additions. Now read it to someone else and ask for their feedback.

Somerset Maugham is quoted as saying, "There are three rules for writing; unfortunately, no one knows what they are."

There are lots of rules for teachers, volunteers and visitors who go inside prison that are delivered by a representative of the prison or the governing corrections department. Heed them and add one more: Be true to yourself. If you feel uncomfortable in the prison environment, let someone else do the teaching or volunteering or visiting.

Prison policy has been decided by voters who listened to political arguments that said we needed to get tough on crime. We tried controlling illegal drugs by locking up persons who use and/or sell them. We created an industrial prison complex that consumes a huge portion of our tax dollars. I believe we can turn back the tide of mass incarceration by investing more of our tax dollars in intervention, especially in early education for all communities and all ethnicities at all income levels.

I will close with one final note for correctional educators: Maintain a sense of humor. Pick your battles. Stop to take a deep breath. Trust your instincts. Trust that the students who are committed to making it out in the real world will help you cope with those who aren't ready to do the work.

| Afterword |

There are many thoughtful and informative books and articles available about the criminal justice system in the U.S. Most writers agree that there is serious racial disparity in our prisons; some suggest the way to address that problem is by investing in very early education in low income inner city areas where criminal acts are often a rite of passage into adulthood.

One organization, the Justice Mapping Center, uses computer mapping known as Geographic Information Systems (GIS) to locate and map neighborhoods where corrections spending is the highest. You can read about their services, policies and funding at their website listed in the "Read More About ..." section at the end of Resources.

I begin this listing with books and materials for use with parenting and family programs inside prisons. That remains my first interest in the complex criminal justice system.

I end with information about some of my own work. As I write this I am continuing to develop materials for use inside prisons. One set of materials, titled "Teach Inside" is written for adult basic education level students as individual lessons. They are intended for use in jails where offenders' time may be short, and where instruction is often self-guided. With that in mind, I created those lessons with five components: Read, Think, Write, Discuss and Share. The overview of the work suggests students read, think about the material and write their thoughts first. Once they've done that, they are urged to discuss the material with others and then share the material with family and friends outside.

| Resources |

Parenting and Family Resources (search the web for additional information)

All Alone in the World: Children of the Incarcerated, Nell Bernstein, The New Press, 2005.

Annie E Casey Foundation/ National Institute of Corrections – www.nicic.gov

Children & Families of the Incarcerated: The National Resource Center on Children and Families of the Incarcerated – www.nrccfi.camden.rutgers.edu

Children of Incarcerated Parents: A Bill of Rights: San Francisco Partnership for Incarcerated Parents – www.sfcipp.org

Children with Incarcerated Parents – Considering Children's Outcomes in the Context of Complex Family Experiences:

Children's Mental Health eReview – University of Minnesota Extension,2013 – www.extension.unm.edu/.../June2013ereview.pdf

Family and Corrections Network – www.fcnetwork.org

Parenting Connection newsletter – www.ceawisconsin.org

Parenting from a Distance: Your Rights and Responsibilities – Third Edition, Jan Walker, Plicata Press LLC, 2011 – www.plicatapress.com

"Raising Babies in Prison," Abby Quillen article on Washington
Corrections Center for Women (WCCW)
Residential Parenting Program, *YES! Magazine*, 2011 –
www.yesmagazine.org/issues

Books to Supplement Parenting and Family Coursework
*Family Ties That Bind: A Self-Help Guide to Change Through Family of
Origin Therapy*, Dr. Ronald W. Richardson, Self-Counsel Press
Fourth Edition, 2011. (The author suggests this for helping
students create genograms.)
Goddesses in Everywoman, Jean Shinoda Bolen, M.D., HarperCollins.
Available as an eBook 2009.
(The author used select information with incarcerated women in
family history and patterns coursework.)
Gods in Everyman, Jean Shinoda Bolen, M.D., HarperCollins, Revised
2014. (The author used select information with incarcerated
men in family history and patterns coursework.)
Growing Up Again: Parenting Ourselves, Parenting Our Children, Jean
Illsley Clarke and Connie Dawson, Hazeldon Second Edition,
1998. (The author adapted the material for use inside prison
classrooms. Highly recommended.)
Helping Children Cope with Separation and Loss, Claudia L. Jewett,
Harvard Common Press Revised 1994. (The author used this as
supplementary material for parenting coursework.)
Please Understand Me: Character & Temperament Types, David Keirsey,
Prometheus Nemesis Book Company, 1998. See also
www.Keirsey.com (The author's students used this work in
conjunction with spouses and other family members who
studied the work on the outside.)

Books About Prison and Doing Time (A select few of many
available on this topic.)
A Plague of Prisons: The Epidemiology of Mass Incarceration in America,
Ernest Drucker, The New Press, 2013.

Chasing Gideon: The Elusive Quest for Poor People's Justice, Karen
   Houppert, The New Press, 2013.
The Collapse of American Criminal Justice, William J. Stuntz, The
   Belknap Press of Harvard University Press, 2011.
Doing Time: 25 Years of Prison Writing, Bell Gale Chevigny, Editor,
   Arcade Publishing, 1999.
Inside the Criminal Mind, Stanton E. Samenow, Ph.D., Times Books,
   1984.
It's About Time: America's Imprisonment Binge, John Irwin and James
   Austin, Wadsworth Publishing Company, 1994.
The New Jim Crow: Mass incarceration in the Age of Colorblindness,
   Michelle Alexander, The New Press, 2012.
Prison Profiteers: Who Makes Money from Mass Incarceration, Tara Herivel
and Paul Wright, Editors, The New Press, 2009
   (Author's Note: The works by Drucker, Stuntz and Alexander
   are especially informative regarding the current prison
   situation.)

General Prison Resources

"Banking on Bondage: Private Prisons and Mass Incarceration,"
   American Civil Liberties Union, November 2022 – .
   www.aclu.org/files/assets/bankingonbondage_20111102.pdf
"Caging of America," *The New Yorker*, Adam Gopnic, January 30,
   2012 – www.newyorker.com/arts/critics/atlarge/2012
Education Content Package Descriptions, iPEP Tablets for
   Incarcerated Learners, Correctional Education Association –
   www.cea.org
How Effective is Correctional Education, and Where Do We Go from Here?
   The Results of a Comprehensive Evaluation, The Rand Corporation,
   2014 – www.rand.org
"Prisoners in 2013," U.S. Department of Justice, Office of Justice
   Programs, Bureau of Justice Statistics, E. Ann Carson, Ph.D.,
   BJS statistician, Revised September 30, 2014
   www.bjs.gov/content/pub/pdf/p13.pdf

"Mass Incarceration: The Whole Pie, Prison Policy Initiative" –
    www.prisonpolicy.org/reports/pie.html
"Trends in U.S. Corrections" – The Sentencing Project –
    www.sentencingproject.org/

Read More About ...

Correctional Education Association – www.cea.org
Critical Thinking – www.criticalthinking.org
George Orwell and his essay, "Shooting an Elephant." –
    www.online-literature.com/orwell/887/
"Holder Endorses Proposal to Reduce Drug Sentences in Latest
    Sign of Shift," Matt Apuzzo, *The New York Times*, March 2014 –
    www.nytimes.com/2014/03/14/us/politics/holder
McNeil Island Corrections Center History –
    www.doc.wa.gov/facilities/prison/micc/mcneilhistory.asp
"National Justice Atlas of Sentencing and Corrections," the Justice
    Mapping Center – www.justicemapping.org
"Personalized Instruction," James W. Keefe and John M. Jenkins,
    Phi Delta Kappa International – www.pdkintl.org
Rotary, Gig Harbor Club, Rotary Women's Prison Program –
    www.rotarywomen'sprison.com A new effort to launch a series
    of programs serving the women at WCCW. Includes Reentry
    Employment Training, scholarships for continued learning,
    mentoring and the use of a jobs/skills database to assist in
    securing employment. (Email at rotarywomensprison@gmail.com)
"Still a Huge Wound: Remembering Green River Killer's Victims,"
    Sara Jean Green, *The Seattle Times*, March 19, 2013 –
    www.seattletimes.com/html (includes quotes from Dave
    Reichert, U.S. Congressman and former King County WA
    sheriff.)
Washington State Department of Corrections Prison Life –
    www.doc.wa.gov/family/ (Every state has information about
    their prison system and outreach to families.)
"Women, Trauma and PTSD" – PTSD: National Center for PTSD
    – www.ptsd.va.gov/public

Author Jan Walker's Prison Related Books

An Inmate's Daughter, Raven Publishing Inc., 2006 – Young adult
novel called "true fiction" about a 13-year-old girl with a father
doing time at McNeil Island Corrections Center. Addresses
telling children the truth about an incarcerated parent, visiting a
parent inside prison, and an incarcerated father who is parenting
his children from behind bars. ISBN 978-0-9714161-9-2

Parenting from a Distance: Your Rights and Responsibilities – Third Edition,
Plicata Press LLC, 2011 – Resource for incarcerated parents
who are committed to remaining involved with their children
and willing to accept the responsibilities associated with
parenting from inside prison. Includes information on preparing
for reentry and reuniting with family. ISBN 978-0-9828205-1-3

Romar Jones Takes a Hike:Missing Person or Runaway, Second Edition,
licata Press LLC, 2015 – A ninth grade boy about to get
dumped on new foster care relatives walks out of his Oregon
high school to search for his mother in a Washington prison.
Includes visiting inside Washington Corrections Center for
Women, completing high school course work online and teen
being granted independent living status. ISBN 978-0-9848400-2-1

| About the Author |

Jan Walker is a retired community college instructor who taught inside adult women's and men's prisons for 18 years. She developed parenting, family relationships and social responsibility curriculum specific to the needs of incarcerated students. After retiring she volunteered inside a women's reentry prison for several years where she worked with offenders and their family members as they prepared for the woman's release.

Walker is known for strong character and setting development in both fiction and nonfiction, and as an accomplished speaker at professional education and writers' conferences. She wrote *Parenting From a Distance: Your Rights and Responsibilities,* a text for incarcerated students, early in her prison teaching career, and has updated it over the years. She is the author of nine books and publisher at Plicata Press, an independent press founded to assist local writers bring their works to print. You can read more about Jan Walker and her work and events at www.TeachInside.com